The Trauma of Racism

Alisha Moreland-Capuia

The Trauma of Racism

Exploring the Systems and People Fear Built

 Springer

Alisha Moreland-Capuia
Psychiatry
McLean Hospital-Harvard Medical School.
Belmont, MA, USA

ISBN 978-3-030-73435-0   ISBN 978-3-030-73436-7   (eBook)
https://doi.org/10.1007/978-3-030-73436-7

This Springer imprint is published by the registered company Springer Nature Switzerland AG
The registered company address is: Gewerbestrasse 11, 6330 Cham, Switzerland

This book is dedicated to my husband and children who are a boundless, relentless source of inspiration, motivation, and hope for me. They support my core belief that I am here on this earth to do good, serve others, and reduce human suffering. My love and gratitude for them run wide and deep.

Acknowledgments

I am so incredibly grateful to my husband Daniel Capuia for his unwavering support of me in writing this book. His global perspective, value of global community, and his unwavering commitment to help his native country of Angola, Africa, have been and continue to be a rich source of motivation and inspiration for me and my work. Thank you to my children who challenge, teach, and love me deeply, and I am so blessed to be their mother and hope that I can continue to make them proud. To my family, friends, community, and mentors, thank you so much for your continued belief in me. From my King Elementary School days in NE Portland, I hold fast and live out this part of the school's daily pledge that read: "If it is to be, it is up to me." To whom much is given, much is expected, a responsibility I take seriously.

Special thank you to Jaime Vilasanta and Daniel Capuia for helping me to think thoughtfully through the chapter in this book on Angola, Africa. Thank you to my mentor Dr. Kerry J. Ressler, M.D., Ph.D., at McLean Hospital/Harvard Medical School for his boundless wisdom and support of my scholarship and humanity.

I am so grateful to be working with the bold and brilliant illustrator Audrey A. Tran once more. Audrey, you are amazing. Your illustrations tell stories through art and articulate so clearly and profoundly that which cannot be adequately articulated verbally. Thank you.

Book Description

2020 has been uniquely challenging with the COVID-19 pandemic and heightened racial tension in the context of a tumultuous geopolitical environment. Within a year, a multicultural, multigenerational coalition came together to tackle the COVID-19 pandemic with the construction of a vaccine and a commitment to continued learning and adjustment to prevent needless death from the disease. Meanwhile, the persistent pandemic of racism, which is preventable, rages and ravages whole communities, systems, and societies. Because racism is systemic and structural, the approach to dismantling must also be systemic and structural. Racism is a form of trauma. Because trauma is perpetuated systemically and structurally, healing must be facilitated systemically and structurally. This book explores the intersection of history, philosophy, politics, psychology, neurobiology, and the role of fear in influencing traumatic structural-systemic racism. This book respectfully challenges the reader to identify individual, systemic, and societal fear, fear-on-fear interactions and their relationship to the trauma of racism. Finally, Chapter 10, the last chapter of this book, highlights three African countries, Angola, Kenya, and South Africa, and the deleterious and traumatic impact of colonialism, civil war, European supremacy, and each country's respective path toward truth, reconciliation, and healing. This book is for any person, system, or society that is ready to identify fear and temper it; acknowledge, contain, and treat the persistent pandemic of racism; and poised to make a commitment to continued learning and adjustment to prevent needless death from racism and steadfast in a desire to facilitate healing.

Contents

1 The Ecosystem of Fear – Predator and Prey – Which Involves Maintenance of Hierarchy and Ecosystems and Survival/Survival of the Fittest 1

   1.1 Primitive Origins of Fear and Its Power to Transform Ecosystems 2

   1.2 How Fear in (Nature) Ecosystems Mirrors Fear in the Environment of Humans and How Fear-Driven Practices Like Racism Impact People and Systems 5

   1.3 Brain and Fear 5

   References 8

2 The Role of Fear in the Founding of the United States: A Historical and Philosophical Perspective 13

   2.1 A Government and Founding Documents Powerfully Shaped by Fear 16

   2.2 John Adams and Fear 18

   2.3 George Washington and Fear 19

   2.4 Benjamin Franklin and Fear 20

   2.5 Alexander Hamilton and Fear 20

   2.6 James Madison, John Jay, and Fear 21

   2.7 Thomas Jefferson and Fear 21

   2.8 The Inhumanity of Slavery and Fear 23

   2.9 Persistence of Fear in State Constitutions, Laws, Policies, and Practices: The Oregon Story in Brief 24

   2.10 Fear Begets Fear – The Chinese Exclusion Act 26

   References 27

3 The Role of Fear in Politics, Politicians, Government, and Society .. 35

   3.1 Fear and Politics 36

   3.2 Nixon and Fear 37

   3.3 Hoover and Fear 38

   3.4 Franklin D. Roosevelt and Fear 40

3.5   McCarthy and Socially Constructed Fear   41
3.6   Social Constructivism   44
3.7   The Power of False Negative Narratives and Social Constructs
      in Influencing Harmful Behavior Toward Blacks
      and the Unfortunate Backing of Research in Perpetuating
      and Accentuating Harmful Behavior Toward Blacks.   47
3.8   The Birth of a Nation and Negative Social Constructs   47
3.9   Social Construct of Black Women as Mammy's
      and Aunt Jemimah   48
3.10 The Social Construct of the Bell Curve.   48
3.11 The Social Construct of and Narrative Around Black Pain   49
3.12 Truman and Fear   49
3.13 Johnson and Fear   51
3.14 Nixon and Fear.   51
3.15 Reagan and Fear.   52
3.16 Obama and Fear.   53
3.17 Trump and Fear   54
References.   56

4   **Fear and Poverty**.   63
4.1   Fear-Based Narrative, Race, and Poverty   65
4.2   Economic Downturn and Poverty   65
4.3   Poverty and Its Impact on Brain Development   67
4.4   Poverty and Nutrition.   68
4.5   Poverty Is Structural.   69
4.6   Poverty + Environmental Injustice.   70
4.7   Poverty and Unemployment, Underemployment,
      Low Skills, and the Technological Divide   70
4.8   Fear and Toxic Stress   71
References.   72

5   **Education, Fear, and Trauma**   79
5.1   History of Education, in Brief   79
5.2   Civil War, Reconstruction Era, and Civil Rights
      Act of 1964 and Its Impact on Education   80
5.3   The Department of Education, Title 1, and No Child Left
      Behind (NCLB)   81
5.4   Education as a Determinant of Health   84
References.   86

6   **Law Enforcement/Policing and Fear**.   91
6.1   Hatred Undergirded by Fear Grows When Unchecked   92
6.2   Disproportionality in Black Men and Women Killed by Police . . .   93
6.3   Slave Patrols.   95
6.4   Law Enforcement During the Reconstruction Era.   95
6.5   Twentieth-Century Policing   96

6.6   Conditioned Fear, Perception of Threat/Extremism,
         and Behavior Modification.   97
6.7   Classical Conditioning and Fear Conditioning   98
6.8   Attitudes Toward the Police and Fear   99
References.   101

7   **Fear, Trauma, and Racism**   107
7.1   Racism – Structural Impact (Employment, Economic,
         and Housing)   109
7.2   Disparities in Wages.   110
7.3   Housing Disparities   110
7.4   Adverse Childhood Experiences (ACEs).   110
7.5   Philadelphia ACEs and Racism   112
7.6   Culturally Informed Adverse Childhood Experiences – C-ACEs . .   113
7.7   Racism and Trauma   113
7.8   Making the Connection Between Trauma in Individuals,
         Organizations, and Society   115
References.   115

8   **Healthcare, Fear, Discrimination, and Racism**.   119
8.1   The Relationship Between Fear, Discrimination, Racism,
         and Its Health Impact.   119
8.2   Disparities in Pain Management Due to Perception of
         Discrimination   122
8.3   Cardiovascular Health Disparities   123
8.4   Disparities in Cancer Detection, Treatment, and Management   124
8.5   Racial Disparities in Mental Health Diagnosis and Treatment   126
8.6   Structural Components to Health Disparities   127
8.7   Attitudes of Healthcare Providers and Clinicians   128
References.   129

9   **Historical and Structural Fear Compounded**   135
9.1   A Novel Virus, Absene of Leadership and Fear Intensified.   137
9.2   Argument Over the Economy Versus Health and Safety   140
9.3   Disparities Rise to the Top amid Crisis: 1918   140
9.4   Historical Fear: Tuskegee Experiment and Other
         Experiments on Black People   141
9.5   Regions Hit Harder Than Others: Real-Life Examples
         of the Disproportionate Impact of COVID-19.   142
9.6   Los Angeles Health Workers, EMTs, and Vicarious Trauma.   143
9.7   Vaccination Disparities Well Before COVID.   144
9.8   COVID-19 Pandemic, Structural Disparities and Fear
         Compounded   145
References.   146

10 **The Trauma of Colonialism, European Supremacy, Truth,
    and Reconciliation**. 151
    10.1   The Scramble for Africa. 151
    10.2   Colonialism and European Supremacy 153
    10.3   Angola, Africa 153
    10.4   Portuguese Influence in Angola. 154
    10.5   Queen Njinga Mbande Pushes Back against Portuguese
           Colonial Powers. 155
    10.6   Angolan Independence. 156
    10.7   Kenya, Trauma and Healing. 158
    10.8   South Africa, Apartheid, White Supremacy, Truth,
           and Reconciliation 160
    10.9   Apartheid 161
    10.10 Trauma of Apartheid 163
    10.11 Truth and Reconciliation 163
    References. 164

Index. 171

About the Author

Alisha Moreland-Capuia (Dr. AMC) graduated from Stanford University in 2002 with a B.S. in biological sciences and a minor in urban studies. She earned her Doctor of Medicine from the George Washington University School of Medicine in 2007. She completed 4 years of psychiatry residency and an addiction fellowship at Oregon Health and Science University. She is board certified in addiction and general adult psychiatry and is currently faculty at McLean Hospital-Harvard Medical School.

She is an expert in trauma-informed systems change and has worked with multiple systems to include education, not-for-profit organizations, clinics and hospitals, and government and community-based organizations to facilitate trauma-informed change. She has committed significant time and effort to facilitating trauma-informed change in various aspects of the criminal justice and government. She has served on the Portland Community Oversight Advisory Board, charged with monitoring the implementation of the City of Portland's settlement agreement with the U.S. Department of Justice to enact reform to Portland Police Bureau (PPB) policies and training. She has partnered with the Federal Judicial Center and the National Judicial College to provide training for Federal Judges and Probation Officers and State Supreme Court Judges, respectively.

Dr. AMC has trained U.S. Senators and staffers in applying a trauma-informed lens to policies and legislation. She is training various U.S. Probation and Pretrial Service District Offices to facilitate trauma-informed change in U.S. presentencing and sentencing guidelines and post-prison supervision. Dr. AMC has assisted with policy and training with the Multnomah County District Attorney's office over the span of three elected district attorneys as well as extensively with Portland's local judiciary. She has also trained the Multnomah County Probation Office and other local law enforcement agencies and personnel in Oregon.

While in residency training, Dr. AMC built Healing Hurt People-Portland (HHP), a trauma-informed, hospital-based, community-focused youth violence prevention program.Dr. AMC's trauma-informed efforts are global as she works in Angola, Africa, at their family clinic Centro Medico Bom Samaritano, and is the co-founder of The Capuia Foundation. Additionally she is partnering with a team in Scotland for global trauma-informed change.She is currently establishing an institute for trauma-informed systems change at McLean Hospital-Harvard Medical School. She is the sole author of *Training for Change: Transforming Systems to be Trauma-Informed, Culturally Responsive, and Neuroscientifically Focused* published by Springer in 2019.

She is purpose driven and holds the conviction that her purpose in life is to do good, serve others, and reduce human suffering.

She lives in Cambridge, Massachusetts, with her husband and children.

About the Illustrator

Audrey A. Tran received her B.A. at Wellesley College, *magna cum laude,* in biochemistry with a minor in music. She then worked as a research assistant in Boston, MA, and became enamored with stem cell and CRISPR genome editing technology. She matriculated into medical school in 2017 and completed her master's degree in clinical research in 2020.

Her passion for science is coupled with a drive to share what she has learned through creative approaches. This led her to develop a style of tutoring that incorporates intuitive, illustrative, and color-coded study guides, which are now permanently housed in the OHSU Library Archives. She has been recognized by her peers and faculty for her illustrations and is now working with OHSU faculty to develop illustrative videos for patient education.

She is committed to advancing racial justice and believes that education is the first step to empowerment, self-actualization, and effective advocacy. To stay creative, she writes music, and is working on producing an album chronicling her experiences in medical school. She can likely be found harmonizing to your favorite song.

Chapter 1
The Ecosystem of Fear – Predator and Prey – Which Involves Maintenance of Hierarchy and Ecosystems and Survival/ Survival of the Fittest

A brief Google search on the word "fear" produces close to half a million undupli-cated hits. There are thousands upon thousands of quotes about fear. "Fear not" is a command used in the bible over 365 times. Franklin D. Roosevelt popularized and paraphrased the saying: "There is nothing to fear but fear itself" – the country was at the height of the Great Economic Depression of the 1920s, emerging from World War I, suicide rates increased in the context of unemployment during the Great Depression, and fear and uncertainty were off the charts (José & Ana, 2009; Sydenstricker, 1934). The leader of the free world told the country not to fear, yet fear was all consuming as it had encroached upon every single aspect of human life during the Great Depression. Fear leaves an impression on the body, soul, and spirit and is passed down through generations (Braga, Mello, & Fiks, 2012; Dietz et al., 2011; Yehuda, Engel, Brand, et al., 2005). A study by Warner et al. investigated the role of fear and anxiety in the familial risk for major depression across three genera-tions, and several other studies demonstrated that fear can be passed down through generations (Biederman et al., 2006; Hirshfeld-Becker et al., 2012; Warner, Wickramaratne, & Weissman, 2008). Fear is powerful.

For the last decade, I have had the honor of facilitating healing in systems and people by working to help systems and people identify fear in systems, recognize the relationship between fear and trauma, and manage fear through employing trauma-informed practices. I have consistently witnessed this sentiment – where there are humans there too is fear and trauma – and have concluded that every sys-tem and every human being benefit from trauma-informed practices and approaches: it costs nothing and changes everything.

If we pause and ponder deeply some of the unfortunate things currently happen-ing in our world to include but not limited to children being detained and separated from their parents at the border, anti-immigrant sentiment, partisan politics, law enforcement brutality and excessive use of force in minority populations, racism and hatred, poverty, limited access to healthcare, disparate and discriminatory edu-cation systems, discriminatory housing, and economic inequity, the pretext, subtext, and context are fear – fear of losing status and/or esteem, a false perception of threat, fear of someone mattering more or most, fear of losing power or the perception thereof, and fear of living and dying. Fear.

1.1   Primitive Origins of Fear and Its Power to Transform Ecosystems

Fear is an incredibly commanding emotion that can drive actions and behaviors. Fear is as primitive and poignant as human evolution itself. Let's consider for a moment the concept of predator and prey which involves maintenance of hierarchy in various ecosystems and survival. The ecology of fear is a conceptual framework describing the psychological impact predator-governed stress experienced by animals has on populations and ecosystems. Biologists write about the fear factor in ecosystems explaining how this powerful emotion is responsible for transforming landscapes. It is theorized that terror experienced by prey establishes a colossal and underappreciated behavioral phenomenon – one that powerfully shapes myriad ecosystems. It (terror and fear) is so powerful that it has been observed to impact the behavior of prey in the absence of predators – the conditioned anticipation of the potential presence of a predator robustly influences behavioral patterns of prey, illustrating the power of fear (Zanette, White, Allen, & Clinchy, 2011).

Biologists Zanette and Clinchy penned a paper entitled "Ecology of Fear" describing a fear-based shift in feeding times and patterns of racoons. Fear of being preyed upon has more impact on an ecosystem than the actual predation itself (Zanette & Clinchy, 2019; Zanette et al., 2011). Racoons are noted to operate mostly at night – this is functionally necessary for their survival and optimal avoidance of predators (Zanette & Clinchy, 2019). However, it was observed that in the absence of predators, racoons shifted their grazing presence to day time – they became nomadic, moving away from the forest and into exposed tidal flats to search for expanded cuisine options – they felt safe enough to venture out of the forest in the absence of the threat of predators (Zanette & Clinchy, 2019). Raccoons' daytime feeding patterns obstructed how other species and vegetation could thrive – shift in eating location, time of day, and frequency began to have a deleterious impact on the population of worms, red rock crabs, and clams (Zanette & Clinchy, 2019). This is a working example of how fear in ecosystems can have deleterious downstream cascading impact.

Several ecologists and biologists who study the role of fear in ecosystems have highlighted that even when predators aren't killing anything, their tracks, smells, and sounds can instill fear in their prey (Zanette & Clinchy, 2019; Suraci, Clinchy, Dill, et al., 2016; Preisser, Bolnick, & Benard, 2005; Brown, Laundré, & Gurung, 1999). This creates what ecologists call a "landscape of fear" – a mental map of risk that affects how hunted animals move over physical terrain (Zanette & Clinchy,

2019; Suraci et al., 2016; Preisser et al., 2005; Brown et al., 1999). This speaks to both the function and dysfunction of predation on maintaining and sustaining ecosystems (Zanette & Clinchy, 2019; Suraci et al., 2016; Preisser et al., 2005; Brown et al., 1999).

Just the anticipatory fear of being preyed upon has profound impact on wildlife populations even when predators are not directly killing them. This is a significant observation in nature and has implications for what is observed in human behavior.

Direct killing affects prey numbers, but predators lasting scare (traumatic memory) of prey causing prey to live in daily fear of being consumed is theorized to be just as important as direct killing in terms of reducing prey populations. To further demonstrate the impact of traumatic memory/lasting scare/daily fear of prey subject to predation, Zanette and colleagues investigated nesting patterns of song sparrows (Zanette et al., 2011). The birds were isolated, and different groups of birds were exposed to different sounds – non-threatening sounds were control, and threatening predatory sounds were the test – for four months these sounds were predominant. The birds that were exposed to predatory sounds produced 40% less offspring compared to the control group that were exposed to natural, non-threatening sounds (Zanette et al., 2011). Fear of predators had downstream and direct impact on population size of prey, not just by killing them, but by scaring them further illustrating the profound impact that fear has in shaping environments.

Historically, think about the impact of slavery, exclusion, lynchings on populations of marginalized systems, and the fear produced and maintained therefore. Fear-on-fear interactions have real impact. If we can appreciate this phenomenon in nature, then we certainly can appreciate it real time, human to human, system to system. What is understood about predation (predator-prey interactions) is that it (predation) influences animal behavior, and antipredator defenses have physical and behavioral costs. The amount of time occupied by prey concerned with protecting themselves manifest as avoidance of certain high-risk situations – these behavioral impacts come at a high cost to an ecosystem or environment.

Meredith Palmer, Fieberg, Swanson, Kosmala, and Packer (2017) further illustrate the impact of antipredation behavior of prey and its impact on an ecosystem with their work in African large mammal communities – working to understand how they employ a suite of antipredator behaviors of avoidance to temper risks of harm and death (Palmer et al., 2017). This manifest as prey not foraging in an area that has plenty of food for them – this change in foraging behavior has both upstream and downstream implications (Palmer et al., 2017). While there are compensatory mechanisms to include prey changing the time of day, they forage an area to avoid prey; prey may use more of the landscape to forage, for example – these behavioral changes marked by time and energy shifts (focused more on survival as opposed to thriving and living), avoidance, and fear can depress and/or improve an ecosystem (Palmer et al., 2017). The bottom line though is when fear is accounted for in a system, it is shown to consistently and profoundly impact ecosystems (Frank,

Blaalid, Mayer, Zedrosser, & Steyaert, 2020; Zaguri & Hawlena, 2020; Palmer et al., 2017; Palmer, Menninger, & Bernhardt, 2010). One study showed that predators drove a lizard population to extinction without eating them (Pringle et al., 2019). The fear predators evoke in prey can set off a domino effect, reshaping ecosystems in the process (Pringle et al., 2019). Over the years, Pringle and colleagues studied three local lizard populations in the Bahamas. One of the three lizard species was a long-time native brown anole (*Anolis sagrei*) of the Bahamas, and the other two species introduced were the non-native tree-dwelling green anole (*Anolis smaragdinus*) and the curly-tailed lizard (*Leiocephalus carinatus*), which is a known predator of anoles and insects. Brown anoles and curly-tailed lizards behaviorally frequent the forest amid myriad predators (Pringle et al., 2019). In the absence of a known predator, the green and brown anoles functioned in peace, together, harmoniously. They occupied different spaces in the shared ecosystem as green anoles remained in the forest canopy, eating on arboreal beetles, and brown anoles ate cockroaches on the forest floor. It was hypothesized that because of this behavior, the native brown anole population would decrease – they were in the presence of a known predator (the curly-tailed lizard and other forest predators). The working theory was that as the native brown anole lizard species would decrease, the non-native green anole species would increase and thrive. According to Pringle and colleagues, a green anole (*Anolis smaragdinus*) resides primarily in tree canopies, munching on insects, like beetles, that live in the leaves. The working theory was debunked – the green anoles (non-native species) declined, not because they were being eaten, but because brown anoles were afraid of being eaten so they left the forest and began to inhabit the trees (Pringle et al., 2019). The migration of brown anoles from the forest to the trees crowded out the green anoles from their historical habitat of trees, rendering them homeless, vulnerable, and ultimately extinct. Pringle and colleagues demonstrated that in the absence of physical harm, a predator can significantly change the behavior of prey based on anticipation of harm – a conditioned fear response that has profound upstream and downstream impact, changing an entire ecosystem (Pringle et al., 2019). *Predators exert significant effects on prey not just through killing but also by scaring them* (Fardell, Pavey, & Dickman, 2020; Zanette & Clinchy, 2019; Pringle et al., 2019; Suraci et al., 2016).

Living under constant threat of being preyed upon is stressful; several studies and animal models of predatory-prey dynamics show the deleterious physiologic and behavioral changes that accompany the stress of being eliminated, the fear imposed on prey by predators (Gross & Canteras, 2012; Mervis et al., 2012; Mobbs, Hagan, Dalgleish, Silston, & Prévost, 2015; Laundre et al., 2010; Liana and Clinchy, 2019). The role of fear is observed and appreciated in nature – its impact on animal behavior and its capacity to change an entire ecosystem. Fear can transform an entire ecosystem.

1.2   How Fear in (Nature) Ecosystems Mirrors Fear in the Environment of Humans and How Fear-Driven Practices Like Racism Impact People and Systems

If the phenomenon of predator and prey holds true in any ecosystem, then it should not be too farfetched to conceptualize fear as an underlying driver of much of human behavior and to appreciate its role in impacting human ecosystems. If you want to understand human behavior, observe it and study it in the context of fear. This book will address what I refer to as "fear-on-fear" interactions, how they have shaped and continue to influence human behavior, decision-making, policies, and practices and how we might address them as a means of moving toward as a society in a more humane, inclusive way and facilitate trauma-informed practice and policy transformation and healing. Healing in this book is referred to as spiritual, psychological, and physical wellness. There is greater opportunity for healing when and where we begin to ask and identify, "Where is the fear?" "What is the fear?"

Our human existence is a protracted exercise of seeking safety and learning how to modulate fear so that it is not all consuming, so that we might survive and thrive as humans. This human phenomenon of prioritizing safety is observed in "how" the human brain develops with the survival part of our brains being the most prominent and impacting subsequent brain development when humans are first born.

1.3   Brain and Fear

The brain develops from the bottom up and the inside out (see Fig. 1.1) – this means that the most developed part of our brain when we are first born is the brain stem. The brainstem is the bottom, primitive part of our brain that is responsible for our literal survival – responsible for our hearts beating, lungs breathing, and consciousness. It has a role in sleep, reflexes, and blood pressure too. The brainstem is connected to the spinal cord which allows for messages from the brain to be sent throughout the body – this is a critical connection. The brainstem is made of the following sections: the diencephalon, midbrain, pons, and medulla oblongata (Basinger & Hogg, 2020; Angeles Fernandez-Gil et al., 2010; Nicholls and Patton, 2009).

Diencephalon – contains the thalamus (sensory, sending information) and the hypothalamus (regulatory, integrating function) (Chatterjee & Li, 2012).

Midbrain – plays a role in motor functions like eye movement and also in visual processing and hearing (Caminero & Cascella, 2020).

Pons – houses several cranial nerves, responsible for coordinating the work of breathing in sleep, may play a role in rapid eye movement or REM sleep, coordinates other important functions including posture, swallowing, bladder regulation, hearing, facial sensation, equilibrium, taste, eye movement, and facial expressions (Huot, 2015).

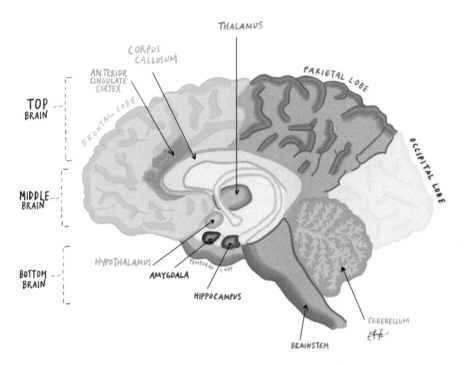

Fig. 1.1 The brain develops from the bottom up and the inside out. The way the brain develops has implications for behavior. Bottom – survival mode. Top – regulation of emotions, judgment, and behavior

Medulla oblongata – responsible for coordinating signals between the spinal cord and the brain, is considered the lowest aspect of the brain, and has a key role in breathing and regulation of heartbeat (Mohanakumar & Sood, 1980).

There are various nuclei along the brain stem; raphe nuclei are distributed near the midline of the brainstem. The serotonergic projections participate in the regulation of different functions (motor, somatosensory, limbic) (Hornung, 2003; Kinney, Broadbelt, Haynes, Rognum, & Paterson, 2011).

The locus coeruleus located in the brainstem plays a role in mediating the fear response and has several projections (functional connections) to the entire neocortex, the thalamus, limbic structures such as the amygdala and the hippocampus, the pallidum, and the cerebellum, as well as other neuromodulatory nuclei controlling the release of norepinephrine (Samuels & Szabadi, 2008).

The reticular formation consists of unified group of nuclei within the brainstem. It plays a role in arousal promotion and consciousness (Mangold & Das, 2020).

Note that the brainstem coordinates with specific parts of the brain responsible for human survival and is intimately and intricately attached to multiple sensations to include vision and hearing (sensory components). External sensory cues are critical in triggering the fear response which directly impacts how the brain functions and develops, how memory is formed, how seeking safety is prioritized, and how behavior is mightily shaped.

The brainstem is powerfully influenced by sensory inputs from the external environment during the third trimester of pregnancy– this has implications for brain function, growth, and connection trajectory (Bouyssi-Kobar et al., 2016; Vasung et al., 2019; Wang, Kloth, & Badura, 2014). Our human existence, from the very beginning, is centered around seeking safety (getting basic needs met) and modulating fear. The ability to learn to modulate fear as opposed to being overcome by fear is strongly connected to basic needs being met (food, water, shelter) and attainment of secure attachments. When basic needs are met, fear is tempered, safety is prioritized, and trajectory for healthy brain development is preserved. John Bowlby's attachment theory highlights the fact that attachments are critical for survival and human beings are primed for connection (Bowlby, 1969). It is also understood that the attachment system is an evolved brain system that produces and governs a human need to be protected (safe) and comforted and regulates distress and fear (Bowlby and Ainsworth, 1966; Bowlby, 1969; Bell, Lewenstein, Shouse, & Feder, 2009; Perry & Sullivan, 2014).

The fear system is tied into perception to detect danger, memory to remember dangerous places and situations and the capacity to avoid and escape danger. When the fear response is appropriately tempered, safety is established. Secure attachment, where basic needs like love, attention, food, and care from primary caregiver are provided, helps to temper the fear response and reduce stress (Ainsworth & Bell, 1970; Ukezono, Nakashima, Sudo, Yamazaki, & Takano, 2015).

Humans were born with the proclivity for survival, and the goal of healthy development and maturation in our society involves learning how to modulate fear and learning to seek safety.

Fear is meant to be a time- and threat-limited response.

Fear that doesn't turn off is trauma (Moreland-Capuia, 2019).

The brainstem is profoundly influenced by external sensory inputs, which has profound implications for modulation of the fear response, subsequent brain development and attachment.

Toxic stress and fear have deleterious impact on the brain and the body.

Fear shapes the developmental process – brain, body, and behavior.

If we understand the pervasive, ubiquitous nature of fear and its ecological, biological, sociological, psychological, physical, and behavioral impact, we can begin to think about how we might approach systems to help them help. Healing must involve identifying the fear, tempering it, and centering safety.

Fear of fear can drive an entire species extinct – this is powerful. Fear translated and superimposed on the human condition is even more amplified – fear-on-fear interactions have resulted in persistent deleterious behavioral, physical, psychological, and societal outcomes – even disproportionate death in some communities.

Making the connection between fear, trauma, and racism. One way to understand the neurobiological underpinnings of trauma: trauma is fear that doesn't turn off. Persons subject to racism are often in a chronic state of toxic stress and fear, which is trauma. Racism is traumatizing. In our world, racism (undergirded by fear) is the predator, and it (racism) has dramatically impacted many of the systems humans have come to rely on. Several studies have effectively demonstrated the link between racism and its deleterious impact on the physical and mental well-being of racial/ ethnic minority groups subject to it, leaving many in a constant state of stress and fear (actual and literal fear for their lives) and the social harms of systems that perpetuate fear and racism (Bennett, Merritt, Edwards, & Sollers, 2004; Branscombe, Schmitt, & Harvey, 1999; Bryant-Davis & Ocampo, 2005; Carter, 2007; Carter, Forsyth, Mazzula, & Williams, 2005; Contrada et al., 2001). There is an entire chapter dedicated to the trauma of racism in this book, but it is critical to highlight perpetuators of racism (based in a fear of loss of status among other things) and persons subject to racism (living in a constant state of fear) as a fear-on-fear interaction worthy of greater exploration. Additionally, this book aims to uncover the spaces, places, and systems that fear built and maintains. It is more likely to improve a thing when it is readily identified.

I will conclude this chapter like how I began, with Roosevelt's popularized quote that "we have nothing to fear but fear itself." There lies some truth in this statement – fear unchecked and unrecognized is destructive. Fear-on-fear interactions powerfully and poignantly shape and shift behavior and impact environments, whole ecosystems, and societies – fear in nature and humanity deleteriously impacts human behavior, systems, and society: this is where this book begins.

References

Ainsworth, M. D., & Bell, S. M. (1970). Attachment, exploration, and separation: Illustrated by the behavior of one-year-olds in a strange situation. *Child Development, 41*(1), 49–67. https:// doi.org/10.2307/1127388.

Angeles Fernández-Gil, M., Palacios-Bote, R., Leo-Barahona, M., & Mora-Encinas, J. P. (2010, Jun). Anatomy of the brainstem: A gaze into the stem of life. *Seminars in Ultrasound, CT, and MR, 31*(3), 196–219.

Basinger, H., & Hogg, J. P. (2020, January). Neuroanatomy, Brainstem. [Updated 2020 May 23]. In *StatPearls* [Internet]. Treasure Island (FL): StatPearls Publishing. Available from: https:// www.ncbi.nlm.nih.gov/books/NBK544297/

Bell, P., Lewenstein, B., Shouse, A. W., & Feder, M. A. (2009). *Learning science in informal environments: People, places, and pursuits*. Washington, DC: National Academies Press.

Bennett, G. G., Merritt, M. M., Edwards, C. L., & Sollers, J. J. (2004). Perceived racism and affective responses to ambiguous interpersonal interactions among African American men. *American Behavioral Scientist, 47*(7), 63–76.

Biederman, J., Petty, C., Faraone, S. V., Henin, A., Hirshfeld-Becker, D., Pollack, M. H., de Figueiredo, S., Feeley, R., & Rosenbaum, J. F. (2006, August). Effects of parental anxiety disorders in children at high risk for panic disorder: A controlled study. *Journal of Affective Disorders, 94*(1–3), 191–197. https://doi.org/10.1016/j.jad.2006.04.012. Epub 2006 Jun 6. PMID: 16753222.

Bouyssi-Kobar, M., du Plessis, A. J., McCarter, R., Brossard-Racine, M., Murnick, J., Tinkleman, L., Robertson, R. L., & Limperopoulos, C. (2016, November). Third trimester brain growth in preterm infants compared with in utero healthy fetuses. *Pediatrics, 138*(5), e20161640. https:// doi.org/10.1542/peds.2016-1640. PMID: 27940782; PMCID: PMC5079081.

Bowlby, J., & Ainsworth, M. (1966). *Maternal care and mental health*. New York: Schocken Books.

Bowlby, J. (1969). Attachment and Loss, Vol. 1: Attachment. Attachment and Loss. New York: Basic Books.

Braga, L. L., Mello, M. F., & Fiks, J. P. (2012). Transgenerational transmission of trauma and resilience: a qualitative study with Brazilian offspring of Holocaust survivors. *BMC Psychiatry, 12*, 134. https://doi.org/10.1186/1471-244X-12-134.

Branscombe, N. R., Schmitt, M. T., & Harvey, R. D. (1999). Perceiving pervasive discrimination among African-Americans: Implications for group identification and well-being. *Journal of Personality and Social Psychology, 77*, 135–149.

Brown, J. S., Laundré, J. W., & Gurung, M. (1999). The ecology of fear: Optimal foraging, game theory, and trophic interactions. *Journal of Mammalogy, 80*, 385–399.

Bryant-Davis, T., & Ocampo, C. (2005). Racist-incident-based trauma. *The Counseling Psychologist, 33*(4), 479–500.

Caminero, F., & Cascella, M (2020, January). Neuroanatomy, Mesencephalon Midbrain. [Updated 2020 Nov 2]. In: *StatPearls* [Internet]. Treasure Island (FL): StatPearls Publishing. Available from: https://www.ncbi.nlm.nih.gov/books/NBK551509/

Carter, R. T. (2007). Racism and psychological and emotional injury: Recognizing and assessing race-based traumatic stress. *The Counseling Psychologist, 35*(1), 13–105. https://doi.org/10.1177/0011000006292033.

Carter, R. T., Forsyth, J., Mazzula, S., & Williams, B. (2005). Racial discrimination and race-based traumatic stress. In R. T. Carter (Ed.), *Handbook of racial-cultural psychology and counseling: Training and practice* (Vol. 2, pp. 447–476). New York: Wiley.

Chatterjee, M., & Li, J. Y. (2012). Patterning and compartment formation in the diencephalon. *Frontiers in Neuroscience, 6*, 66. https://doi.org/10.3389/fnins.2012.00066.

Contrada, R. J., Ashmore, R. D., Gary, M. L., Coups, E., Egeth, J. D., Sewell, A., et al. (2001). Measures of ethnicity-related stress: Psychometric properties, ethnic group differences, and associations of well-being. *Journal of Applied Psychology, 31*, 1775–1820.

Dietz, D. M., et al. (2011). Paternal transmission of stress-induced pathologies. *Biological Psychiatry, 70*(5), 408.

Fardell, L. L., Pavey, C. R., & Dickman, C. R. (2020). Fear and stressing in predator-prey ecology: Considering the twin stressors of predators and people on mammals. *PeerJ, 8*, e9104. https://doi.org/10.7717/peerj.9104.

Frank, S. C., Blaalid, R., Mayer, M., Zedrosser, A., & Steyaert, S. M. J. G. (2020). Fear the reaper: Ungulate carcasses may generate an ephemeral landscape of fear for rodents. *Royal Society Open Science, 7*(6), 191644. https://doi.org/10.1098/rsos.191644.

Gross, C. T., & Canteras, N. S. (2012). The many paths to fear. *Nature Reviews Neuroscience*.

Hirshfeld-Becker, D. R., Micco, J. A., Henin, A., Petty, C., Faraone, S. V., Mazursky, H., Bruett, L., Rosenbaum, J. F., & Biederman, J. (2012, November). Psychopathology in adolescent offspring of parents with panic disorder, major depression, or both: A 10-year follow-up. *The American Journal of Psychiatry, 169*(11), 1175–1184. https://doi.org/10.1176/appi.ajp.2012.11101514.

Hornung, J. P. (2003, December). The human raphe nuclei and the serotonergic system. *Journal of Chemical Neuroanatomy, 26*(4), 331–343. https://doi.org/10.1016/j.jchemneu.2003.10.002.

Huot, P. (2015). The pons and human affective processing—Implications for Parkinson's disease. *eBioMedicine, 2*(11), 1592–1593. https://doi.org/10.1016/j.ebiom.2015.10.031.

José A. Tapia Granados and Ana V. Diez Roux (2009, October 13). Life and death during the Great Depression. *PNAS, 106*(41), 17290–17295. https://doi.org/10.1073/pnas.0904491106.

Kinney, H. C., Broadbelt, K. G., Haynes, R. L., Rognum, I. J., & Paterson, D. S (2011, July). The serotonergic anatomy of the developing human medulla oblongata: implications for pediatric disorders of homeostasis. *Journal of Chemical Neuroanatomy, 41*(4), 182–199. https://doi.org/10.1016/j.jchemneu.2011.05.004. Epub 2011 May 27. PMID: 21640183; PMCID: PMC3134154.

Laundre, J., Hernandez, L., & Ripple, W. (2010). The landscape of fear: Ecological implications of being afraid. *The Open Ecology Journal, 3*, 1–7. https://doi.org/10.2174/1874213001003030001.

Liana, Y. Z., & Clinchy, M. (2019). Ecology of fear. *Current Biology, 29*(9), R309–R313. https://doi.org/10.1016/j.cub.2019.02.042. ISSN 0960-9822.

Mangold, S. A., & Das, J. M. (2020, January). Neuroanatomy, reticular formation. [Updated 2020 Aug 15]. In *StatPearls* [Internet]. Treasure Island (FL): StatPearls Publishing. Available from: https://www.ncbi.nlm.nih.gov/books/NBK556102/

Mervis, C. B., Dida, J., Lam, E., Crawford-Zelli, N. A., Young, E. J., Henderson, D. R., Onay, T., Morris, C. A., Woodruff-Borden, J., Yeomans, J., et al. (2012). Duplication of GTF2I results in separation anxiety in mice and humans. *American Journal of Human Genetics, 90*, 1064–1070.

Mobbs, D., Hagan, C. C., Dalgleish, T., Silston, B., & Prévost, C. (2015). The ecology of human fear: Survival optimization and the nervous system. *Frontiers in Neuroscience, 9*, 55. https://doi.org/10.3389/fnins.2015.00055.

Mohanakumar, K. P., & Sood, P. P. (1980, December). Histological and histoenzymological studies on the medulla oblongata and pons of hedgehog (Paraechinus micropus). *Acta Morphologica Neerlando-Scandinavica, 18*(4), 291–304.

Moreland-Capuia, A. (2019). *Training for change: Transforming systems to be trauma-informed, culturally responsive and neuroscientifically focused* (377 p). Springer Nature.

Nicholls, J. G., & Paton, J. F. (2009). Brainstem: neural networks vital for life. *Philosophical Transactions of the Royal Society of London. Series B, Biological Sciences, 364*(1529), 2447–2451. https://doi.org/10.1098/rstb.2009.0064.

Palmer, M. A., Menninger, H. L., & Bernhardt, E. (2010). River restoration, habitat heterogeneity and biodiversity: A failure of theory or practice? *Freshwater Biology, 55*, 205–222. https://doi.org/10.1111/j.1365-2427.2009.02372.x.

Palmer, M. S., Fieberg, J., Swanson, A., Kosmala, M., & Packer, C. (2017). A 'dynamic' landscape of fear: prey responses to spatiotemporal variations in predation risk across the lunar cycle. *Ecology Letters, 20*(11), 1364–1373.

Perry, R., & Sullivan, R. M. (2014). Neurobiology of attachment to an abusive caregiver: Short-term benefits and long-term costs. *Developmental Psychobiology, 56*(8), 1626–1634. https://doi.org/10.1002/dev.21219.

Preisser, Bolnick, D. I., & Benard, M. F. (2005). Scared to death? The effects of intimidation and consumption in predator-prey interactions. *Ecology, 86*, 501–509.

Pringle, R. M., Kartzinel, T. R., Palmer, T. M., Thurman, T. J., Fox-Dobbs, K., Xu, C. C. Y., Hutchinson, M. C., Coverdale, T. C., Daskin, J. H., Evangelista, D. A., Gotanda, K. M., A Man In 't Veld N, Wegener, J. E., Kolbe, J. J., Schoener, T. W., Spiller, D. A., Losos, J. B., Barrett, R. D. H. (2019, Jun). Predator-induced collapse of niche structure and species coexistence. *Nature, 570*(7759), 58–64. https://doi.org/10.1038/s41586-019-1264-6. Epub 2019 Jun 5. PMID: 31168105.

Samuels, E. R., & Szabadi, E. (2008). Functional neuroanatomy of the noradrenergic locus coeruleus: Its roles in the regulation of arousal and autonomic function part I: principles of functional organisation. *Current Neuropharmacology, 6*(3), 235–253. https://doi.org/10.2174/157015908785777229.

Suraci, J., Clinchy, M., Dill, L., et al. (2016). Fear of large carnivores causes a trophic cascade. *Nature Communications, 7*, 10698. https://doi.org/10.1038/ncomms10698.

Sydenstricker, E. (1934). Health and the depression. *Milbank Memorial Fund Quarterly, 11*, 273–280.

Ukezono, M., Nakashima, S. F., Sudo, R., Yamazaki, A., & Takano, Y. (2015). The combination of perception of other individuals and exogenous manipulation of arousal enhances social facilitation as an aftereffect: Re-examination of Zajonc's drive theory. *Frontiers in Psychology, 6*, Article 601. https://doi.org/10.3389/fpsyg.2015.00601.

Vasung, L., Abaci Turk, E., Ferradal, S. L., Sutin, J., Stout, J. N., Ahtam, B., Lin, P. Y., & Grant, P. E. (2019). Exploring early human brain development with structural and physiological neuroimaging. *NeuroImage, 187*, 226–254. https://doi.org/10.1016/j.neuroimage.2018.07.041.

Wang, S. S., Kloth, A. D., & Badura, A. (2014). The cerebellum, sensitive periods, and autism. *Neuron, 83*(3), 518–532. https://doi.org/10.1016/j.neuron.2014.07.016.

Warner, V., Wickramaratne, P., & Weissman, M. M. (2008, November). The role of fear and anxiety in the familial risk for major depression: A three-generation study. *Psychological Medicine, 38* (11), 1543–1556. https://doi.org/10.1017/S0033291708002894. Epub 2008 Feb 14. PMID: 18275630; PMCID: PMC2904071.

Yehuda, R., Engel, S. M., Brand, S. R., et al. (2005). Transgenerational effects of posttraumatic stress disorder in babies of mothers exposed to the World Trade Center attacks during pregnancy. *The Journal of Clinical Endocrinology and Metabolism, 90*, 4115–4118.

Zaguri, M., & Hawlena, D. (2020). Odours of non-predatory species help prey moderate their risk assessment. *Functional Ecology, 34*(4), 830–839. https://doi.org/10.1111/1365-2435.13509.

Zanette, L. Y., White, A. F., Allen, M. C., & Clinchy, M. (2011). Perceived predation risk reduces the number of offspring songbirds produce per year. *Science, 334*(6061), 1398–1401. https://doi.org/10.1126/science.1210908.

Zanette, L.Y., Hobbs, E.C., Witterick, L.E. et al. Predator-induced fear causes PTSD-like changes in the brains and behaviour of wild animals. *Sci Rep, 9*, 11474 (2019). https://doi.org/10.1038/s41598-019-47684-6.

Chapter 2
The Role of Fear in the Founding of the United States: A Historical and Philosophical Perspective

Fear has been a driving force behind policy development and key decision points that birthed the United States of America. The country was birthed by fear. Martha Nussbaum, a philosopher, professor, and author, penned the book *The Monarchy of Fear: A Philosopher Looks at Our Political Crisis* – she wrote postelection of the United States' 45th President. She spoke of the role of fear in the election process, writing "there is a lot of fear around the US today, and this fear is often mingled with anger, blame and envy" (Nussbaum, 2018). Nussbaum goes on to highlight the depth and width of fear, referring to fear's ability to interrupt rational deliberation, usurp hope, and compromise cooperation (Nussbaum, 2018). As described in Chap. 1 of this text, fear is a primitive response that helps humans appropriately seek safety. One could describe fear as a breach of safety (real and/or perceived). Where there is lack of safety, there is survivalist behavior, and further, fear begets fear. When individuals are afraid of losing something, whether it is other people, esteem, status, position, or perception of power, they will do everything they can to prevent loss even if it involves violence and death (Jochim, 2020; Nussbaum, 2018).

In 2020, at the height of the COVID-19 public health crisis, the top 1% of the country have continued to make gains as the gap between the haves and have nots has increased exponentially (Scigliuzzo, 2021; Economist, 2020). Approximately 10% of Americans (and growing) do not know where their next meal is coming from (Cohen, 2020). Food banks are overwhelmed by the enormous need – individuals who have never experienced food lack before are now in need of their services (Cohen, 2020). Joblessness and homelessness rates have intensified (Hsu, Ashe, Silverstein, et al., 2020; Parker, Minkin, & Jesse Bennett, 2020). The virus shut down small business resulting in massive loss of health insurance – many are uninsured and/or underinsured (Kapman & Zuckerman, 2020). The main street has suffered violently, and Wall Street has continued to make tremendous gains (Scigliuzzo, 2021; Economist, 2020). Worst fears realized. It is under these conditions that fear-on-fear interactions are more likely. To be hungry, tired, chronically stressed, uncertain, and facing a major public health threat render more fear. Where there is fear there is survival – folks will do what they must in order to survive (Mobbs, Hagan, Dalgleish, Silston, & Prévost, 2015).

There is a relationship between fear, trauma, and toxic stress. Fear is a powerful emotion, driven primarily by a small almond-like structure in the midbrain called the amygdala. Where there is threat and/or perception of threat, both the brain and the body engage to help humans appropriately seek safety. The mechanism of being fearful and seeking safety involves several brain structures (see Fig. 2.1) like the amygdala (fear processing center), the hippocampus (it helps to remember the things that made you afraid so that you can avoid them in the future, insuring future

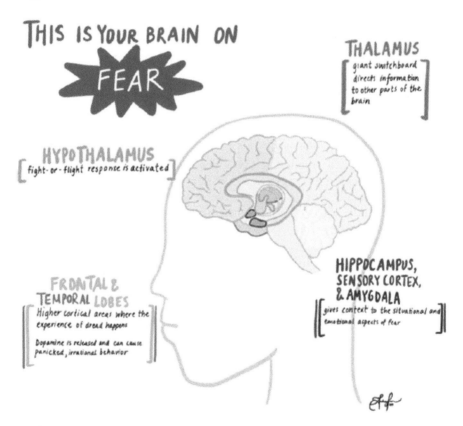

Fig. 2.1 *Brain on fear.* The mechanism of being fearful and seeking safety involves several brain structures to include the amygdala (fear processing center), the hippocampus (it helps to remember the things that made you afraid so that you can avoid them in the future, insuring future safety), the frontal and temporal lobes (allow for the cognitive awareness that something doesn't feel safe, responsible for the sense of doom), and the hypothalamus (through its relationship with the pituitary and adrenal glands produces the stress hormones required to "survive" the threat)

safety), the frontal and temporal lobes (allow for the cognitive awareness that something doesn't feel safe, responsible for the sense of doom), and the hypothalamus (through its relationship with the pituitary and adrenal glands produces the stress hormones required to "survive" the threat). Fear is designed to be a time- and threat-limited response that helps humans appropriately seek safety in the face of threat (Adolphs, 2013). When the threat leaves, the body and brain are expected to go back to a kind of baseline. Research demonstrates the connection between a prolonged fear response and trauma – a fear response that doesn't quite turn off is one way to think of the neurobiological underpinnings of trauma (Carroll, Cohen, & Marsland, 2011; Danese et al., 2008; Danese et al., 2009; Felitti et al., 1998; Franke, 2014; Gunnar, Morison, Chisholm, & Schuder, 2001; Johnson, Riley, Granger, & Riis, 2013; Meewisse, Reitsma, de Vries, Gersons, & Olff, 2007; Sherin & Nemeroff, 2011; Slopen, McLaughlin, & Shonkoff, 2014; Vermetten & Bremner, 2002).

Trauma (fear unchecked or that doesn't turn off) is related to toxic stress (Johnson et al., 2013; Meewisse et al., 2007; Slopen et al., 2014). Toxic stress, where stress hormones are not as regulated, can contribute to increased inflammation in the body resulting in higher risk for chronic medical and behavioral health conditions (Danese et al., 2008; Danese et al., 2009). This is what "fear" can do. There are myriad conditions and circumstances that result in individuals being in a locked fear state – fear can compromise judgment, undermine rational thinking, and impair executive functioning. According to the National Center for Injury Prevention and Control, Division of Violence Prevention (2020):

- Approximately 61% of adults surveyed across 25 states reported that they had experienced at least one type of ACE.
- Nearly one in six reported they had experienced four or more types of ACEs.
- The impact and implications of preventing ACEs – estimates demonstrate that up to 1.9 million cases of heart disease and 21 million cases of depression could have been potentially avoided by preventing ACEs.
- Women and several racial/ethnic minority groups were at greater risk for having experienced four or more types of ACEs.
- The economic and social costs to families, communities, and society total hundreds of billions of dollars each year (National Center for Injury Prevention and Control, Division of Violence Prevention, CDC, 2020).

Trauma is ubiquitous and can be found just about everywhere, experienced by many humans and seen in and across myriad systems. When humans are stressed, it is more likely that systems are stressed too. When humans are fearful and engaging with systems shaped by fear, fear is compounded. It is a cycle.

Let us consider the role of fear (and subsequent trauma) in shaping America and how it has contributed to persistent and deleterious societal fear and trauma.

Hope didn't build systems, fear did. The systems and policies that fear built continue to have dire and deadly consequences on entire communities and societies. When Barack Obama ran for office, he employed the platform of hope. Hope was the subtle reminder that we had been and have been driven by fear as a nation and that, in order to progress, fear must be acknowledged and reconciled and blotted out by hope. He spoke to hope as a remedy for the sins of a nation but fell short in speaking to both real and constructed fear.

2.1 A Government and Founding Documents Powerfully Shaped by Fear

Our founding documents to include the Declaration of Independence, Articles of Confederation, and the Constitution represented and codified intentional exclusion and epitomized fear. "We hold these truths to be self-evident" and "We, the people" didn't include people of color, immigrants, women, and others (Foner, 2019; Rothstein, 2018).

We hold these truths to be self-evident, that all men are created equal, that they are endowed by their Creator with certain unalienable Rights, that among these are Life, Liberty and the pursuit of Happiness. (Jefferson, 2018).

Historians like Jack Rakove in his textbook *Original Meanings: Politics and Ideas in the Making of the Constitution* (1996) contend that "we the people" was not a reference to individual rights, but about the rights of colonies – arguing that through a game of metaphorical telephone, the meaning of "all men are created equal" has been taken out of its original context (Rakove, 1996). I would posit that whether the statement referred to individuals and/or colonies, colonies were made up of individuals who possessed a moral frame and way of thinking with a predisposition for othering and devaluing. Colonies and/or individuals, the Constitution yet and still perpetuated and codified exclusion and limited who was expected to and could have a voice in democracy and government.

Of great complexity and contradiction is that pre-declaration of independence the colonies were not yet legally deemed the United States of America (Armitage, 2004; Lutz, 1989). This means that a good majority of the individuals who established and signed the Declaration of Independence were not technically born in the United States, which would render them immigrants; framers of the US Constitution were born in colonies that eventually became the United States.

Additional context surrounding the Declaration of Independence, Thomas Jefferson, Benjamin Franklin, John Adams, and others fought for independence from British control and feared being subject to a monarchy – an official announcement by a community demanding the capacity to shape and determine their own government (Cogliano, 2017; Forde, 1992; Tyron, 1948). Yet, what would become the United States was constructed by aristocracy and maintained by oligarchy – the early framers built what they feared.

Thomas Jefferson's influence and voice were predominant in the construction of the Declaration as it has been noted that he lifted myriad sections of the document from Virginia's Declaration of Rights constructed by George Mason; Section 1 of Virginia's Declaration read:

> That all men are by <u>nature equally free</u> and independent and have <u>certain inherent rights</u>, of which, when they enter into a state of society, they cannot, by any compact, deprive or divest their posterity; namely, <u>the enjoyment of life and liberty</u>, with the means of acquiring and possessing property, and <u>pursuing and obtaining happiness and safety.</u> (Virginia Convention, 1776; Lee, 1776).

The underlined sections were changed by Thomas Jefferson and added to the US Declaration of Independence. This further points to individuals (who were part of colonies) shaping policies and legislation bent toward fear and intentional exclusion. According to historian and scholar Yohuru Williams, there was evidence that Thomas Jefferson (a slave owner) placed a bid to include direct and specific language in the Declaration of Independence that condemned the British elevation of the slave trade – Thomas was overruled by the committee, and this clause of condemnation was removed (Williams, 2020). The founding fathers were fighting for freedom – just not for everyone.

Of greater interest, once the colonies moved mightily toward independence from the British, they desperately needed structure and direction for how they would proceed and govern. Men (referred to as the founding fathers) gathered to discuss the Articles of Confederation, and they brought their fears to the negotiating table. Mild hope was represented also, but mostly fear. There was keen recognition that while they were free, there existed a weak central government allowing unbalanced and dangerous power to rest with the colonial entities. Out of a desire to strengthen, organize, and unify government came the Articles of Confederation (deemed the pre-draft of the US Constitution), the inspiration for what we now understand as our Federal government. Amid the eruption of the Revolutionary War, there were 13 loosely associated American colonies (weakly linked) that desperately needed a binder in the absence of and to strongly dissociate from the British system – the Articles of Confederation were established in this context. It is estimated that the Articles were written at the height of the American Revolutionary War, between 1776 and 1777 (Merrill, 1959; Rakove, 1988). The pre-US colonists were afraid (and at one point expressed fear) of being enslaved by the British (Ammerman, 1976).

The Articles of Confederation charted/centered the components of the national government of the United States upon freedom and independence from Great Britain. The 13 Articles in brief: Article 1, established the name United States of America; Article 2, provided states independence, freedom, and power; Article 3, established that states would defend one another against hostility; Article 4, allowed movement between states; Article 5, determined stating voting power; Article 6, declared that there must be one central Army as a federal government entity and not state entity; Article 7, allowed states to elect military officials; Article 8, established a mechanism for states to contribute to the centralized/federal government system financially; Article 9, outlined that only Congress could wage war against another country, not the states; Article 10, established guidelines for executive committees; Article 11, established that at least 9/13 states had to approve any new states joining the confederation and statehood was offered to Canada; Article 12, established that all states would assume responsibility for national debt in advance of the war;

Article 13, established that all states would abide by the laws as outlined by the Confederation (Feinberg, 2002; Yale Law School, 2008).

The Articles of Confederation and subsequently the US Constitution were penned by men who in part were influenced and motivated by fear. The US Constitution reads: "we the people of the United States, in Order to form a more perfect Union, establish Justice, ensure domestic tranquility, provide for the common defense, promote the general Welfare, and secure the Blessings of Liberty to ourselves and our Posterity, do ordain and establish this Constitution for the United States of America" (US Constitution, Preamble). We the people did not include women, Black people, and/or chronically marginalized populations (Forkosch, 1968; Ratcliffe, 2013). According to some scholars, we the people was designed to benefit and buoy approximately 6% of the US population when it was written and subsequently signed in September of 1787 benefitting primarily White male property owners (Forkosch, 1968; Ratcliffe, 2013). Let's consider the men, framers, founding fathers, and the fears that drove their writing and decision-making at the time. Seven figures in review: John Adams, Benjamin Franklin, Alexander Hamilton, John Jay, Thomas Jefferson, James Madison, and George Washington played critical, substantive roles in the formation of the United States. What did they fear?

2.2   John Adams and Fear

In the summer of 1776, when the Declaration was signed, the population of the nation was estimated to have been about 2.5 million. (Today the population of the United States is more than 300 million.) The constitutional convention was held on May 25, 1787, in Philadelphia, where the core values and laws that gave birth to America were debated. The proverbial room where it happened consisted of a few powerful men who brought mostly their fears to the negotiating table.

John Adams, second president, Constitution writer and supporter, openly expressed his fear of what he called the powerful elite class in America – he was fearful that this disproportionately wealthy, powerful class posed a threat to the republic and went further to deem them a threat facing republics. Adams was concerned about executive authority undermining and obstructing the government's ability to optimally function (Mayville, 2016; "Adams Time Line", 2009; McCullough, 2008). He feared that unchecked power and influence of the rich and powerful in politics, a small number of individuals wielding incredible power over systems and nations, could destroy and divide a nation (Mayville, 2016; "Adams Time Line", 2009; McCullough, 2008).

Adams fear was accounted for in the Constitution by producing counters for power – a strong emphasis was placed on the structure centered around the idea of separation and division of powers functionally, normatively, and territorially. The Constitution broadly outlines the limitations of powers of state agencies and office holders. The spirit of the Constitution was penned to address a commitment to equitable distribution of power (political and economic) among many rather than few – referred to as an anti-oligarch constitution. Many would argue that Adams' greatest fear, that he originally attempted to protect against, has been realized and is core to the widespread suffering of many. Winters J and Page B penned a perspectives piece on oligarchy in the United States and argued that the US political system can be characterized as an oligarchy based on wealth distribution (Winters & Page, 2009). There is varied and collective argument that individuals of great wealth are more likely to possess political influence (Bottomore, 1964; Cammack, 1990; Dye, 2002; Edwards & Bourne, 2019; Oklopcic, 2019; Regilme, 2019). Look at Jeff Bezos, Bill and Melinda Gates, Mark Cuban, and Mark Zuckerberg, for example. The wealthiest 1% of families in the United States holding about 40% of all wealth and the bottom 90% of families holding less than one-quarter of all wealth (Edwards & Bourne, 2019). A New York Times piece written by Michael Tomasky in 2019 entitled "Is America Becoming an Oligarchy?: Growing inequality threatens our most basic democratic principles" highlights that economic health and equal and fair participation in the economy have always been synonymous with democracy itself as defined by John Adams and Thomas Jefferson (Tomasky, 2019). To elevate this point, Tomasky reminds us that upon Thomas Jefferson completely penning the Declaration of Independence, as a member of the Virginia House of delegates, he sponsored legislation to put an end to large inheritances being passed down across generations within families – demonstrating his core conviction that excess inherited wealth was mismatched with democracy (Tomasky, 2019).

2.3 George Washington and Fear

George Washington (a general who stopped the French from assuming Ohio and ran the British out of New York) feared that he was not good enough to be president, that he would not be able to build a republic, that the expectations of the people were far beyond his capacity to succeed in building a nation.

According to the National Archives, in 1787, George Washington attended a convention in Philadelphia, PA, to determine the future of the new country and revise the Articles of Confederation (George Washington to Benjamin Harris, National Archives, 2018; John Jay to George Washington, National Archives, 2018). Washington was the moderator over the convention, and his quiet leadership (which stemmed from his fear of being inadequate) helped to guide a group of men in constructing what we now know as the Constitution. Washington believed in central government with a single executive leader (George Washington to Benjamin Harris, National Archives, 2018; John Jay to George Washington, National Archives, 2018).

George Washington also feared demagogues – individuals who would appeal to the lowest form of humanity, capitalize on prejudice and fear to influence large masses of people (sound familiar?). Washington was afraid that if demagogues gained political power, they posed an existential and real threat to democracy (Van Cleve, 2019; Bartoloni-Tuazon, 2014; Ketchum, 1974). Constitutionally, Washington and colleagues adopted the power of impeachment (Van Cleve, 2019;

Bartoloni-Tuazon, 2014; Ketchum, 1974). There was keen recognition, at the founding of our country, that fear combined with immorality and misinformation could undo an entire democracy, and therefore this reality is mitigated constitutionally with impeachment as form of checks and balances. The Constitution's check on power spoke to an acknowledgement that freedom is most effective when prejudice and appetites are tempered. It is a process by which Congress can check power in the context of treason, bribery, and other high crimes and misdemeanors. Alexander Hamilton referred to impeachment to check the powerful when they violate public trust (Hamilton, 2012).

2.4   Benjamin Franklin and Fear

Benjamin Franklin's fear – demonstrated very early anti-immigrant sentiment with his profound fear that individuals of German ancestry would overtake American and fundamentally change and threaten American values and republic (CATO Institute, 2018; Davis, 2010; Yglesias, 2008; Frantz, 1998). Fear is incredibly powerful as it can inspire irrational and contradictory thinking. By way of reminder, the founders of the United States were immigrants and/or born to parents of immigrants. However, in a twist of fate, circa 1855, Benjamin Franklin (of immigrant status himself) expressed grave concern about Germans' presence in North America. Part of his letter read: "Those who come hither are generally of the most ignorant stupid sort of their own nation; and as few of the English understand the German language, and few of their children in the country learn English; they import many books from Germany..." (Franklin, 1970; Frantz, 1998; Hodgson, 1991). Franklin was an early model for how to "other" as he emphasized the word alien as he referred to Germans. Bringing his fear to the table, Benjamin Franklin made certain that laws were designed to control immigration. Eventually, Franklin was able to speak to the importance of immigration as a means of growth for the nation, conceding that he was not completely against German immigration, but wanted to make certain that there were predictable levers of their population growth in the Americas (CATO Institute Policy Report, 2018).

2.5   Alexander Hamilton and Fear

Alexander Hamilton's fears – that America would not have a robustly functional central government or a modern economy (Hamilton, Madison, & Jay, 2009; Harold & Cooke, 1957; Moramarco, 1967). Hamilton feared that if ultimate power rested with the states, the nation's ability to be economically upwardly mobile would be compromised (Hamilton et al., 2009; Harold & Cooke, 1957; Moramarco, 1967). It is this fear that inspired the Federalist papers and a fierce drive to prioritize a federal government in the construction of the US Constitution. In 1788, three men wrote urgently to inspire the ratification of the US Constitution. Authors Alexander Hamilton, James Madison, and John Jay had a core thesis that decentralization of power would result in a weak, ineffective, and vulnerable government that would be at the mercy of the world (Hamilton et al., 2009). The Federalist Papers were a direct response to the Articles of Confederation, which Hamilton, Madison, and Jay argued didn't go far enough in terms of procuring and protecting American power, influence, and interest (Hamilton et al., 2009). They made a robust argument for a centralized, federal government. The Federalist Papers (all 85 essays) were a critical persuasive tool that aided in the ratification of the US Constitution.

2.6 James Madison, John Jay, and Fear

James Madison's fear – a breakup of the union and national bankruptcy. The fear was tempered with a desire to have an institutional framework in place, such as a strong central government and a federal banking system. John Jay fear – disunity among the colonies and that too much independence would result in violence. Jay held the core conviction that the only conditions under which America would thrive and lead is if it were unified. Jay, along with Hamilton, penned a few of the Federalist Papers and believed that a centralized-federal government was critical, and so it is.

2.7 Thomas Jefferson and Fear

Thomas Jefferson feared the concentrated, monopolizing power – a threat to democracy (Mayer, 1994). Jefferson feared that banks and institutions would overpower and overwhelm the power of the people. Jefferson spoke about the importance of centering and fearing the people as a form of a good government and a means of tempering concentrated, monopolizing power (Malone, 1974; Mayer, 1994; Nock, 1926).

Each of the founding fathers' fear had a core thread – the fear of concentrated, monopolizing power crushing democracy. The preamble to the Constitution represents a structured communication to calm and temper the fear as it starts with "We the people."

We the People of the United States, in Order to form a more perfect Union, establish Justice, insure domestic Tranquility, provide for the common defense, promote the general Welfare, and secure the Blessings of Liberty to ourselves and our Posterity, do ordain and establish this Constitution for the United States of America. ("The Constitution of the United States," Preamble).

Fear or being overpowered was accentuated by individual desire to maintain power – natural contradictions and conflicts arise. While fears of demagogues, immigrants, oligarchy, and monarchy were central themes among the framers, there was little room to recognize that they themselves represented the few, their power was concentrated, and they had profound influence in their respective states and what would become the United States. In some sense, they were what they feared – power personified and concentrated.

Through the process of time, historians, philosophers, and sociologists would point out that the founding documents excluded so many individuals, groups, and communities. While there was a knowing that the people should be empowered and centered (as stated by many of the original framers), the original ratified construction of the US Constitution forgot about the people, which is why states came back with feedback that suggested amendments be adopted. Circa the fall of 1789, the first round of amendments was submitted/introduced by the First Congress – these first ten amendments are what we now understand to be the Bill of Rights and were ratified on December 5, 1791. They surefire individual basic rights and civil liberties that protect US citizens and included things like the right to free speech, assembly, religion, and press – essentially to allow US citizens to have voice. This voice would be another mechanism to temper monopolistic, concentrated power and move the country closer to adhering to its preamble "we the people."

The question of citizenship – who was considered a citizen, who could participate in democracy – was limited. The legislative, constitutional walls of exclusion were thick, wide, and impermeable to some. Upon the founding of the United States of America, slavery was still legal and active. As noted earlier in this chapter, framers like Thomas Jefferson and Benjamin Franklin both owned slaves (Freehling, 1972). Alexander Hamilton had moral reservations about slavery (Sowell, 2013; Pettit, 2002); however, history would have it that he did broker slave transactions for his wife's family. How can a group of men be thought leaders centering the rights of people and reducing human suffering yet would participate in such dehumanizing acts?

Slavery was on what is now called the US shores well before the founding of the country in 1776 is outlined by myriad historians (Berlin, 2004; Tetlow, 2002; Finkelman, 2001; Morgan, 2000; Berry, 1988; Freehling, 1972). Unfortunately, slavery was a European practice that long preceded America (Eltis, 1993). Europeans, inspired by Greeks and Romans, justified slavery as a means of punishing who they deemed as prisoners of war (Fenoaltea, 1984; Tarn, 1952; Watson, 1987; Trümper, 2009). They felt that coerced labor and maltreatment were better than death or being killed. Of relevance to this textbook on fear and the fear that systems built, slaves were core to the economic success of the southern colonies as they were needed to work in rice, tobacco, and sugarcane fields. It is estimated in 1745–1750 that 25% of the population in American colonies (with an estimated total population of ~1.5 million circa 1750) were Black slaves (Menard, 2000; Wells, 1974).

2.8   The Inhumanity of Slavery and Fear

When the conditions under which Black slaves were brought to the Americas is considered, it is difficult not to appreciate the inhumanity, violence, profound disregard for psychological, physical and emotional safety and pain inflicted. Slavery was a known entity as it was accepted and violently perpetuated by Great Britain in the early fifteenth and sixteenth centuries. While the founding fathers demonstrated their commitment to move away from the monarchy and rule of the British, they did not abandon all British practices to include slavery. Slavery, the ultimate dehumanizing display of profoundly sick power, persisted in the colonies and then in the Americas and among some of the founding fathers. The fear of allowing slaves to be free and participate in the larger global economy meant that the South would lose economic power – fear of any type of loss breeds greater fear and hate. It took a Civil War and the political will of persons like Abraham Lincoln (a former slave owner who eventually signed the Emancipation Proclamation to free slaves – it just gets more and more complicated). Lincoln was elected in 1860 – the election was controversial and divisive. Seven of the Southern states withdrew from the union and formed Confederate States of America. The base of the Southern economy was slavery; they feared that the end of slavery would place a hole in their economic prosperity which translated into power. In 1861, the Civil War commenced and was representative of the growing differences between Northern and Southern states' view on slavery, the right of states, and expansion. In 1863, Lincoln issued an executive order in the form of the Emancipation Proclamation which mandated the freeing of slaves in Confederate states during the Civil War, but it wasn't enacted and didn't outlaw slavery completely. The Civil War lasted four long years, ending in 1865, culminating in significant death (over half million dead and/or injured) and the Confederate surrendering. One of the first acts by Lincoln was to finish what he started, to codify the precepts of the Emancipation Proclamation through the ratification of the 13th Amendment on January 31, 1865, abolishing slavery (making slavery illegal). Less than three months after ratifying the 13th Amendment, Lincoln was assassinated on April 15, 1865. The chaos of his death, the leadership gap, and the desperate need to pull a divided country back together threw us into what we now know to be the "Reconstruction Period" – there were some who believed that Southern states should be punished for withdrawing, and others were of the mind that the country just needed to get back on one accord. President Andrew Jackson succeeded Lincoln and had to determine how to reconcile with what were formerly their enemies (their Southern neighbors and counterparts). The Reconstruction Acts of 1867 established a process by which Southern states could reenter the union, and in 1868, the 14th Amendment granted Black slaves' citizenship (equal protection under the law), and subsequently in 1870, the 15th Amendment was ratified which granted Black men the right to vote. The 13th, 14th, and 15th have been deemed "Reconstruction Amendments" by historians – it is explained that while the Bill of Rights protected people from government, the "Reconstruction Amendments" protected people from the government of their states.

It took ammendments to the Constitution (which was constructed as the law of the land) to effectively widen the bench of inclusion for Black slaves and women. Women too were excluded from the original "we the people" as their subsequent constitutional inclusion came through in the form of the 19th Amendment in the 1920s. Some states were slow to fully adopt the laws of the land.

In 1877, when Federal troops withdrew, many of the states defaulted to pre-Civil War/Confederacy conditions. Many Southern states annulled Black voting rights, interstate travel for Blacks was restricted, and economic and housing discrimination and interference increased.

Fear grew big and overwhelmed White southerners. The appearance of segregation and "Jim Crowism" and the Ku Klux Klan was robust. The intentional, inhumane murdering of Black people through lynching peaked, and the rhetoric of fear took root. The fight for citizenship and inclusion for Blacks was prominent from the end of Reconstruction through the Civil Rights Movement of the 1950s–1960s to the present day.

The question that is worthy of deeper exploration is what were folks so afraid of? There was literal panic that a way of living and thriving would be compromised if Blacks and other marginalized groups could participate in opportunities of economic advancement. In other words, fear and lack and loss of power (perceived and real) were critical drivers of inhumane, unjust behavior, policies, and practices. The answer might be found again in Martha Nussbaum's dissertation on the monarchy of fear. Speaking of fear, Nussbaum sums it up nicely: "It can consequently seem all too attractive to convert that sense of panic and impotence into blame and the 'othering' of outsider groups" (Nussbaum, 2018). Put differently, fear has traditionally and historically been the default, convenient, and attractive driver. Unfortunately, the way Europeans and Whites associated power (as modeled by the Greeks, Romans, and the British) and maintenance thereof is through the subjugation of persons they deemed mattered less. There has always been fear cloaked in a drive to maintain power and status.

2.9   Persistence of Fear in State Constitutions, Laws, Policies, and Practices: The Oregon Story in Brief

As mentioned, several states rolled back federal protections constitutionally outlawing Blacks and other marginalized groups. I am from the State of Oregon, so will employ Oregon as a case example for states that were slow to adopt federal laws and mandates in the areas of capacity to live in the state and own property and equal protection under the law to voting rights. To give greater context: as noted earlier in this chapter, the Reconstruction era from 1865 to 1876 represented the rebuilding of America post-Civil War, but there was legislative, systemic exclusion and marginalization of specific groups. The rise of Jim Crowism began and lasted up until the period of the Civil Rights Movement. Before the Black Lives Matter Movement, there was the Harlem Renaissance, Langston Hughes' *I too, am America* (1920s–1930s), which sociologists and historians would contend was a period where Black citizens, through art and poetry, were asking to be seen, heard, and included. Half a century after the ratification of the 13th Amendment, people of color were still imploring to be included. The Civil Rights Movement of 1965 (not that long ago) helped to swing the door wide open for women and other marginalized groups. Almost 200 years after the abolishment of slavery and there are still disproportionate groups of individuals in this country begging to be included.

Oregon decided to move at its own pace, fear was centered. In 1844, the provisional government of the territory passed a law banning slavery and, at the same time, required any African-American in Oregon to leave the territory. In 1857, Oregon adopted a state constitution that banned Black people from coming to the state, residing in the state, or holding property in the state (Bancroft & Victor, 1886, 1888; Brownell, 1962; Dodds, 1977). Oregon Statehood granted, February 14, 1859 – explicitly forbade Black people from living in its borders (and was the only state to do so) (McLagan and the Oregon Black History Project, 1980; Dodds, 1977; Brownell, 1962; Bancroft & Victor, 1886, 1888). In 1922, Governor Walter M. Pierce (a Democrat) was an open, vocal Klan supporter (and was photographed with Klansmen) (Camhi, 2020; Mangum, 2008). In 1926, Black exclusion laws were repealed in Oregon (McLagan and the Oregon Black History Project, 1980; Little, 1978). In the early 1940s – World War II – African-Americans came to Oregon to work in shipyards (Little & Weiss, 1978). In 1948, the Columbia River flooded – Vanport Flood – wiping out a predominantly African-American community (approximately 6300), unnecessarily. Modern day would be likened to Hurricane Katrina (lack of infrastructure, lack of political will) (Geiling, 2015; Maben, 1987). The 13th, 14th, and 15th amendments passed, which meant that Oregon's state laws were superseded by national law; however, Oregon did not ratify the 14th Amendment to give Black people equal protection under the law until 1973. Oregon didn't ratify the 15th Amendment to give Black people the right to vote until 1959 (which made it one of the six states that refused to ratify the amendment when it initially passed at the federal level). In the 1960s, Portland, Oregon, like many urban cities at this time where predominantly Black families and communities lived, undertook "urban renewal" projects that strategically displaced Black people (most prominent is the building of the Legacy Emanuel Hospital and the I-5 corridor) (Pedro-Xuncan, 2019; Goodling, Green, & McClintock, 2015; Bates, 2013; Gibson, 2007). It wasn't until the early 2000s, under the leadership of the first Black woman to serve in the Oregon State legislature, that racist and discriminatory language was removed from the State Constitution (Camhi, 2020). This is how present, close, and active fear is and how robustly it lingers.

2.10   Fear Begets Fear – The Chinese Exclusion Act

There are several unfortunate examples in history of hate undergirded by fear-inspired policies and practices composed to mitigate irrational fear. Chinese and Japanese migrants labored as railroad and agricultural specialist in the late nineteenth and twentieth centuries (National Archives, Chinese Immigration and the Chinese in the United States). There was fear that Asian immigrants would competitively take jobs from Americans and taint the cultural makeup of the country (Ong, 1993). Policies and practices were constructed to mitigate these fears. The Chinese Exclusion Act of 1882, designed to reduce the arrival of Chinese immigrants to the United States (namely, in California), suspended immigration for almost a decade and deemed Chinese immigrants disallowed for naturalization (Dufour, 2012; Ferrelly, 1894; Li, 2007). Then there was the Geary Act of 1892 (inspired by Thomas J. Geary, a Californian congressman), which extended exclusion for an additional decade and required Chinese residents to carry special certificates of residence issued by the Internal Revenue Service (National Archives, Chinese Immigration and the Chinese in the United States). In 1893, the Geary Act was upheld by the Supreme Court in the landmark Fong Yue Ting v. United States case – Chinese immigration was permanently illegal (National Archives, Chinese Immigration and the Chinese in the United States). In 1924, the Immigration Act was passed. It wasn't until 1943, through the Magnuson Act, that anti-Chinese immigration laws were abolished (National Archives, Chinese Immigration and the Chinese in the United States).

Anti-immigrant sentiment was seen in Benjamin Franklin (one of the founding fathers) with the Germans – his sentiment was driven by fear at the inception of the United States. That similar and familiar fear permeated policies and practices and persisted through the centuries, at the state and federal levels. That similar and familiar fear can be identified in current anti-immigrant sentiment. Myriad literature link fear as a driver of anti-immigrant sentiment (Avdagic & Savage, 2019; Buzby, 2018; Hirschman, 2014; Huntington, 2004; Malhotra, Margarlit, & Mo, 2013; Meseguer & Kemmerling, 2018; Wilson, 1999). Americans fear loss of American identity which includes maintaining English as the core language, fear of job loss and economic competition, and fear that the country will be "fundamentally changed" in a way that will exclude them (Bouvier, 1992; Brimelow, 1995; Huntington, 2004). Historically, there have been two central components of anti-immigrant sentiment to include fear over job competition and the fiscal burden – manifest as resentment over having to pay for the social services used by immigrants and their families. A study by Hainmueller and Hiscox demonstrated that job/economic competition may be less salient compared to the cultural components that shape anti-immigrant sentiment. Further that attitudes are more favorable toward high-skilled versus low-skilled immigrants (I find this stratification troubling, but it does offer a window into the depth and width of strongly clung-to ideologies) (Hainmueller & Hiscox, 2007). The study was conducted in late 2007, early 2008, and included 2285 American citizens – it found that approximately one third of all people strongly disagreed with the United States having low-skilled immigrants enter the country (Hainmueller & Hiscox, 2007), whereas one third of Americans strongly agreed with having high-skilled immigrants (Hainmueller & Hiscox, 2007). The level of valuing and devaluing demonstrated in this study is fear-based: the fear of losing something – status, legal, cultural, economic, and social dominance. This level of sentiment was prominent during the 2016 US Presidential elections where #45 described Latinos as rapists and gang members and Haiti and African countries as s-hole countries and rallied his base when he proclaimed that not only would he build a border wall between the United States and Mexico, but that he would make Mexico pay for such wall. We see history repeating itself as demonstrated by fear and building walls. East Germans were kept in by the Berlin Wall, and it kept what were perceived as threats out. The Berlin Wall was a formidable symbol for the Cold War. Walls are built to keep people out and offer the illusion of safety and protection for those inside the wall. Walls built by hate and fear tend to propagate more fear for those inside and outside of them.

This chapter began by highlighting men, the founding fathers of the United States of America who brought some hope, but mostly their fear, to the negotiating table. Their individual and collective fear gave birth to and shaped the culture of America. Fear was represented constitutionally by the initial exclusion of Black citizens, women, and immigrants – it took amendments to initiate the process of mitigating some of the fear. The fear gave rise to more fear as evidenced by the Reconstruction era, rise of Jim Crowism, and the Civil Rights Movement up to the Black Lives Matter Movement of the twenty-first century. Isn't it ironic that few men of influence (at the time) determined the trajectory of America and then feared that few individuals would hoard power and deviate from democracy? The irony and the contradiction. Irrationality is at the center of fear. Black citizens and immigrants live in constant fear of being harmed and even killed. This level of fear exists because of a constructed fear that includes racism but was birthed in 1776. Constructed fear is the fear established by humans in their daily lives, and it helps make meaning out of experiences (good and/or not so good) (Glassner, 1999). Whether the fear is constructed and/or real, it has powerfully impacted people, policies, practices, laws, and societies from the inception of the United States of America to present day. Fear-on-fear interactions are the unspoken, profound threat to American democracy, government, and politics, and these interactions must be addressed. The possibility for sustained positive change might come from identifying and acknowledging fear in people, systems, and society.

References

Adams Time Line. (2009). *Massachusetts historical society. Archived from the original on March 24, 2009.* Retrieved from http://www.masshist.org/2012/adams/printable-timeline February 9, 2021.

Adolphs, R. (2013). The biology of fear. *Current Biology: CB, 23*(2), R79–R93. https://doi.org/10.1016/j.cub.2012.11.055.

Ammerman, D. (1976). The British Constitution and the American Revolution: A Failure of Precedent. *William & Mary Law Review, 17*, 473. https://scholarship.law.wm.edu/wmlr/vol17/iss3/4.

Armitage, D. (2004, April). The declaration of independence in world context. *OAH Magazine of History, 18*(3), 61–66. https://doi.org/10.1093/maghis/18.3.61.

Avdagic, S., & Savage, L. (2019). Negativity Bias: The impact of framing of immigration on welfare state support in Germany, Sweden and the UK. *British Journal of Political Science*, 1–22. https://doi.org/10.1017/S0007123419000395.

Bancroft, H. H., & Victor, F. F. (1886). *History of Oregon, Volume One*. The History Company.

Bancroft, H. H., & Victor, F. F. (1888). *History of Oregon, Volume Two*. The History Company.

Bartoloni-Tuazon, K. (2014). *For fear of an elective king: George Washington and the presidential title controversy of 1789*. Ithaca, NY/London: Cornell University Press. Retrieved December 12, 2020, from http://www.jstor.org/stable/10.7591/j.ctt1287fj1

Bates, L. (2013). *Gentrification and displacement study: implementing an equitable inclusive development strategy in the context of gentrification*. Commissioned by the City of Portland's Bureau of Planning and Sustainability. Retrieved from www.portlandoregon.gov/bps/article/454027

Berlin, I. (2004). American slavery in history and memory and the search for social justice. *The Journal of American History, 90*(4), 1251–1268. https://doi.org/10.2307/3660347.

Berry, M. F. (1988). Slavery, the constitution, and the founding fathers. *Update on Law Related Education, 12*(3).

Bottomore, T. B. (1964). *Elites and society*. New York: Penguin Books.

Bouvier, L. F. (1992). *Peaceful invasions*. Lanham, MD: University Press of America.

Brimelow, P. (1995). *Alien nation: Common sense about America's immigration disaster*. New York: Random House.

Brownell, J. (1962). *Negroes in Oregon before the civil war*. Oregon Historical Society. Unpublished Manuscript.

Buzby, A. (2018). Locking the borders: Exclusion in the theory and practice of immigration in America. *International Migration Review, 52*(1), 273–298. https://doi.org/10.1111/imre.12291.

Camhi, T. (2020, June 9) *A racist history shows why Oregon is still so white*. OPB. Retrieved from https://www.opb.org/news/article/oregon-white-history-racist-foundations-black-exclusion-laws/ February 10, 2021.

Cammack, P. (1990). A critical assessment of the elite paradigm. *American Sociological Review, 55*(3), 415–420.

Carroll, J. E., Cohen, S., & Marsland, A. L. (2011). Early childhood socioeconomic status is associated with circulating interleukin-6 among mid-life adults. *Brain, Behavior, and Immunity, 25*(7), 1468–1474.

CATO Institute Policy Report. (2018). *Immigration: Setting the record straight*. Retrieved from https://www.cato.org/policy-report/january/february-2018/immigration-setting-record-straight on February 10, 2021.

Cogliano, F. (2017). John Adams and the fear of oligarchy; John Adams's Republic: the one, the few, and the many. *Intellectual History Review, 27*(2), 279–282. https://doi.org/10.1080/17496977.2017.1292640.

Cohen, S. (2020, December 7). *Millions of hungry Americans turn to food banks for 1st time*. Associated Press. Retrieved from https://apnews.com/article/race-and-ethnicity-hunger-coronavirus-pandemic-4c7f1705c6d8ef5bac241e6cc8e331bb February 9, 2021.

Danese, A., Moffitt, T. E., Harrington, H., Milne, B. J., Polanczyk, G., Pariante, C. M., Poulton, R., & Caspi, A. (2009). Adverse childhood experiences and adult risk factors for age-related disease: Depression, inflammation, and clustering of metabolic risk markers. *Archives of Pediatrics & Adolescent Medicine, 163*. https://doi.org/10.1001/archpediatrics.2009.214.

Danese, A., Moffitt, T. E., Pariante, C. M., Ambler, A., Poulton, R., & Caspi, A. (2008). Elevated inflammation levels in depressed adults with a history of childhood maltreatment. *Archives of General Psychiatry, 65*(4), 409–415.

Davis, K. C. (2010). *Anti-immigrant rage is older than the nation itself.* National Public Radio. Retrieved from https://www.npr.org/templates/story/story.php?storyId=126565611 on February 10, 2021.

Dodds, G. B. (1977). *Oregon: A history.* W. W. Norton & Company.

Dufour, J. Comp. (2012, November–December). Case Study of Chinese Exclusion Act Enforcement. *Social Education, 76*(6), 306–311.

Dye, T. R. (2002). *Who's running America? The bush restoration* (7th ed.). Englewood Cliffs, NJ: Prentice-Hall.

Edwards, C., & Bourne, R. (2019, November 5). *Exploring wealth inequality* (Policy analysis no. 881). Washington, DC: Cato Institute. https://doi.org/10.36009/PA.881.

Eltis, D. (1993). Europeans and the rise and fall of African slavery in the Americas: An interpretation. *The American Historical Review, 98*(5), 1399–1423. https://doi.org/10.2307/2167060.

Feinberg, B. S. (2002). *The Articles of Confederation: The first constitution of the United States.* Brookfield, CT: Twenty-First Century Books.

Felitti, V. J., Anda, R. F., Nordenberg, D., Williamson, D. F., Spitz, A. M., Edwards, V., Koss, M. P., & Marks, J. S. (1998). Relationship of childhood abuse and household dysfunction to many of the leading causes of death in adults. *American Journal of Preventive Medicine, 14*, 245–258.

Fenoaltea, S. (1984). Slavery and supervision in comparative perspective: A model. *The Journal of Economic History, 44*(3), 635–668. Retrieved February 10, 2021, from http://www.jstor.org/stable/2124146

Ferrelly, M. J. (1894). The United States Chinese Exclusion Act. *American Law Review, 28*, 734.

Finkelman, P. (2001). *The founders and slavery: Little ventured, little gained* (Vol. 13, p. 413). Yale J.L. & Human.

Foner, E. (2019, September 17). *The second founding: How the civil war and reconstruction remade the constitution* (304 pages). W. W. Norton & Company. History.

Forde, S. (1992). Benjamin Franklin's autobiography and the education of America. *The American Political Science Review, 86*(2), 357–368. https://doi.org/10.2307/1964225.

Forkosch, M. D. (1968). Who are the "People" in the Preamble to the Constitution. *Case Western Reserve Law Review, 19*, 644. Available at: https://scholarlycommons.law.case.edu/caselrev/vol19/iss3/8.

Franke, H. A. (2014). Toxic stress: Effects, prevention and treatment. *Children (Basel, Switzerland), 1*(3), 390–402. https://doi.org/10.3390/children1030390.

Franklin, B. (1970). Observations concerning the increase of mankind, peopling of countries, Etc. *Perspectives in Biology and Medicine, 13*(4), 469–475. https://doi.org/10.1353/pbm.1970.0036.

Frantz, J. (1998). Franklin and the Pennsylvania Germans. *Pennsylvania History: A Journal of Mid-Atlantic Studies, 65*(1), 21–34. Retrieved February 10, 2021, from http://www.jstor.org/stable/27774077.

Freehling, W. (1972). The founding fathers and slavery. *The American Historical Review, 77*(1), 81–93. https://doi.org/10.2307/1856595.

Geiling, N. (2015, February 18). *How Oregon's Second Largest City Vanished in a Day: A 1948 flood washed away the WWII housing project Vanport—but its history still informs Portland's diversity.* Smithsonian Magazine. Retrieved from https://www.smithsonianmag.com/history/vanport-oregon-how-countrys-largest-housing-project-vanished-day-180954040/ February 10, 2021.

George Washington to Benjamin Harrison, 18 January 1784, *Founders Online*, National Archives, last modified June 13, 2018, http://founders.archives.gov/documents/Washington/04-01-02-0039.

Gibson, K. (2007). Bleeding Albina: A history of community disinvestment, 1940–2000. *Transforming Anthropology, 15*(1), 3–25.

Glassner, B. (1999). The Construction of Fear. *Qualitative Sociology, 22*, 301–309. https://doi.org/10.1023/A:1022055604426.

Goodling, E., Green, J., & McClintock, N. (2015). Uneven development of the sustainable city: Shifting capital in Portland, Oregon. *Urban Geography, 36*(4), 504–527. https://doi.org/10.108 0/02723638.2015.1010791.

Gunnar, M. R., Morison, S. J., Chisholm, K., & Schuder, M. (2001). Salivary cortisol levels in children adopted from Romanian orphanages. *Development and Psychopathology, 13*(3), 611–628.

Hainmueller, J., & Hiscox, M. (2007). Educated preferences: Explaining attitudes toward immigration in Europe. *International Organization, 61,* 399–442.

Hamilton, A. (2012). *The federalist papers.* Dutton/Signet.

Hamilton, A., Madison, J., & Jay, J. (2009). Federalist No. 84. In *The federalist papers.* New York: Palgrave Macmillan. https://doi.org/10.1057/9780230102019_53.

Harold, C. S., & Cooke, J. E. (1957). The papers of Alexander Hamilton. *The Historian, 19*(2), 168–181. https://doi.org/10.1111/j.1540-6563.1957.tb01801.x.

Hirschman, C. (2014). Immigration to the United States: Recent trends and future prospects. *Malaysian journal of economic studies: journal of the Malaysian Economic Association and the Faculty of Economics and Administration, University of Malaya, 51*(1), 69–85.

Hodgson, D. (December 1991). Benjamin Franklin on population: From policy to theory. *Population and Development Review, 17*(4), 639–661.

Hsu, H. E., Ashe, E. M., Silverstein, M., et al. (2020). Race/ethnicity, underlying medical conditions, homelessness, and hospitalization status of adult patients with COVID-19 at an urban safety-net medical center — Boston, Massachusetts, 2020. *MMWR Morbidity and Mortality Weekly Report, 69,* 864–869. https://doi.org/10.15585/mmwr.mm6927a3externalicon.

Huntington, S. L. (2004). *Who are we? The challenges to America's national identity.* New York: Simon and Schuster.

Jefferson, T. (2018). *The papers of Thomas Jefferson, volume 1: 1760 to 1776* (p. 315). Princeton University Press. ISBN 978-0-691-18466-1

Jochim, J. (2020). The monarchy of fear: A philosopher looks at our political crisis. *Contemp Polit Theory, 19,* 149–152. https://doi.org/10.1057/s41296-018-00305-9.

John Jay to George Washington, 27 June 1786, *Founders Online,* National Archives, last modified June 13, 2018, http://founders.archives.gov/documents/Washington/04-04-02-0129.

Johnson, S. B., Riley, A. W., Granger, D. A., & Riis, J. (2013). The science of early life toxic stress for pediatric practice and advocacy. *Pediatrics, 131*(2), 319–327. https://doi.org/10.1542/peds.2012-0469.

Kapman M, Zuckerman S (2020, November 6). *ACA offers protection as the COVID-19 pandemic erodes employer health insurance coverage.* Urban Institute. Retrieved from https://www.rwjf.org/en/library/research/2020/11/aca-offers-protection-as-the-covid-19-pandemic-erodes-employer-health-insurance-coverage.html February 9, 2021.

Ketchum, R. M. (1974). *The world of George Washington.* American Heritage Publishing Company, Inc.: New York.

Lee, T. L. Virginia Declaration of Rights, 1776. Accession 21539. Personal papers collection. The Library of Virginia, Richmond, Va. 23219.

Li, C. Y. (2007). The other Great Wall: A study of the enforcement of the Chinese Exclusion Act. *Honors College Theses.* Paper 63. http://digitalcommons.pace.edu/honorscollege_theses/63

Little, W. A., & Weiss, J. E. (1978). *Blacks in Oregon: A statistical and historical 87 report.* Portland: Portland State University.

Lutz, D. S. (1989, Winter). The declaration of independence as part of an American national compact. *Publius: The Journal of Federalism, 19*(1), 41–58. https://doi.org/10.1093/oxfordjournals.pubjof.a037772.

Maben, M. (1987). *Vanport.* Portland, OR: Oregon Historical Society Press.

Malhotra, N., Margarlit, Y., & Mo, C. (2013). Economic explanations for opposition to immigration: Distinguishing between prevalence and magnitude. *American Journal of Political Science, 57*(2), 391–410.

Malone, D. (1974). *Jefferson and his time.* Boston: Little, Brown and Company.

Mangum, K. (2008). The Ku Klux Klan are still scrapping here: African American response to the Oregon Klan, 1922–1924. In W. H. Alexander, C. L. Newby-Alexander, & C. H. Ford (Eds.), *Voices from within the veil: African Americans and the experience of democracy* (pp. 254–286). Newcastle Upon Tyne, UK: Cambridge Scholars Publishing.

Mayer, D. N. (1994). *The constitutional thought of Thomas Jefferson.* Charlottesville: University Press of Virginia.

Mayville, L. (2016). *John Adams and the Fear of American Oligarchy.* Princeton/Oxford: Princeton University Press. https://doi.org/10.2307/j.ctt1q1xr8h.

McCullough, D. G. (2008). *John Adams.* New York: Simon and Schuster Paperbacks.

McLagan, Elizabeth, and Oregon Black History Project. (1980). *A peculiar paradise: A history of Blacks in Oregon, 1778–1940.* Georgian Press.

Meewisse, M. L., Reitsma, J. B., de Vries, G. J., Gersons, B. P., & Olff, M. (2007). Cortisol and post-traumatic stress disorder in adults: Systematic review and meta-analysis. *The British Journal of Psychiatry, 191,* 387–392.

Menard, R. (2000). Slave demography in the lowcountry, 1670–1740: From frontier society to plantation regime. *The South Carolina Historical Magazine, 101*(3), 190–213. Retrieved February 10, 2021, from http://www.jstor.org/stable/27570447.

Merrill, J. (1959). *The articles of confederation* (p. 37). University of Wisconsin Press. ISBN 978-0-299-00204-6.

Meseguer, C., & Kemmerling, A. (2018). what do you fear? Anti-immigrant sentiment in Latin America. *International Migration Review., 52*(1), 236–272. https://doi.org/10.1111/imre.12269.

Mobbs, D., Hagan, C. C., Dalgleish, T., Silston, B., & Prévost, C. (2015). The ecology of human fear: survival optimization and the nervous system. *Frontiers in Neuroscience, 9,* 55. https://doi.org/10.3389/fnins.2015.00055.

Moramarco, F. (1967). Hamilton and the historians: The economic program in retrospect. *Midcontinent American Studies Journal, 8*(1), 34–43. Retrieved February 10, 2021, from http://www.jstor.org/stable/40640678.

Morgan, K. (2000). George Washington and the problem of slavery. *Journal of American Studies, 34*(2), 279–301. Retrieved February 10, 2021, from http://www.jstor.org/stable/27556810

National Archives. Chinese immigration and the Chinese in *the United States.* Retrieved from https://www.archives.gov/research/chinese-americans/guide February 10, 2021.

National Center for Injury Prevention and Control, Centers for Disease Control and Prevention. (2020). *Adverse Childhood Experiences (ACE's).* Retrieved from https://www.cdc.gov/violenceprevention/acestudy/.

Nock, A. J. (1926). *Jefferson.* New York: Brace &.

Nussbaum, M. C. (2018). *The monarchy of fear: A philosopher looks at our political crisis* (p. 272). New York: Simon & Schuster.

Oklopcic, Z. (2019). Imagined ideologies: Populist figures, liberalist projections, and the horizons of constitutionalism. *German Law Journal, 20*(2), 219.

Ong, H. B. (1993). *Making and remaking Asian America through immigration policy 1850–1990.* Stanford: Stanford University Press.

Parker, K., Minkin, R., & Jesse Bennett, J. (2020, September 24). *Economic fallout from COVID-19 continues to hit lower-income Americans the hardest.* Pew Research Center. Retrieved from https://www.pewsocialtrends.org/2020/09/24/economic-fallout-from-covid-19-continues-to-hit-lower-income-americans-the-hardest/ February 9, 2021.

Pedro-Xuncax, D. J. (2019). Portland Oregon's "right to return" policy & its relation to urban renewal: A community psychology approach. *University Honors Theses,* paper 715. https://doi.org/10.15760/honors.732

Pettit PhD, M. H. (2002). Slavery, Abolition, and Columbia University. *Journal of Archival Organization, 1*(4), 77–89. https://doi.org/10.1300/J201v01n04_06.

Rakove, J. N. (1988). The Collapse of the Articles of Confederation. In J. J. Barlow, L. W. Levy, & K. Masugi (Eds.), *The American founding: Essays on the formation of the constitution* (pp. 225–245).

Rakove, J. N. (1996). *Original meanings: Politics and ideas in the making of the constitution*. New York: Alfred A. Knopf.

Ratcliffe, D. (2013). The Right to Vote and the Rise of Democracy, 1787–1828. *Journal of the Early Republic, 33*(2), 219–254. Retrieved February 9, 2021, from http://www.jstor.org/stable/24768843

Regilme, S. S. F. (2019, May). Constitutional order in oligarchic democracies: Neoliberal rights versus socio-economic rights. *Law, Culture and the Humanities*. https://doi.org/10.1177/1743872119854142.

Rothstein, R. (2018). *The color of law*. Liveright Publishing Corporation.

Scigliuzzo, D. (2021, January 17). *The rich are minting money in the pandemic like never before*. Bloomberg Wealth. Retrieved from https://www.bloomberg.com/news/articles/2021-01-17/the-rich-are-minting-money-in-the-pandemic-like-never-before February 9, 2021.

Sherin, J. E., & Nemeroff, C. B. (2011). Post-traumatic stress disorder: The neurobiological impact of psychological trauma. *Dialogues in Clinical Neuroscience, 13*(3), 263–278. https://doi.org/10.31887/DCNS.2011.13.2/jsherin.

Slopen, N., McLaughlin, K. A., & Shonkoff, J. P. (2014). Interventions to improve cortisol regulation in children: A systematic review. *Pediatrics, 133*, 312–326. https://doi.org/10.1542/peds.2013-1632.

Sowell, J. (2013). *The Alexander Hamilton and Slavery Debate* (Vol. 38). History Class Publications. https://scholarlycommons.obu.edu/history/38.

Tarn, W. W. (1952). *Hellenistic Civilization* (3rd ed.). London.

Tetlow, T (2001–2002). The founders and slavery: A crisis of conscience. 3 Loyola Journal of Public Interest Law 1.

The Constitution of the United States. Preamble.

The Economist. (2020). *Some rich people are getting even richer during the pandemic*. Retrieved from https://www.economist.com/graphic-detail/2020/10/23/some-rich-people-are-getting-even-richer-during-the-pandemic on February 9, 2021.

Tomasky, M. (2019, April 14). Is America Becoming an Oligarchy?: Growing inequality threatens our most basic democratic principles. *The New York Times*. https://www.nytimes.com/2019/04/14/opinion/america-economic-inequality.html

Trümper, M. (2009). *Graeco-Roman slave markets: Fact or fiction?* Oxford.

Tryon, W. S. (1948, December). *The Puritan Oligarchy: The Founding of American Civilization*. By Thomas Jefferson Wertenbaker. (New York: Charles Scribner's Sons, 1947. xiv + 359 pp. Illustrations and index. $5.00.). *Journal of American History, 35*(3), 493–495. https://doi.org/10.2307/1897698.

Van Cleve, G. (2019). *We have not a government: The articles of confederation and the road to the constitution*. Chicago: University of Chicago Press.

Vermetten, E., & Bremner, J. D. (2002). Circuits and systems in stress. II. Applications to neurobiology and treatment in posttraumatic stress disorder. *Depression and Anxiety, 16*, 14–38.

Virginia Convention. (1776: May 6–July 5). Proposed amendments to the Declaration of Rights, 1776 June 12. Accession 30003, State government records collection, The Library of Virginia, Richmond, Virginia.

Watson, W. A. J. (1987). *Roman Slave Law*. Baltimore

Wells, R. (1974). Household Size and Composition in the British Colonies in America, 1675–1775. *The Journal of Interdisciplinary History, 4*(4), 543–570. https://doi.org/10.2307/202712.

Williams, Y. (2020, June 29) *Why Thomas Jefferson's Anti-Slavery Passage Was Removed from the Declaration of Independence*. Retrieved from https://www.history.com/news/declaration-of-independence-deleted-anti-slavery-clause-jefferson on February 9, 2021.

Wilson, T. D. (1999). Anti-Immigrant Sentiment and the Process of Settlement among Mexican Immigrants to the United States: Reflections on the Current Wave of Mexican Immigrant Bashing. *Review of Radical Political Economics, 31*(2), 1–26. https://doi.org/10.1177/048661349903100201.

Winters, J., & Page, B. (2009, December). Oligarchy in the United States? *Perspectives on Politics, 7*(4), 731–751. https://doi.org/10.1017/S1537592709991770.

Yale Law School: Lillian Goldman Law Library. (2008). *Articles of Confederation: March 1, 1781.* http://avalon.law.yale.edu/18th_century/artconf.asp. Accessed February 2021. https://ushistoryscene.com/article/articles-of-confederation/

Yglesias, M. (2008). *Swarthy Germans.* The Atlantic. Retrieved from https://www.theatlantic.com/politics/archive/2008/02/swarthy-germans/48324/ February 10, 2021.

Chapter 3
The Role of Fear in Politics, Politicians, Government, and Society

Whether humans are conscious of it or not, the core of human existence revolves around being safe, feeling safe, and/or seeking safety (Wanless, 2016). David Altheide would concur with the notion that safety is central to human existence as he wrote: "My 'compass' is the discourse of fear or the pervasive communication, symbolic awareness, and expectation that danger and risk are a central feature of everyday life" (Altheide, 2003). Fear is a potent emotion that possesses the clout to move masses, change minds, alter decision-making, and compromise judgment. Behavioral and social scientist would likely tell you that if you want to understand human behavior, study in the context of heightened fear. Fear is the antithesis of safety. Fear leaves individuals in survival mode – the drive to seek and secure safety is so incredibly powerful that humans will do what they must to secure it. Fear is uncompromising. The primitive intent of fear is to help humans appropriately (in a time- and threat-limited manner) respond to threat, survive it, and eventually get back to some form of thriving/living (Adolphs, 2013). Appreciate the brain on fear – the top cortical part of the brain is responsible for modulated thinking, exercising good judgment, and intact motor and executive functioning – all which are not operating optimally when humans are afraid. In a fear response, the amygdala (fear center) becomes prominent (see Fig. 3.1), increases stress in the body, and compromises top-brain-cortical functioning to include perception, attention, memory, and decision-making (Baars, 2005; Holland & Gallagher, 1999; Feinstein, Adolphs, Damasio, & Tranel, 2011; Debiec & LeDoux, 2004).

As demonstrated in Chap. 1 of this textbook, in a predator-prey relationship, the power of threat and fear and even the perception/anticipation of it can profoundly impact various animal species and ecosystems. Fear is taught, passed down, adapted and associated with survival and persistence. A form of tribalism flows from fear – appreciated from predator-prey relationships. Michael Shermer writes about tribalism and fear in Scientific American and describes it as "sharing intentionality and the ability to share mental representations of tasks" as a means of species persisting and surviving (Shermer, 2012). From the beginning of time, the powerful emotion

A. Moreland-Capuia, *The Trauma of Racism*,
https://doi.org/10.1007/978-3-030-73436-7_3

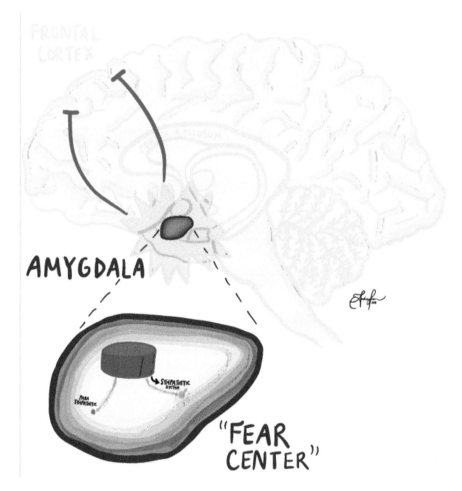

Fig. 3.1 The amygdala (a subcortical, almond-like structure) is the fear center. When humans are experiencing fear, the amygdala (survival mode, stress state) is more pronounced, and the cortex (top cortical, rational, emotion regulatory part of the brain) is less pronounced

of fear has influenced behavior, a phenomenon observed in politics too. Politicians realized very early on that in order to move the masses and shift the thoughts of and influence constituents, fear must be employed (Ahmed, 2003).

3.1 Fear and Politics

Politics involve constructing conflict and conjuring fear to attain and maintain power and to contain and manipulate behavior. Politics and fear have been written about extensively. Sarah Ahmed explores the role of the politics of fear in containing others and acting as an affective economy of truth objectifying humans and contributing to the construction of alternative truths via crisis – this is fear (Ahmed, 2003). Neocosmos, in an article on the politics of fear and fear of politics, asserts that poverty and deprivation (conditions of lack and powerlessness) create the conditions for fear to thrive and undergird chaos and violence (Neocosmos, 2008). Gerard writes about how developing countries took advantage of the stressed conditions of lack. In postcolonial Africa, tenuous governments plus elevated fear among ethnic groups plus the fear of falling under unscrupulous, dangerous leadership translated to stressed conditions – these stressed conditions compelled a good portion of the population to support a ruler who made massive reductions in welfare (highlighting the unfortunate reality that folks can be so afraid that they vote against their own interests) (Miquel, 2007). Former Vice President Al Gore wrote about politics and fear too, explaining that fear is misused often and "its specific goal is to distort the political reality of a nation by creating fear in the general population that is hugely disproportionate to the actual dangers…" (Gore, 2004). Gore was speaking about terrorism and the behavioral tactics employed to shape a predominant narrative and move the masses to accept an action (justified or not).

Shirlow and Pain wrote: "There is no denying the substance of fear in terms of media coverage, political manipulation and public discourse. Fear, whether it is quelled and or stimulated, provides the capacity to both control and manipulate a variety of social and political discourses" (Shirlow & Pain, 2003). Altheide's writing on fear and politics posits that fear is, through the process of time and conditioning, inextricably linked with matters and topics that impact humans daily – to the extent that fear becomes like the air we breathe, we cannot see it, but it is there and a part of our daily living. Altheide describes fear as "the invisible hyphen" added to every feeling and word (Altheide, 2003), highlighting the pervasiveness of it.

3.2 Nixon and Fear

Richard Nixon famously said: "People react to fear, not love—they don't teach that in Sunday School, but it's true" (Altheide, 2003). Historians contend that Nixon's keen understanding of fear and how it works to influence people was core to his method for pursuing the Presidency. Nixon campaigned at the height of the turmoil of the Civil Rights Movement in the late 1960s, the United States was in a war in Vietnam (that was not going so well and many Americans disagreed with the premise to go to war), two key civil rights leaders were murdered (Martin Luther King Jr. and shortly thereafter Robert F. Kennedy), racial tensions had reached a boiling point – Nixon played to the vulnerability of this moment in time. Americans were afraid. Nixon was convinced that "people react to fear, not love" so fear became his platform. He began a successful crusade of othering and fear mongering based on a keen understanding of the emotional underpinnings of human behavior and fear. Humans model and pass on fear – humans will always move in the direction of seeking safety in the face of threat (perceived and/or real) – and when fear is present, it can compromise perception, attention, memory, and decision-making (Baars, 2005).

Tim Weiner wrote in his book *One Man Against the World: The Tragedy of Richard Nixon* that Nixon was consumed by fear and further that fear begets fear-driven behavior which included domestic spying, breaking into the Democratic National Committee headquarters and constructing suboptimal sociopolitical and policy decisions (Weiner, 2015). Morgan's book alluded to Nixon's personal insecurities and fear that he was not enough (not smart enough, not good enough, not well liked), and these fears shaped his interpersonal and political interactions and decisions (Morgan, 1996). In the end, Nixon was led by fear. Nixon, however, wasn't the only president and/or politician led by fear.

3.3   Hoover and Fear

Chapter 2 of this text spoke extensively about the fear of the founding fathers and early presidents of the United States to include George Washington, John Adams, Thomas Jefferson, James Madison, and Abraham Lincoln. Because it is well understood that crisis breeds greater fear, let us consider the events and presidents and political leaders who led amid some of the United States greatest crisis marked by fear in our nation's history (Coles, 1967; Kliman, Bichler, & Nitzan, 2011). United States 31st President Herbert Hoover led during the Great Depression from 1929 to 1933, reminiscent of the 2007–2008 economic crisis (unemployment rates were far worse than during the Great Depression) and 2020 COVID-19 economic crisis. The Great Depression lasted nearly a decade from 1929 to 1939. Economic historians like Lester Chandler speak to the harsh realities of what he refers to as "America's greatest depression" (Chandler, 1970). While there does not exist consent among historians and/or economists on how the great precipitous market decline of 1929 happened, it contributed to great panic, was detrimental to industrial productivity and employment, and contributed to exceptional and robust increases in poverty, joblessness, and homelessness and profound and protracted global suffering (Chandler, 1970).

Hoover had a history of early childhood trauma of losing both his parents to illness and subsequently becoming orphaned. He eventually transformed his pain into power. He was diligent and disciplined enough to make his way through Stanford University. Status post-World War I, he established an organization that helped to target and reduce starvation in Europe. Hoover was no stranger to suffering. His story of rising above and succeeding against all odds is what won him favor and accolades as a leader. When the peak of his success culminated as the President of the United States in 1929, during the height of a profound economic recession, it was almost as if he forgot about his own intimate experience with suffering as demonstrated by his inability to alleviate the economic, physical, and psychological suffering of the citizens of the United States at the time. Hoover had been elevated to superhuman status, and the expectations of his leadership were great. The Great Depression was deemed a significant economic disaster – citizens anticipated that Hoover's humanitarian proclivities would be employed as President and that he would ease the hurt, calm the fears of lack, and ease suffering. As a matter of historical record, Hoover campaigned on reducing and eliminating fear and poverty. In an ironic twist of fate, upon seizing office, a great economic crash hit, and when the true test of leadership and putting words into action was upon him, he could not quite reach the benchmark. Hoover was deemed ambivalent and ineffective during this time of crisis. He was characterized as cold and lacking empathy.

While history may not look kindly and/or objectively on Hoover's leadership, when you dig beneath the surface of what appeared as indifference and lack of empathy, there was fear. Hoover understood and even appreciated suffering; however, he feared that if he spoke directly to the reality of the suffering, it would contribute to greater suffering. Equally, before Hoover assumed office, it is postulated that he was afraid that his reputation of excellence and leadership far exceeded the reality of his capacity to lead. He was burdened by and feared the expectations placed on him – this reality paralyzed him in some ways (McElvaine, 1984; F.A. Hayek to Paul Samuelson, 1980; Hoover, 1951).

While historians make mention of Hoover's early childhood loss through the tragic death of both his parents, it is quickly overshadowed by his subsequent success and rise to power. From current and evolving understanding of childhood trauma and its impact on the brain and body, it is not outside of the realm of possibility that Hoover's drive for success and his leadership style were powerfully shaped by his trauma history and intimate knowledge of fear. One could conjecture that Hoover's worst fear was loss, rejection, and abandonment, a recapitulation of his childhood trauma of being orphaned. Bearing witness to exceptional, widespread suffering in the context of not having ever had the space of processing and understanding one's own trauma can certainly look like ambivalence and feel like being stymied or in fight, freeze, flight mode.

Studies on early childhood trauma confirm that the body keeps the score in the context of trauma as shown by classical conditioning theory, highlighting that learned behavior is based on previous experiences (Kirsch, Lynn, & Vigorito, 2004). Maier and colleagues drive home this theory as they demonstrate learned helplessness in animal models by placing animals under conditions of uncontrollable shock and witnessing their seemingly inability to escape the suffering and subsequently have pronounced fear responses, social isolation, and poor health (Maier & Watkins, 2005). The seminal adverse childhood experiences (ACEs) study by Felitti and Anda shows that early exposure to childhood trauma to include but not limited to neglect and abandonment increases the risk for chronic physical and mental health conditions (Felitti et al., 1998). The impact of early trauma cannot be underestimated on its potential long-term impact on the manifestation of fear and how it can show up behaviorally and physically in humans (Al-Shawi & Lafta, 2015; De Bellis & Zisk, 2014).

A study by van Duin and colleagues investigated the association of ACEs and severe challenges later in life. Over 11 ACEs were surveyed (i.e., breakdown in familial structure/loss; physical, emotional, and sexual abuse; exposure to poverty; substance use and/or mental health; limited access to basic needs). Over 640 men between the ages of 18 and 27 consented to the use of retrospective psychiatric case register data and completed questionnaires. Statistical analysis of this retrospective data revealed that participants who were subject to psychological challenges in their families and/or grew up in single-parent homes were more likely to have employed mental healthcare. The overarching conclusion was that ACEs have a long-term negative impact on psychological functioning, notably in the context of emotional abuse and emotional neglect (van Duin et al., 2019). ACEs were not well studied and/or understood in the early twentieth century – retrospectively analyzing Hoover's experience and behavior through the lens of ACEs helps to identify where fear and trauma may have been operating at very high levels. There are no excuses here, but an explanation and a different lens to view humans in crisis and managing crisis.

3.4 Franklin D. Roosevelt and Fear

Franklin D. Roosevelt, the 32nd US President, succeeded Hoover, serving from 1933 to 1945. President Roosevelt was credited for helping to bring the United States out of the depths of the Great Depression. Roosevelt came into leadership at the peak of a nation's uncertainty, poverty, and abject suffering. Several studies point to the relationship between economic downturn and its deleterious impact on mental health in the form of increased psychiatric hospitalizations, suicide rates, fear, and stress (Brenner, 1973, 1990; Durkheim, 1951; Hamermesh & Soss, 1974; Horwitz, 1984; Trainor, Boydell, & Tibshirani, 1987; Zivin, Paczkowski, & Galea, 2011). Roosevelt was expected to lead a depressed nation, literally and figuratively. Roosevelt was the author of the New Deal, which created jobs by building and rebuilding America's infrastructure (bridges, roads, highways). The New Deal came in the form of a Federal Emergency Relief Administration that subcontracted with states to create jobs and build America, to buoy the economy (Badger, 1989; Borgwardt, 2005). Roosevelt came from great wealth and opportunity. Wealth and privilege do not shield humans from trauma and the traps of fear. Historian Doris Kearns-Goodwin researched and wrote extensively about Franklin D. Roosevelt. She revealed that in his childhood, Roosevelt witnessed his Aunt's body aflame from an accident with an alcohol lamp (Kearns-Goodwin, 1994). This image and experience of his Aunt on fire, etched in his psyche, fundamentally changed him. Kearns-Goodwin shared that Roosevelt never locked the doors to his residence, but instead had secret service men patrolling the front door to respond to any and everything (Kearns-Goodwin, 1994). Roosevelt was persistently on guard, and this high level of vigilance stemmed from his fear of fire – a trauma response.

When Roosevelt's early childhood trauma exposure and manifestation of this trauma and fear are juxtaposed with his leadership style, it leaves tremendous room for interpretation and seeming contradiction. At the peak of suffering and the height of collective fear, Franklin D. Roosevelt, in his 1933 inaugural speech, uttered these words (paraphrased): "This is preeminently time to speak the truth boldly and honestly, nor need we shrink from facing the conditions of country….let me assert my firm belief that the only thing we have to fear is fear itself" (Roosevelt & Zevin,

1946). Roosevelt went on to characterize the nation's fear as "unjustified terror." (Roosevelt & Zevin, 1946). Roosevelt lacked awareness on how his own fear and trauma shaped his leadership style and life. From the speech, one could postulate that there was recognition that trauma and fear had concentrated the nation, hence his specificity in addressing it with such directed veracity in his inaugural speech. One could interpret this as Roosevelt's unconscious attempt to project how he had desired to work through his internal fears. In other words, fear was something that had to be tackled head on, not processed. This approach subsequently influenced his construction of the New Deal, which marked the beginning of and is credited for lifting American citizens out of despair. According to historians and economists, the New Deal established legal minimum wage; unemployment insurance; relief programs for persons unemployed; improved regulation of labor, agriculture, and finance; and significant social services and resources for single-parent families, persons living in poverty, and persons differently abled (Brinkley, 1995). Much of the country's infrastructure to include highways, bridges, roads, and sewage systems were built under the umbrella of the New Deal, which created jobs and stimulated the economy (Brinkley, 1995). These structural adjustments and boosts to the economy didn't mean that fear didn't abound. According to Nicholas Crafts and Peter Fearon, "New Dealers were totally opposed to 'dole' payments, which they feared would lead to a dependency culture" (Crafts and Fearon, 2010). There was also fear that banks would build reserves in excess and too expansively and rapidly lend. There was fear of repeat recession (Peppers, 1973). It is most unfortunate that an individuals' inability to recognize their own fear and trauma results in inadvertent (seemingly) invalidation of others potential trauma experiences. When Roosevelt hit office, suicide rates and depression were high, alcohol and drug use increased significantly, and folks were in survival mode because they had lived through four years of inaction, uncertainty, starvation, joblessness, and homelessness – there was nothing unjustified about fear. Research on the impact of the Great Depression demonstrated that self-medication with alcohol and other substances served as a means of coping with significant job, social, and psychic losses (Elder, 1974; Richman et al., 2012; Institute of Medicine, 1996). Roosevelt's declaration that there is nothing to fear in the face of insurmountable and real fear is a historical example of a fear-on-fear encounter and a reminder that just because fear and trauma weren't recognized doesn't mean they didn't exist.

3.5   McCarthy and Socially Constructed Fear

Lodged between the presidency of Franklin Roosevelt and Harry Truman was a controversial leader and philosophy shaped and stoked by fear, McCarthy and McCarthyism respectively. The theme of fear can be identified at nearly every point in history and in most notable politicians. Tense points in history and leaders most robustly highlight how fear is passed down and employed to generate and motivate behavior. Joseph McCarthy, US Senator from Wisconsin for a decade (1947–1957), served up fear daily and often. He was well known for what historians refer to as the red scare – a constructed fear-based narrative about the prospect of the rise of communism and persons skeptical of authority and rejecting of hierarchy (anarchy) (Schrecker, 1988; UKEssays, 2018; Rimmington, 1998). The conditions that have been theorized to lend themselves to this massive propagation of fear included the conclusion of World War I, which increased anti-immigrant sentiments and nationalism, and the Bolshevik Revolution in Russia which flamed even more anti-immigrant sentiment as Americans feared that immigrants from Russia and Europe intended to overtake the US government (Schrecker, 1988; UKEssays, 2018; Rimmington, 1998). McCarthy took advantage of the political atmosphere and emotional state of Americans and fanned the flames of fear by accusing government employees and elites of treason in the absence of proof. Many workers falsely accused of treason lost their jobs, and American fear continued to mount in the early 1950s. McCarthy's fear tactic proved effective as it was documented that by 1952, a good proportion of Americans held the conviction that communists were operating in the United States and must be identified and eliminated. So, the rise of McCarthyism began – defined as lacking evidence, making false claims of treason and rebellion, and stoking fear (Schrecker, 1988; UKEssays, 2018; Rimmington, 1998).

More on the conditions that gave air to McCarthy and McCarthyism. World War II started in 1939 and lasted until about 1945 – which was during the last four years of Franklin Roosevelt's presidency. Roosevelt's leadership was flanked by tragedy as he began by taking office in 1933, during the height of the Great Depression, and ended by joining with Great Britain, France, and several other world powers to temper Germany and Hitler's invasion of Poland. World War II ended in 1945, and the Cold War began approximately two years later in 1947. The Cold War marked a time of poignant strain between the United States and the Soviet Union (Crockatt, 2009; Fleming, 1966; Pickett, 2006). The strain hinged on a desire to be powerful both politically and globally, fear of the emergence of nuclear weapons, and demonstrable fear of communism in the United States (Downing, 2003; Crockatt, 2009; Fleming, 1966; Pickett, 2006). Historians contend that the Cold War influenced American foreign policy and political dogma; it had domestic economic implications and was noted to have contributed to the establishment of expected conformity by Americans (Crockatt, 2009; Fleming, 1966; Pickett, 2006). The relative disruption of the Cold War contributed to subsequent advancement of economic growth for the United States and strengthened the United States' relationship with allies and supports (Crockatt, 2009; Fleming, 1966; Pickett, 2006). The Cold War lasted until 1991 and was culminated by the disbanding of the Soviet Union (Schmemann, 2006). Circa 1966, Fleming highlighted in a piece on "The Costs and Consequences of the Cold War" that at the conclusion of World War II, there was a preeminent shift to "global containment of communism in the United States" (Fleming, 1966). Fleming asserts that "by making anticommunism our life motive, we have fostered rightist fanaticism" (Fleming, 1966).

The Cold War and its impact traversed other poignant, tense moments in American history to include the Civil Rights Movement (which began around 1954, almost seven years into the Cold War) and the Vietnam War (began in 1955, almost eight years into the Cold War). 1954 marked the acme of the Civil Rights Movement where Black Americans coordinated and strategized to fight for equal rights and treatment and desegregation in the United States as was constitutionally mandated but not universally recognized. While legal and constitutional mandates for social, political, economic, and educational equality existed, they were not being enforced consistently and/or evenly by states. Discrimination, hate, and fear were centered in some states' resistance to equality resulting in the dehumanization and erasure of Black Americans. The relentless political and social movement of the Civil Rights era influenced the passing of the Civil Rights Act of 1964, which forbids discrimination based on race, color, religion, sex, or national origin and in schools, public accommodation, and federally assisted programs. Also, important to mention is the Brown v. Board of Education of Topeka, Kansas, Supreme Court decision in 1954 (at the inception of the Civil Rights Movement), which ruled that state-sanctioned segregation of public education was unconstitutional – this decision is said to have spurred the Civil Rights Movement. The historical relationship between fear and education will be discussed in greater detail in a subsequent chapter in this book. Of critical note, two years after the landmark Civil Rights Act was passed, in 1966, an activist named James Meredith established a colossal demonstration called the "March Against Fear" (Bausum, 2017). The demonstration took place in the South (from Memphis, Tennessee, to Jackson, Mississippi, with an anticipated distance of nearly 270 miles within a timeframe of 21 days) and was constructed for the purpose of buoying the efforts of the Civil Rights Movement and to counter persistent racism in the South (despite federal legislation banning it) and to encourage Black Americans to register to vote (Bausum, 2017). Of interest is the fact that Meredith called it a "March Against Fear" – Meredith was referring to the fear of Whites who struggled with the idea of relinquishing and/or sharing power with individuals they deemed subhuman not worthy of rights and the respondent fear of Black Americans who were chronically subject to racism and avoided situations that were unsafe, like voting at that time.

In 1955, just one year after the inception of the Civil Rights Movement in the United States and almost a decade into the Cold War, the Vietnam War ensued, and scholars and historians contend that it was an extension of the fear of communism (Gartner, Segura, & Wilkening, 1997; Gawthorpe, 2020; Herring, 2004; Lawrence, 2008). The war was fought between North Vietnam (supported by China, the Soviet Union, and communist associates) and South Vietnam (supported by Australia, Thailand, the United States, and other anti-communist associates). The Vietnam War ended (or the beginning of the end) in 1973 when Richard Nixon ordered withdrawal of troops in the context of poignantly divided Americans – many questioned the basic premise of the war. Equally contributing to the end of the war was when in 1975 Communist forces detained control of South Vietnam and unified.

It can be argued that McCarthyism was a form of constructed fear, consistent with the phenomenon of social constructivism. Social constructivism is a framework employed to understand how human develop meaning and procure core beliefs and worldviews from their life experiences (Marin, Benarroch, & Jimenez, 2000). Erol defines social constructivism as groups collectively build meaning for one another while concomitantly establishing shared subcultural understandings (Erol, 2015). Humans move toward simplification which can often look like the establishment of neat narratives that can be sorted, packed, and retrieved as needed (Howard & Hussain, 2018; National Research Council, 1988; Star, 1983). Much literature points to the evolution of human fear – a notable transition from human's fear of nature tempered by the influx of technology. Fears of nature were replaced with other forms of fear like fear (primarily constructed) of having to share power with individuals and/or groups of individuals who they believe are undeserving. Philosopher Seneca famously stated (paraphrasing) that human imaginations of the potential things that frighten them are much greater than the reality of the things that are scary (Seneca & Campbell, 1969). Sociologists assert that whether the fears are constructed (perceived or imagined), the constructed fear stems from narrative established by individuals in power (Adler, 1997; Jung, 2019; Tudor, 2003). Barry Glassner, in *The Culture of Fear*, warns (paraphrased) that humans must find a way to manage their overblown fears less they be consumed (Glassner, 1999).

3.6   Social Constructivism

Human's derivation of meaning from experiences can be powerfully shaped by narrative which influences perception. Studies demonstrate that narrative is inherently persuasive as it pronounces experiences as opposed to general truths (Dahlstrom, 2014). Literature on narrative and educating audiences suggests that it is powerfully persuasive when fictional (Green & Brock, 2000). It is noted that even though a narrative might be fictional, it typically contains some elements of truth, and it is through the lens of fictional narrative that individuals employ information to answer critical questions about the world around them (Appel & Richter, 2007; Dahlstrom & Ho, 2012; Marsh, Meade, & Roediger, 2003; Wyer, Read, & Miller, 1995).

Studies on perception and dynamics inform that individuals do not completely process all the local information in their environment at one time (Frith & Frith, 1999; Wick, Alaoui Soce, Garg, Grace, & Wolfe, 2019). Instead, individuals' home in on some objects and/or regions rendering those areas more fully processed than other areas in an environment (Wick et al., 2019). Further, critical for the survival of humans is the ability to infer the intentions of others – it has been suggested that neural mechanisms to detect biological motion have evolved to fulfill this survival mechanism in humans (Frith & Frith, 1999).

Social constructivism, narrative, and perception have a relationship with fear conditioning. Fear is a response to external influences (perceived and/or real threats) – threat and fear can be constructed; this construction can be powerfully shaped by narrative – all of which have roles in survival functioning in humans as described by Frith and Frith (1999). Fear conditioning is the mechanism that underpins associative learning of threat and safety – see Fig. 3.2 (Guimarãis, Gregório, Cruz, Guyon, & Moita, 2011). The process of fear conditioning/learning (a form of classical conditioning/associative learning – see Fig. 3.3) involves a robust initiation

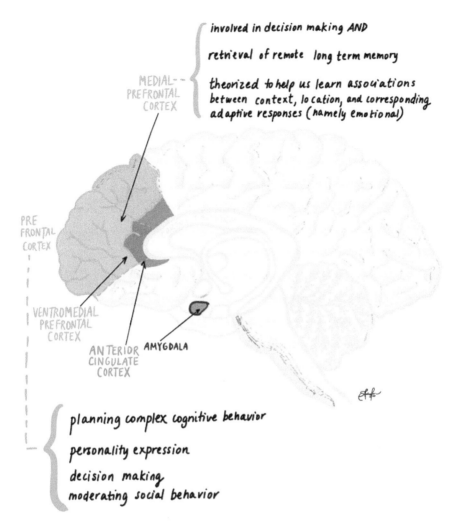

involved in decision making AND

retrieval of remote long term memory

theorized to help us learn associations
between context, location, and corresponding
adaptive responses (namely emotional)

MEDIAL--
PREFRONTAL
CORTEX

PRE
FRONTAL
CORTEX

VENTROMEDIAL
PREFRONTAL
CORTEX

ANTERIOR AMYGDALA
CINGULATE
CORTEX

planning complex cognitive behavior

personality expression

decision making
moderating social behavior

Fig. 3.2 Fear conditioning is the mechanism by which humans identify, recognize, remember, and forecast things in the external environment that cause fear and establish behaviors to help them avoid fear-inducing things in the future. The parts of the brain involved in fear conditioning are the amygdala (the fear processing center); the anterior cingulate cortex (plays a role in emotion regulation, impulse control, personality expression, empathy); the hippocampus (plays a role in memory); and the ventromedial prefrontal cortex (plays a role in decision-making and retrieval of long-term memory)

of a learned fear state and the expression of learned fear-related behaviors. The fear conditioning process also involves the ignition of fear and the extinction of it. Studies suggest that extinction does not erase fear learning, it only allows for the creation of new learning to counter the fear learning (Shechner, Hong, Britton, Pine, & Fox, 2014). The interface between fear conditioning and extinction of fear influences behavior at critical points of development when the impact of learning is deep

Fig. 3.3 Classical (Pavlovian) conditioning made simple: it involves taking a stimulus and/or thing that does not cause fear (considered neutral) and blending it with something that does cause fear (considered antagonistic). The result of such a combination is that the initial neutral stimulus (now associated with an aversive one) is associated with the antagonistic stimulus effectively changing behavioral and psychological responses (what was initially neutral now inspires fear). This is called associative learning and has been traditionally explained by Pavlovian classical conditioning theory as illustrated above

(Gdalyahu et al., 2012; Guimarãis et al., 2011; Shechner et al., 2014). The amygdala is the epicenter of the fear conditioning process (Barrett, Mesquita, Ochsner, & Gross, 2007; LaBar, Gatenby, Gore, LeDoux, & Phelps, 1998).

3.7   The Power of False Negative Narratives and Social Constructs in Influencing Harmful Behavior Toward Blacks and the Unfortunate Backing of Research in Perpetuating and Accentuating Harmful Behavior Toward Blacks

Negative, fear-based narrative about Black Americans was prominent in the 1950s and 1960s of Black Americans. Black Africans were forcibly taken from their home land, made subject to the treacherous conditions of the transatlantic slave trade to subsequently become the economic engine for an emerging society – valuable worker, devalued subhuman. From the inception of America, Black Africans and eventually Black Americans were relegated to "the help, the servant." The narrative on Blackness was socially constructed to be the antithesis of Whiteness. The emergence of things like Black face, the dancing fool, minstrel, and clown combined with the image of being disparate, impoverished, needy, differently abled, and non-- threatening because it met a need for wild entertainment was stark. Of note is the way Black face produced an image and narrative that had the effect of putting Black people in their place. Minstrel culture constructed a narrative about who Black folks were and could be and attached it to the image of being down in the dumps, power-less and palatable only when comical and knowing their place. The minstrel culture picked up after the Civil War (Blair, 1990).

3.8   The Birth of a Nation and Negative Social Constructs

The Birth of a Nation in the early twentieth century, after the Civil War, amid the Reconstruction era, a silent film depicting Black American males predominantly as violent, unrestrained (sending the subliminal message that they required restraint) brute beast to be feared, was featured. Boskin highlighted the fact that several silent films at the height of the twentieth century depicted Blacks as coons and slaves and reinforced words like the "N" word (there was actually a 1915 movie called "The Nxxxer"). These films constructed narratives and further established and reinforced dangerous and inaccurate stereotypes about Blacks (Boskin, 1986). The negative and overwhelmingly false social construct of intellectual inferiority – unfortunately supported by science – was also heavily featured in the late nineteenth and early twentieth century (Plous & Williams, 1995). Researchers like Morton, Bean, and Mall studied the size of skulls and brains of Whites and Blacks asserting that the size of skulls determined intelligence (Bean, 1906; Mall, 1909; Morton, 1839). These studies drew conclusions that Blacks were less intelligent and sophisticated because of smaller skulls and brains. Specifically, in Bean's comparison of White and Black brains, he focused on the corpus callosum and inferred that Whites had a larger prefrontal cortex compared to Blacks which rendered them smarter (Bean, 1906). Bean also made claims that men had bigger brains than women (Bean, 1906). While this may seem incredibly absurd, his research was widely published and legitimized by a major research journal at the time.

3.9 Social Construct of Black Women as Mammy's and Aunt Jemimah

Jewell highlights the characterization of the happy-while suffering (enslaved) Black women – depicted as midnight dark-skinned with pearly white teeth, large body habitus, fiercely independent – also known as Mammy (Jewell, 1993). Mammy transitioned to Aunt Jemimah, characterized as the help who cooks and cleans. These stereotypes are profound, pervasive, and persistent. Pine-Sol commercials in the 1990s portrayed a heavy-set Black woman with braids as the face of the cleaning product – a reinforced monetized stereotype that now has economic implications as Pine-Sol is a top cleaning product purchased by Black Americans (Fuller, 2001).

3.10 The Social Construct of the Bell Curve

In the 1990s, psychologist Richard Herrnstein and political scientist Charles Murray studied and widely published on the Bell Curve. They controlled for equality with the false assumption that it had been achieved while making the argument that merit and innate ability influenced by genetics determine intellectual advantage or disadvantage (Hernstein & Murray, 1994). The Bell Curve suggested that there is an increased chance of intellectual advantage if individuals mate with genetically similar individuals. The book used terms like illegitimate mothers and had social, economic, and IQ correlates based on their working definition of illegitimate mothers. Advantage and disadvantage plus genetics became the euphemism for Black and White and further perpetuated racist ideology and constructs. The Bell Curve theory is contentious, and its claims have been countered by many researchers (Conley & Dominque, 2016).

3.11   The Social Construct of and Narrative Around Black Pain

There even exists a longstanding narrative that Blacks don't feel pain or have higher thresholds for pain, which was used as justification for maltreatment during slavery. Bourke outlined the extensive history of this unfortunate construct in a piece entitled "Pain sensitivity: an unnatural history from 1800 to 1965" revealing the thread from slave plantations and the medical field that held the conviction that African-Americans had less sensitive nervous systems and were easily swayed emotionally (Bourke, 2014). The perception that Blacks experience less and/or no pain is a profound and prevalent stereotype that shows up in medical settings in the twenty-first century, and multiple studies speak to the foundation of the myth and demonstrate how it plays out in disparate health outcomes and treatment (Cintron & Morrison, 2006; Dore, Hoffman, Lillard, & Trawalter, 2014; Hoffman, Trawalter, Axt, & Oliver, 2016; Waytz, Hoffman, & Trawalter, 2014).

These fear-based socially constructed narratives have resulted in death. According to data compiled through the Equal Justice Initiative (EJI), researchers documented 4075 racial terror lynchings of African-Americans in 12 Southern states between 1877 and 1950. EJI highlights the violent and traumatizing nature of lynchings – it left Black people in America afraid and traumatized, and this form of racial terror was endured by state and federal officials (Equal Justice Initiative, 2017). According to EJI, "this form of racial terror strengthened a narrative of racial difference and a legacy of racial inequality" (Equal Justice Initiative, 2017). These shared and constructed narratives are commanding and have shaped white racial attitudes and their perception of Blacks (Fossett & Kiecolt, 1989). The power of public opinion and its great influence on narratives and policy are not only a matter of historical record, but well studied (Burstein, 2003; Giles & Evans, 1985).

3.12   Truman and Fear

Harry Truman, US President from 1945 to 1953, channeled McCarthy's fear. Truman held the conviction that communism was America's greatest threat and should be prioritized as such (Kernell, 1976; Merrill, 2006). He convinced a large cohort of Americans that the United States was in a profound battle for power, status, culture, military planning and expansion, foreign policy, and identity – the fight and fear were over the Soviet Union potentially usurping the esteem and power of the United States. This fear would come to shape US policies and guidelines for decades to come concerning US-Soviet affairs. Truman was able to overextend the truth and inspire greater fear because Americans had bore witness to communism overtake several Eastern European nations and China. They heard Joseph Stalin, a Soviet Union politician, proclaimed that communists should rule the world. The political milieu had been built and maintained by fear – surveys on attitudes and beliefs from the mid-1940s to mid-1950s demonstrated that many Americans believed the allegations that communists were infiltrating and/or running the US government. Fear. Fear. Fear. Fear subsequently compromised the American legal institution of presumed innocence over guilt. The postwar fear aided in the construction and amplification of greater fear(s). At the conclusion of World War II, communism was a direct peril to free markets and enterprise, and it was believed that it would smother the world economy. A direct response to thwarting the spread of communism was the development of the North Atlantic Treaty Organization (NATO) in 1949. In reaction to NATO, there was the subsequent establishment of the Warsaw Pact in 1955 – a collaboration of Central and Eastern European communist states that ultimately strengthened the Soviet allied defenses.

Joseph S. Davis makes the connection between postwar population growth and economic upward mobility (Davis, 1953). Davis highlights in short order that war produced returns for the United States as evidenced by significant increases in goods and services fashioned by the United States with notable growth in American corporations; rise of the middle class; more robust automobile industry; and increased housing ownership – this economic boom was, in part, theorized to be a direct result of the increase in defense spending related to the Cold War (Davis, 1953).

Lizabeth Cohen, historian and author, wrote and researched extensively about the shift to a mass consumption-driven economy postwar and tied the strength of the economy to political and democratic might (Cohen, 2003; Cohen, 2004). Elaine Tyler May analyzed the connection between Cold War politics and how it shaped the conception and construction of the American family (May, 1996). Historians have highlighted that the culture of family shifted notably in the 1950s as there was greater focus on suburban consumer lifestyles, nuclear family, gracefully delineated gender roles, lowered age of marriage, and a significant population boom (May, 1996).

May also highlights that in the mid-1960s (at the peak of the Civil Rights Movement), over 90 percent of Americans polled in the North and South held the conviction that selling property to Blacks, or any form of redistribution of wealth, was too close to communism, a direct threat to democracy and American freedom (May, 1996). In *Grand Expectations*, James Patterson speaks of the firmly held postwar outlooks about America's proclivity toward establishing boundless opportunity and wealth (Patterson, 1996). The fear of sharing wealth and power did not just have an international focus but took on a local-internal focus too. Americans, predominantly White Americans, began to more sharply define and socially construct who matters more and most and who should be likely (worthy) beneficiaries of American growth and wealth. The increased incidences of othering, dehumanizing, racism, discrimination, and segregation (an outgrowth of anti-immigrant sentiment) were fear-based mechanisms employed to maintain perceived power, opportunity, wealth, and esteem.

3.13 Johnson and Fear

Lyndon B. Johnson was Vice President to President John F. Kennedy. He assumed office in 1963 (completing two years of Kennedy's term and subsequently winning re-election and completing his service in 1969) in the context of the trauma of the assassination of President John F. Kennedy, amid the Civil Rights Movement (strongly supported by John F. Kennedy) and persistent American fear of communism. As history reflects on Lyndon B. Johnson, his leadership style and his core values, he was noted as anxious, focused, a behaviorist (could read the behavior of individuals), transactional, and intellectually and physically intimidating. He possessed the fierce urgency of "now." He grew up in poverty and was determined to construct and move forward an anti-poverty agenda while in office. Johnson believed like his predecessor, Kennedy, that in order to create the conditions for every human to succeed they must be given equal opportunity. Johnson wanted to avoid society ever going back to Great Depression conditions – his working agenda was termed "The Great Society" and was driven by a desire to provide equal opportunity and to buoy a nation. Equally, there was notable compassion and empathy for marginalized communities because he, himself, grew up in poverty – this personal experience provided internal motivation and a moral compass for his anti-poverty and equality efforts. In terms of the Great Society agenda, Johnson and his Congress accomplished myriad things to include but not limited to: 1963, Clean Air Act; 1964, Civil Rights Act of 1964, War on Poverty Act, Housing Act, Food Stamps Act; 1965, Medicare and Medicaid, Voting Rights Act, Immigrations Reform Act, Anti-poverty Program, and Affirmative Action Act; 1966, Child Nutrition Act and Air Pollution Control Act; and 1968, Fair Housing Act. He was noted for taking Martin Luther King Jr.'s vision of equality and executing it legally, which should have been his legacy. However, Johnson's legacy has been marked by his moral indifference on and unfortunate supervision of the Vietnam War.

3.14 Nixon and Fear

If searched for, fear can be found operating in many people, systems, and societies. Nixon took office at the height of racial and political unrest in the late 1960s, and he spoke to White fear by touting crime statistics and telling Americans that things were going to get worse if they weren't proactive. Nixon had a record of appealing to fear. He successfully associated civil rights protests with violence and crime – it was something that mandated control and repair. Nixon was quoted saying that freedom from fear is a basic right of every American and this right must be restored. Nixon successfully employed the image of the White woman as the damsel in distress in need of saving from dangerous, violent Black men and women. Nixon was also effective in convincing White American in the late 1960s (after the polarizing and incredibly threatening work done by LBJ toward anti-poverty and equality) that their ability to maintain power, identity, values, status, and safety was threatened by a vicious leftist agenda (i.e., Civil Rights Movement). Nixon was casting his own internal fears – it is documented that he was so fearful and afraid of what others thought about him that it consumed him. Weiner who wrote the book *One Man Against the World: The Tragedy of Richard Nixon* speaks to Nixon's fear growing into anger and the anger to self-destruction (Weiner, 2015). It has also been documented that Nixon tended to overconsume alcohol. He was tortured. Nixon's presidency culminated with impeachment in the setting of criminal abuse of power and unethical and immoral activity notoriously known as the Watergate scandal.

3.15   Reagan and Fear

Ronald Reagan, the 40th President of the United States serving from 1981 to 1989, was known for his notable complexity and contradictions. Reagan is credited for eloquently and convincingly encouraging Soviet politician Mikhail Sergeyevich Gorbachev to "tear down that wall." Reagan's desire to speak with Soviets to help them end the Cold War is marked in the halls of history. While there were calls for peace and unity abroad, at home conditions were complex. Reagan and the department of justice under his leadership were perceived as anti-affirmative action (which had been established under LBJ in 1965) and non-supportive of government-based social support programs (National Research Council, 1998; Palmer & Sawhill, 1982; US Social Security Administration, 1997). Reagan was Governor of California from 1967 to 1975. In a 1964 speech leading up to his gubernatorial bid entitled "A Time for Choosing (aka 'The Speech')," he provides a window into his views on welfare as threat to democracy and freedom.

> *Those who would trade our freedom for the soup kitchen of the welfare state have told us they have a utopian solution of peace without victory.* (Reagan in Alfred A. Bolitzer et al., eds, 1983).

He feared that the big government that solved social problems was too reminiscent of socialist values. Policy changes flowed from that fear as he slashed Aid to Families with Dependent Children (AFDC) spending and allowed states to require welfare recipients to participate in workfare programs (National Research Council Committee on Population, 1998; Palmer & Sawhill, 1982; US Social Security Administration, 1997). According to a 1984 report by Benenson, under Reagan's leadership, in 1981 and 1982, Congress made changes in the food stamp program that, according to CBO, eliminated about 4 percent or one million people from the rolls (Benenson, 1984). Deferrals in adjustments for inflation affected most people still receiving benefits. Reagan was quoted as saying that welfare rewards and motivates folks not to work. Reagan coined the term "welfare queen" in 1976 and began to shift the narrative and paint a picture of poverty and welfare as a matter of personal responsibility, not a government issue. Reagan's anti-welfare, over-involved government, tax-cutting agenda is what led him to the White House in 1981.

Whether there is merit to Reagan's personal responsibility – pull yourself by your own bootstraps approach or not – the move to reform policies was not driven by a desire to cut government spending alone, the subtext was that welfare programs were helping Black families. The cuts didn't account for unemployment, underemployment, and limited opportunities secondary to racism and sociopolitical discrimination of Black citizens and the stress on Black families (Massey & Denton, 1993). Domestic chaos raged in the 1980s in form of crack cocaine. Golub and Johnson wrote extensively about the widespread raving impact of crack cocaine on nuclear families in inner cities, particularly the Black family (Golub & Johnson, 1997). According to US Census Bureau data in the 1980s, 4.6% of America received welfare benefits, of which 5.1% were women, 3.1% were White, and 12.55 were African-American (US Census Bureau, 1999). The statistics tell the story of who benefit more and most – further proof of how powerful narrative is.

The pervasive negative fear-driven social constructs persist. The goal was not to cover every American President, but rather to provide snapshots of points in history that illustrate how pervasive and destructive fear, fear-based constructs, and narrative have been and are – it is important because of what fear leads to. In 2008, then US Senator Barack Obama of Illinois ran for president of the United States of America. The level of vitriol, racial hate, and fear reared its ugly head. Barack Obama was not the first African-American to run for the Presidency as there was Frederick Douglass who was invited to speak at the 1888 National Republican Convention and subsequently received one vote during the roll call theoretically rendering him a candidate; more famously Shirley Chisholm was a democratic candidate in 1972; and Jesse Jackson in 1984 and 1988 made it to the primaries where he received millions of votes – with Douglass to Chisholm to Jackson, there was a progressive inch closer to the presidency. A plethora of scholars have written about the political, social, and racial implications of a Barack Obama presidency (Alter, 2010; D'Antono, 2017; Dyson, 2016). In summary, Barack Obama appealed to the masses because he was biracial born of a Kenyan father and White mother from Kansas; educated at Ivy League institutions; had a solid marriage and family; waxed eloquent; intelligent; charismatic; and operated set of core values and boundless optimism that resonated with twenty-first-century America.

3.16 Obama and Fear

Barack Obama was seeking office at the height of a recession and the war in Iraq. There are several factors that can contribute to a recession to include but not limited to dips in housing sales and prices, lack of leadership, crashing stock markets, and high interest rates. Deregulation of the financial industry, a housing bubble, predatory lending, and defaults on mortgages were among some of the main contributors of the Great Recession of 2008 (Reference). As a matter of historical and public record, President Bush petitioned Congress to allocate over seven hundred billion dollars to absorb defaulted mortgage assets as a means of curving the looming financial crisis in 2008. There was much at stake in 2008 – American fear was high given the economic reality of the time. Obama's bid to lead amid an ongoing war and burgeoning economic recession was gutsy. His candidacy and presidency were marked by every single unfortunate narrative and constructed fear about Black Americans. Donald Trump led the birtherism campaign spreading the lie and fear that Barack Obama was not born in America and therefore an immigrant – reminiscent of deep-seated fear dating back to Benjamin Franklin who was afraid that German immigrants would usurp American power; birthright is a symbol of power; that he held far-fetched religious views; that he would push a socialist agenda; and that he was un-American and didn't possess nor would he uphold American values. Trump's claims that Barack Obama was not a citizen is part of a long tradition of othering – anything outside of Christian, White, was constructed as a threat to democracy, freedom, power, and identity. Obama, as a Black American, was operating outside of the historically constructed narrative and role; this posed a real and existential threat to parts of White America. Obama recognized the sense of threat and fear that some Americans felt surrounding his candidacy – he pushed the hope agenda as an anecdote to fear.

While hope was on the agenda, it didn't quite quell or temper the fear held by swaths of Americans. Trump worked diligently to counter the Obama's hope narrative with fear, and there is evidence that he was effective. From the period 2008 to 2016, the number of racial violence, hate crimes, grew. According to a Bureau of Justice Statistics National Crime Victimization Survey, during the 5-year aggregate period from 2011 to 2015, racial bias was the most common motivation for hate crime (48%) (Bureau of Justice Statistics). The US Department of Justice Hate Crime Statistics for 1996–2018 demonstrates a steady increase in hate crimes (US Department of Justice).

Diana Mutz investigated the "left behind" narrative and evidence pertaining to popular narratives for the American public's support for Donald J. Trump in the 2016 presidential election. Mutz sampled persons (White, male, Christian) from 2012 to 2016 who had felt they'd been left out of economic opportunity during the Obama era with job loss and who felt as though they had not been represented for the eight years that Obama was president (Mutz, 2018). Considerations were given to the potential for status threat, the perception that Obama represented a shift in historical hierarchy and growing global diversity (Mutz, 2018). Mutz concluded that the combination of growing domestic racial diversity and globalization underwrote a sense of significant threat, fear, and perceived loss of status and anxiety over this loss of status in the dominant group (Mutz, 2018).

3.17   Trump and Fear

In 2016, Donald Trump initiated his run for president and subsequently won by framing the United States as a nation in descent. Adopting the slogan "Make America Great Again," he set his campaign against a backdrop of loss and declared a mission for reclamation. Numerous analysts claim that his candidacy and rhetoric galvanized White voters who feel left behind by changing times, but few have been able to provide direct evidence of a racialized. My analysis argues that how Whites think about whiteness mattered for their likelihood to support Donald Trump. Others have studied and written about the impact of Trump and his fear-inducing tactic of sounding the alarm that something was stolen and must be recaptured – culminated in "Make America Great Again." Trump's election was driven by fear over the economy and racial antipathy (Bunyasi, 2019). The use of fear and racism in presidential candidates' narrative is not a new phenomenon, but it evolved (Banks & Hicks, 2016; Rhodes & Vayo, 2019). Homolar and Scholz wrote about how Trump manipulated individual's ontological security (individual's sense of being) with his use of crisis talk shaped by anti-establishment crisis narrative – knowing that behavior is motivated by fear and what individuals perceive they lost and/or are losing (Homolar & Scholz, 2019).

Trump powerfully and intentionally crafted his narrative, speaking of deep-seated White American fears of socialism, immigration, loss of status, and identity. He called Mexicans rapist and referred to Haiti and African countries as "s" hole countries. He violated and disrespected women, stole, lied, and cheated, but none of these moral violations were adequate to overcome the overwhelming sense of status loss and fear that parts of White America felt. That fear transformed into violence, and Trumpism was birthed. During Trump's tenure, he stoked racial tensions and woke up the beast of White supremacy. Under his watch and via his influence, a sitting Governor's life was threatened by a group of White male Trump supporters who organized a plan to kidnap her. Under his watch and via his influence, White nationalist descended on Charlottesville with tiki torches reminiscent of the Ku Klux Klan, and he called them "good people." It is under his leadership that hate crimes sharpened. Edwards and colleagues employed time series analysis and demonstrated that Donald Trump's election in November of 2016 was associated with a statistically significant surge in reported hate crimes across the United States, even when controlling for alternative explanations (Edwards & Rushin, 2018).

In 2020, during the general and primary election, Trump did all that he could to incite violence and employ fear. Once again, appealing to a sense of loss and breach of ontological security, he contributed to inciting tremendous violence. A large group of White, predominantly male, domestic terrorists overtook the Nation's Capital – they carried the American and Confederate flag and guns. They beat up cops, broke windows, damaged property, and set it aflame; they constructed a noose and contributed to a handful of deaths. They caused terror in the US legislature. The source of their anger and fear was fueled by Donald Trump, who was operating out of his own deep-seated fear of loss and being characterized as a loser. This book is not about Trump, but it is about the fear narrative and constructs he built that culminated in needless violence, death, and more fear.

Dodd and colleagues investigated the connection between individual variation in physiological and attentional responses to aversive and appetitive stimuli which was correlated with broad political alignments. In short order, an individual's political views are connected to physiologic predispositions, rendering them more threat-sensitive (Dodd et al., 2012; Huddy et al., 2005). Vigil highlighted that there was variation in tendency to perceive threat in faces based on political leanings and psychosocial functioning (Vigil, 2010). There is evidence that physiologic response to threat can be modulated by political attitudes (Oxley et al., 2008).

If one looks beneath the surface of rhetoric, actions, people, and systems, fear is not difficult to identify. The more fear and its influence are addressed, the more likely violence and hate are mitigated. Politically and historically speaking, fear has worked. Should it any longer?

References

Adler, E. (1997). Seizing the middle ground: Constructivism in world politics. *European Journal of International Relations, 3*, 319–363.

Adolphs, R. (2013). The biology of fear. *Current Biology: CB, 23*(2), R79–R93. https://doi.org/10.1016/j.cub.2012.11.055.

Ahmed, S. (2003). The politics of fear in the making of worlds. *International Journal of Qualitative Studies in Education, 16*(3), 377–398. https://doi.org/10.1080/0951839032000086745.

Al-Shawi, A. F., & Lafta, R. K. (2015). Effect of adverse childhood experiences on physical health in adulthood: Results of a study conducted in Baghdad city. *Journal of Family & Community Medicine, 22*(2), 78–84. https://doi.org/10.4103/2230-8229.155374.

Alter, J. B. (2010). *the promise: President Obama, year one.* New York: Simon & Schuster. ISBN 978-1-4391-0119-3.

Altheide, D. (2003). Notes towards a politics of fear. *Journal for Crime, Conflict and the Media, 1*(1), 37–54.

Appel, M., & Richter, T. (2007). Persuasive effects of fictional narratives increase over time. *Media Psychology, 10*(1), 113–134.

Baars, B. J. (2005). Global workspace theory of consciousness: Toward a cognitive neuroscience of human experience. *Progr. Brain Res., 150*, 45–53.

Badger, A. (1989). *The new deal: The depression years, 1933–40* (p. 212). New York: Hill and Wang.

Banks, A., & Hicks, H. (2016). Fear and implicit racism: Whites' support for voter ID laws. *Political Psychology, 37*(5), 641–658.

Barrett, L. F., Mesquita, B., Ochsner, K. N., & Gross, J. J. (2007). The experience of emotion. *Ann. Rev. Psychol., 58*, 373–403.

Bausum, A. (2017). *The March against fear: The last great walk of the civil rights movement and the emergence of black power* (p. 111). National Geographic Books. ISBN 978-1-4263-2665-3.

Bean, R. B. (1906). "Some racial peculiarities of the Negro brain" (PDF). *American Journal of Anatomy, 5*(4), 353–432. https://doi.org/10.1002/aja.1000050402, hdl:2027.42/49594.

Benenson, R. (1984). Social welfare under Reagan. *Editorial research reports 1984* (Vol. I). http://library.cqpress.com/cqresearcher/cqresrre1984030900

Blair, J. (1990). Blackface Minstrels in Cross-Cultural Perspective. American Studies International, 28(2), 52–65. Retrieved May 10, 2021, from http://www.jstor.org/stable/41280771.

Borgwardt, E. (2005). *A new deal for the world: America's vision for human rights* (pp. 7–8). Cambridge, MA: Harvard University Press.

Boskin, J. (1986). *Sambo: The rise and demise of an American jester.* New York: Oxford University Press.

Bourke, J. (2014). Pain sensitivity: An unnatural history from 1800 to 1965. *The Journal of Medical Humanities, 35*(3), 301–319. https://doi.org/10.1007/s10912-014-9283-7.

Brenner, M. (1990). Influence of the economy on mental health and psychophysiological illness: international perspective. *Community Mental Health in New Zealand, 5*, 2–10.

Brenner, M. H. (1973). *Mental illness and the economy*. Cambridge, MA: Harvard University Press.

Brinkley, A. (1995). *The end of reform: New deal liberalism in recession and war* (p. 47). New York: Knopf.

Bureau of Justice Statistics, National Crime Victimization Survey, 2004–2015.

Burstein, P. (2003). The impact of public opinion on public policy: A review and an agenda. *Political Research Quarterly., 56*, 29–40.

Chandler, L. V. (1970). *America's greatest depression, 1929–1941*. New York: Harper & Row.

Cintron, A., & Morrison, R. S. (2006). Pain and ethnicity in the United States: A systematic review. *Journal of Palliative Medicine, 9*(6), 1454–1473.

Cohen, Lizabeth. A consumer's republic: The politics of mass consumption in postwar America (2003).

Cohen, L. (2004). A consumers' republic: The politics of mass consumption in postwar America. *Journal of Consumer Research, 31*(1), 236–239.

Coles, R. (1967). *Children of crisis: A study of courage and fear*. Boston: Little, Brown.

Conley, D., & Domingue, B. (2016). The Bell Curve Revisited: Testing Controversial Hypotheses with Molecular Genetic Data. *Sociological Science, 3*, 520–539. https://doi.org/10.15195/v3.a23.

Crafts, N., & Fearon, P. (2010, Autumn). Lessons from the 1930s great depression. *Oxford Review of Economic Policy, 26*(3), 285–317. https://doi.org/10.1093/oxrep/grq030.

Crockatt, R. (2009). Local consequences of the global Cold War. *Cold War History, 9*(4), 542–543. https://doi.org/10.1080/14682740903268461.

D'Antonio, M. (2017). *A consequential president: The legacy of Barack Obama*. Thomas Dunne Books.

Dahlstrom, M. (2014, September 16). Using narratives and storytelling to communicate science with nonexpert audiences. *PNAS, 111*(Supplement 4), 13614–13620; first published September 15, 2014. https://doi.org/10.1073/pnas.1320645111.

Dahlstrom, M. F., & Ho, S. S. (2012). Ethical considerations of using narrative to communicate science. *Science Communication, 34*(5), 592–617.

Davis, J. (1953). The population upsurge and the American economy, 1945-80. *Journal of Political Economy, 61*(5), 369–388. Retrieved January 7, 2021, from http://www.jstor.org/stable/1827285.

De Bellis, M. D., & Zisk, A. (2014). The biological effects of childhood trauma. *Child and Adolescent Psychiatric Clinics of North America, 23*(2), 185–vii. https://doi.org/10.1016/j.chc.2014.01.002.

Debiec, J., & LeDoux, J. (2004). Fear and the Brain. *Social Research, 71*(4), 807–818. Retrieved December 27, 2020, from http://www.jstor.org/stable/40971979.

Dodd, et al. (2012). The political left rolls with the good and the political right confronts the bad: Connecting physiology and cognition to preferences. Philosophical Transactions of the Royal Society B367640–649. https://doi.org/10.1098/rstb.2011.0268.

Dore, R. A., Hoffman, K. M., Lillard, A. S., & Trawalter, S. (2014). Children's racial bias in perceptions of others' pain. *The British Journal of Developmental Psychology, 32*(2), 218–231.

Downing, D. (2003). *Communism*. Chicago, IL: Heinemann Library. Print.

Durkheim, E. (1951). *Suicide: A study in sociology*. New York: The Free Press.

Dyson, E. D. (2016). *The black presidency: Barack Obama and the politics of race in America*. Boston: Houghton Mifflin Harcourt.

Edwards, G. S., & Rushin, S. (2018, January 14). *The effect of president Trump's election on hate crimes*. Available at SSRN: https://ssrn.com/abstract=3102652 or https://doi.org/10.2139/ssrn.3102652.

Elder, G., Jr. (1974). *Children of the great depression: Social change in life experience*. Chicago: Univ.

Equal Justice Initiative. (2017). *Lynching in America: Confronting the legacy of racial terror* (3rd ed.).

Erol, Ç. C. (2015). New approaches in art education: Moodle learning and content management system-based art education. *Global Journal of Arts Education, 5*(2), 67–71. https://doi.org/10.18844/gjae.v5i2.248.

F. A. Hayek to Paul Samuelson. (1980, December 18). Friedrich A. von Hayek papers, Box 48, Folder 5, Hoover Institution Library & Archives.

Feinstein, J. S., Adolphs, R., Damasio, A., & Tranel, D. (2011). The human amygdala and the induction and experience of fear. *Current Biology, 21*, 34–38.

Felitti, V. J., & Anda, R. F., Nordenberg, D., Williamson, D. F., Spitz, A. M., Edwards, V., et al. (1998). Relationship of childhood abuse and household dysfunction to many of the leading causes of death in adults. The Adverse Childhood Experiences (ACE) Study. *American Journal of Preventive Medicine, 14*, 245–258.

Fleming, D. F. (1966). The Costs and Consequences of the Cold War. *The ANNALS of the American Academy of Political and Social Science., 366*(1), 127–138. https://doi.org/10.1177/000271626636600115.

Fossett Mark, A., & Kiecolt, K. J. (1989). The relative size of minority populations and white racial attitudes. *Social Science Quarterly., 70*, 820–835.

Frith, C. D., & Frith, U. (1999). Interacting minds — A biological basis. *Science, 286*, 1692–1695.

Fuller, L. (2001). Are we seeing things? The Pinesol Lady and the Ghost of Aunt Jemima. *Journal of Black Studies, 32*(1), 120–131. Retrieved January 9, 2021, from http://www.jstor.org/stable/2668018.

Gartner, S. S., Segura, G. M., & Wilkening, M. (1997). All politics are local: Local losses and individual attitudes toward the Vietnam War. *Journal of Conflict Resolution, 41*(5), 669–694. https://doi.org/10.1177/0022002797041005004.

Gawthorpe, A. (2020). Ken Burns, the Vietnam War, and the purpose of history. *Journal of Strategic Studies, 43*(1), 154–169. https://doi.org/10.1080/01402390.2019.1631974.

Gdalyahu, A., Tring, E., Polack, P. O., Gruver, R., Golshani, P., Fanselow, M. S., Silva, A. J., & Trachtenberg, J. T. (2012). Associative fear learning enhances sparse network coding in primary sensory cortex. *Neuron, 75*(1), 121–132. https://doi.org/10.1016/j.neuron.2012.04.035.

Giles, M., & Evans Arthur, S. (1985). External threat, perceived threat, and group identity. *Social Science Quarterly, 66*, 50–66.

Glassner, B. (1999). *The culture of fear: Why Americans are afraid of the wrong things*. New York: NY, Basic Books.

Golub, A., & Johnson, B. D. (1997). Cracks decline: Some surprises across U.S. cities. National Institute of Justice *Research in Brief*, NCJ 165707. Retrieved May 17, 2004, from http://nij.ncjrs.org/publications/pubs db.asp.

Goodwin, D. K. (1994). *No ordinary time: Franklin and Eleanor Roosevelt: The home front in world war II*. New York: Simon and Schuster.

Gore, A. (2004). The politics of fear. *Social Research: An International Quarterly, 71*(4), 779–798. https://www.muse.jhu.edu/article/527358.

Green, M. C., & Brock, T. C. (2000). The role of transportation in the persuasiveness of public narratives. *Journal of Personality and Social Psychology, 79*(5), 701–721.

Guimarãis, M., Gregório, A., Cruz, A., Guyon, N., & Moita, M. A. (2011). Time determines the neural circuit underlying associative fear learning. *Frontiers in Behavioral Neuroscience, 5*, 89. https://doi.org/10.3389/fnbeh.2011.00089.

Hamermesh, D., & Soss, N. (1974). An economic theory of suicide. *Journal of Political Economy., 82*, 83–98.

Herring, G. (2004). The Cold War and Vietnam. *OAH Magazine of History, 18*(5), 18–21. Retrieved February 13, 2021, from http://www.jstor.org/stable/25163717.

Herrnstein, R., & Murray Charles, A. (1994). *The bell curve: Intelligence and class structure in American life*. New York: Simon & Schuster.

Hoffman, K. M., Trawalter, S., Axt, J. R., & Oliver, M. N. (2016). Racial bias in pain assessment and treatment recommendations, and false beliefs about biological differences between blacks and whites. *Proceedings of the National Academy of Sciences of the United States of America, 113*(16), 4296–4301. https://doi.org/10.1073/pnas.1516047113.

Holland, P. C., & Gallagher, M. (1999). Amygdala circuitry in attentional and representational processes. *Trends in Cognitive Sciences, 3,* 65–73.

Homolar, A., & Scholz, R. (2019). The power of Trump-speak: Populist crisis narratives and ontological security. *Cambridge Review of International Affairs, 32*(3), 344–364. https://doi.org/1 0.1080/09557571.2019.1575796.

Hoover, H. (1951). *The memoirs of Herbert Hoover; years of adventure, 1874–1920.* New York: Macmillan.

Horwitz, A. (1984). The economy and social pathology. *Annual Review of Sociology., 10,* 95–119.

Howard, N., & Hussain, A. (2018). The fundamental code unit of the brain: Towards a new model for cognitive geometry. *Cognitive Computation, 10,* 426–436. https://doi.org/10.1007/ s12559-017-9538-5.

Huddy, L., Feldman, S., Taber, C., & Lahav, C. (2005). Threat, anxiety, and support of anti-terrorism policies. *American Journal of Political Science, 49,* 610–625. https://doi. org/10.1111/j.1540-5907.2005.00144.x.

Institute of Medicine (US) Committee on Opportunities in Drug Abuse Research. (1996). *Pathways of addiction: Opportunities in drug abuse research.* Washington, DC: National Academies Press (US). B, Drug Abuse Research in Historical Perspective. Available from: https://www. ncbi.nlm.nih.gov/books/NBK232965/.

Jewell, S. K. (1993). *From mammy to miss America and beyond: Cultural images and the shaping of US policy.* New York: Routledge.

Jung, H. (2019, January). The evolution of social constructivism in political science: Past to present. *SAGE Open.* https://doi.org/10.1177/2158244019832703.

Kernell, S. (1976). The Truman Doctrine speech: A case study of the dynamics of presidential opinion leadership. *Social Science History, 1*(1), 20–44. https://doi.org/10.2307/1170931.

Kirsch, I., Lynn, S. J., & Vigorito, M. (2004). The Role of Cognition in Classical and Operant Conditioning. *Journal of Clinical Psychology, 60*(4), 369–392.

Kliman, A., Bichler, S., & Nitzan, J. (2011). Systemic crisis, systemic fear: An exchange. *Journal of Critical Globalization Studies.* ISSN 2040-8498.

LaBar, K. S., Gatenby, J. C., Gore, J. C., LeDoux, J. E., & Phelps, E. A. (1998). Human amygdala activation during conditioned fear acquisition and extinction: A mixed-trial fMRI study. *Neuron, 20*(5), 937–945.

Lawrence, M. A. (2008). *The Vietnam war: A concise international history.* Oxford, UK: Oxford UP, Print.

Lopez Bunyasi, T. (2019). The role of whiteness in the 2016 presidential primaries. *Perspectives on Politics, 17*(3), 679–698. https://doi.org/10.1017/S1537592719001427.

Maier, S. F., & Watkins, L. R. (2005). Stressor controllability and learned helplessness: The roles of the dorsal raphe nucleus, serotonin, and corticotropin-releasing factor. *Neuroscience and Biobehavioral Reviews., 29,* 829–841.

Mall, F. P. (1909). On several anatomical characters of the human brain, said to vary according to race and sex, with especial reference to the weight of the frontal lobe. *American Journal of Anatomy, 9,* 1–32. https://doi.org/10.1002/aja.1000090102.

Marin, N., Benarroch, A., & Jimenez, G. E. (2000). What is the relationship between social constructivism and Piagetian constructivism? An analysis of the characteristics of the ideas within both theories. *International Journal of Science Education, 22*(3).

Marsh, E. J., Meade, M. L., & Roediger, H. L. (2003). Learning facts from fiction. *Journal of Memory and Language, 49*(4), 519–536.

Massey, D. S., & Denton, D. A. (1993). *American apartheid: Segregation and the making of the underclass.* Cambridge, MA: Harvard.

May, Elaine Tyler. Homeward bound: American families in the cold war era (1996).

McElvaine, R. S. (1984). *The great depression: America, 1929–1941*. New York: Time Books.
Merrill, D. (2006). The Truman Doctrine: Containing Communism and Modernity. *Presidential Studies Quarterly, 36*(1), 27–37. Retrieved February 13, 2021, from http://www.jstor.org/stable/27552744.
Miquel, G. P. (2007). The control of politicians in divided societies: The politics of fear. *Review of Economic Studies, Oxford University Press, 74*(4), 1259–1274.
Morgan, R. (1996). Nixon, Watergate, and the study of the presidency. *Presidential Studies Quarterly, 26*(1), 217–238. Retrieved December 27, 2020, from http://www.jstor.org/stable/27551561.
Morton, S. G. (1839). *Crania Americana; or, a comparative view of the skulls of various aboriginal nations of North and South America: To which is prefixed an essay on the varieties of the human species*. Philadelphia: J. Dobson.
Mutz, D. (2018, May). Status threat, not economic hardship, explains the 2016 presidential vote. *PNAS, 115*(19), E4330–E4339; first published April 23, 2018. https://doi.org/10.1073/pnas.1718155115.
National Research Council (US) Committee on Population; Moffitt, R. A. (Eds.). (1998). *Welfare, the family, and reproductive behavior: Research perspectives*. Washington, DC: National Academies Press (US); . 3, Trends in the Welfare System. Available from: https://www.ncbi.nlm.nih.gov/books/NBK230339/
National Research Council. Division of Behavioral and Social Sciences and Education; Commission on Behavioral and Social Sciences and Education; Committee on Basic Research in the Behavioral and Social Sciences; Gerstein, D. R., Luce, R. D., Smelser, N. J., et al., (Eds.). (1988). *The behavioral and social sciences: Achievements and opportunities*. Washington, DC: National Academies Press (US); 1, Behavior, Mind, and Brain. Available from: https://www.ncbi.nlm.nih.gov/books/NBK546486/
Neocosmos, M. (2008). The Politics of Fear and the Fear of Politics: Reflections on Xenophobic Violence in South Africa. *Journal of Asian and African Studies, 43*(6), 586–594. https://doi.org/10.1177/0021909608096655.
Oxley, D. R., Smith, K. B., Alford, J. R., Hibbing, M. V., Miller, J. L., Scalora, M., Hatemi, P. K., & Hibbing, J. R. (2008 Sep 19). Political attitudes vary with physiological traits. *Science, 321*(5896), 1667–1670. https://doi.org/10.1126/science.1157627.
Palmer, John L., & Isabel V. Sawhill (eds.). (1982). *The Reagan experiment*. The Urban Institute Press.
Patterson, James. Grand expectations: The United States, 1945–1974 (1996).
Peppers, L. (1973). Full employment surplus analysis and structural change: The 1930s. *Explorations in Economic History, 10*, 197–210.
Pickett, C. N. (2006). The cold war reference guide: A general history and annotated chronology, with selected biographies. *Reference Reviews, 20*(8), 49–49.
Plous, S., & Williams, T. (1995). Racial stereotypes from the days of American slavery: a continuing legacy. *Journal of Applied Social Psychology, 25*, 795–817.
Rhodes, J. H., & Vayo, A. B. (2019). The historical presidency: Fear and loathing in presidential candidate rhetoric, 1952–2016. *Presidential Studies Quarterly, 49*(4), 909–931. https://doi.org/10.1111/psq.12512.
Richman, J. A., Rospenda, K. M., Johnson, T. P., Cho, Y. I., Vijayasira, G., Cloninger, L., & Wolff, J. M. (2012). Drinking in the age of the Great Recession. *Journal of Addictive Diseases, 31*(2), 158–172. https://doi.org/10.1080/10550887.2012.665692.
Rimmington, D. (1998). An example of the impact of Mccarthyism and the cold war on the administration of universities. *Minerva, 36*(1), 81–84. Retrieved January 4, 2021, from http://www.jstor.org/stable/41821091.
Ronald, R. (1983). "A time for choosing," 1964. In A. A. Bolitzer et al. (Eds.), *A time for choosing: The speeches of Ronald Reagan, 1961–1982* (pp. 41–57). Chicago: Regnery.
Roosevelt, F. D., & Zevin, B. D. (1946). *Nothing to fear: The selected addresses of Franklin Delano Roosevelt, 1932–1945*. Boston: Houghton Mifflin.

Schmemann, S. (2006). *When the wall came down: The Berlin Wall and the fall of soviet communism.* Boston: Kingfisher. Print.

Schrecker, E. (1988). Archival sources for the study of McCarthyism. *The Journal of American History, 75*(1), 197–208. Retrieved January 4, 2021, from http://www.jstor.org/stable/1889667.

Seneca, L. A., & Campbell, R. (1969). *Letters from a Stoic: Epistulae morales ad Lucilium.* Harmondsworth: Penguin Books.

Shechner, T., Hong, M., Britton, J. C., Pine, D. S., & Fox, N. A. (2014). Fear conditioning and extinction across development: evidence from human studies and animal models. *Biological Psychology, 100*, 1–12. https://doi.org/10.1016/j.biopsycho.2014.04.001.

Shermer, M. (2012, June 1). Evolution Explains Why Politics Is So Tribal: Morality binds us together into cohesive groups but blinds us to the ideas and motives of those in other groups. *Scientific America.* Retrieved from https://www.scientificamerican.com/article/evolution-explains-why-politics-tribal/.

Shirlow, P., & Pain, R. (2003). The geographies and politics of fear. *Capital & Class, 27*(2), 15–26. https://doi.org/10.1177/030981680308000103.

Star, S. (1983). Simplification in Scientific Work: An Example from Neuroscience Research. *Social Studies of Science, 13*(2), 205–228. Retrieved January 7, 2021, from http://www.jstor.org/stable/284590.

The Bichler and Nitzan Archives, Toronto, Iss. 4, pp. 61–118. http://bnarchives.yorku.ca/314/.

Trainor, J., Boydell, K., & Tibshirani, R. (1987). Short-term economic change and the utilization of mental-health facilities in a metropolitan-area. *Canadian Journal of Psychiatry – Revue Canadienne De Psychiatrie, 32*, 379–383.

Tudor, A. (2003). A (Macro) Sociology of Fear? *The Sociological Review, 51*(2), 238–256. https://doi.org/10.1111/1467-954X.00417.

U.S. Census Bureau, Statistical Abstract of the United States: 1999.

U.S. Department of Justice, Federal Bureau of Investigation, *Hate Crime Statistics* for 1996–2018.

U.S. Social Security Administration. (1997). *Social Security Bulletin, 60*(3), unpublished data.

UKEssays. (2018, November). The *Cause and Effects of McCarthyism.* Retrieved from https://www.ukessays.com/essays/politics/the-cause-and-effects-of-mccarthyism.php?vref=1 on February 13, 2021.

van Duin, L., Bevaart, F., Zijlmans, J., Luijks, M. A., Doreleijers, T., Wierdsma, A. I., Oldehinkel, A. J., Marhe, R., & Popma, A. (2019). The role of adverse childhood experiences and mental health care use in psychological dysfunction of male multi-problem young adults. *European Child & Adolescent Psychiatry, 28*(8), 1065–1078. https://doi.org/10.1007/s00787-018-1263-4.

Vigil, J. M. (2010). Political leanings vary with facial expression processing and psychosocial functioning. *Group Process Interg., 13*, 547–558. https://doi.org/10.1177/1368430209356930.

Wanless, S. (2016). The role of psychological safety in human development. *Research in Human Development., 13*(1), 6–14. https://doi.org/10.1080/15427609.2016.1141283.

Waytz, A., Hoffman, K. M., & Trawalter, S. (2014). A superhumanization bias in Whites' perceptions of Blacks. *Social Psychological and Personality Science, 6*(3), 352–359.

Weiner, T. (2015). *One man against the world: The tragedy of Richard Nixon.* New York: Henry Holt and Company.

Wick, F. A., Alaoui Soce, A., Garg, S., Grace, R. C., & Wolfe, J. M. (2019). Perception in dynamic scenes: What is your Heider capacity? *Journal of Experimental Psychology General, 148*(2), 252–271. https://doi.org/10.1037/xge0000557.

Wyer, R. S., Read, S. J., & Miller, L. C. (1995). Stories are fundamental to meaning and memory: For social creatures, could it be otherwise? In R. S. Wyer (Ed.), *Knowledge and memory: The real story* (pp. 139–152). Hillsdale, NJ: Lawrence Erlbaum.

Zivin, K., Paczkowski, M., & Galea, S. (2011). Economic downturns and population mental health: research findings, gaps, challenges and priorities. *Psychological Medicine, 41*(7), 1343–1348. https://doi.org/10.1017/S003329171000173X.

Chapter 4
Fear and Poverty

In sixteenth-century England, Vagabonds was the term used to describe individuals who were without housing and nomadic and often took from others in order to survive (McIntosh, 2005; Rushton & Sigle-Rushton, 2001; Slack, 1988). Vagabonds were feared in English society and viewed as inherently flawed, idle, and criminal (Fritzsche, 1994; Lawrence, 2017). Much of English society was afraid of their presence, fearing that they would cause a rebellion (Fritzsche, 1994; Lawrence, 2017). Vagrancy increased with population growth and inflation. This level of fear led to the Vagabonds Act of 1572 (also called the Poor Law – not very trauma-informed) under the leadership of Queen Elizabeth I (Fritzsche, 1994; Lawrence, 2017). The Act mandated every impoverished and ill person be registered in their respective jurisdictions, and it imposed a community tax for the provision of care for impoverished persons – many historians argue that this is one of the first documented accounts of the development of the welfare state (Fritzsche, 1994; McIntosh, 2005; Rushton & Sigle-Rushton, 2001; Slack, 1988). The responsibility of caring for persons with less economic opportunity extended beyond the church and into the community. However, the Act also increased punishment for persons with less financial opportunity as if they were wandering; they could be subject to physical whippings and/or being burned with a hot iron (Fritzsche, 1994; Lawrence, 2017; McIntosh, 2005; Rushton & Sigle-Rushton, 2001; Slack, 1988). The contradictions and complexity of poverty are observed as early as the sixteenth century, and it appears that attitudes and beliefs have not shifted much in the twenty-first century. William Shakespeare, a prolific English author, playwright, and poet wrote extensively about the social conditions of his time. Romeo and Juliet, a classic Shakespearean love story written circa the sixteenth century, illustrates the dynamics of society and class. Romeo and Juliet both came from wealthy families, but wealth did not insulate them from personal suffering. There is a point in the story where Romeo is emotionally depraved in the context of thinking the love of his life, Juliet, was dead. Romeo goes to purchase poison from a character, Apothecary, with intention to take his own life. Apothecary was afraid to sell poison to Romeo because it was illegal – there was a notable status difference between Romeo and Apothecary (Shakespeare, 2003; Shakespeare & Durband, 1985). To convince Apothecary to sell to him, Romeo reminds Apothecary of his poverty. Here is what Romeo says to Apothecary:

"Famine is in thy cheeks,
Need and oppression starveth in thine eyes,
Contempt and beggary hang upon thy back;
The world is not thy friend nor the world's law:
The world affords no law to make thee rich;
Then be not poor, but break it, and take this." (Shakespeare, 2003; Shakespeare & Durband, 1985).

Taking note of the way that Shakespeare writes about poverty in the sixteenth century (and he makes multiple references to poverty in subsequent writings like in Othello when he writes "to him that ever fears he will be poor"), it is evident from the political and social climate at the time that poverty was feared (to be and/or at risk of being poor). It is no coincidence that words like need, oppression, starvation, and contempt and a snapshot of societal views on poverty are all represented in the above exchange between Shakespeare's characters Romeo and Apothecary. This is the backdrop from which this chapter emerges.

As demonstrated by the history of Vagabonds provided, some attitudes about individuals living in poverty are overwhelmingly negative – these negative attitudes have negative impact. Multiple studies confirm negative attitudes, constructs, and stereotypes of persons living in poverty as subhuman and less competent (Buraschi, Bustillos, & Huici, 2018; Malul, 2020; Olson, McFerran, Morales, & Dahl, 2020; Rodriguez-Bailon et al., 2017). One Swedish study evaluated class stereotypes by surveying Swedish citizens on their views of poor members in their society supported by the welfare system (Lindqvist, Björklund, & Bäckström, 2017). The study employed the Implicit Association Test (IAT). Results of this study revealed that participants linked poverty with low competence and low to medium warmth (Lindqvist et al., 2017). Sweden is known for egalitarianism; however, views on poverty appear consistent with other countries and with historical stereotypes (Cozzarelli et al., 2001; Durante & Fiske, 2017; Heider, 1958).

Many children around the world read the story of Robin Hood, a noble-thief (an oxymoron) who stole from the rich and gave to the poor (Pyle, 1883; Reynolds et al., 2003). The reality of Robin Hood's sixteenth-century English folklore character has been hotly debated among historians (Pyle, 1883; Reynolds et al., 2003). Whether his character is fiction and/or nonfiction, the story left an impression on the psyche of young people all around the world and indicates that the condition of poverty dates back to late antiquity (and perhaps before), but the fact that there is limited data about it suggests a kind of invisibility (invisibility of persons living in poverty) that persists in the current day. Thomas Riis addresses attitudes on poverty and the subsequent invisibility of the poor in the middle ages (the period from circa fifth to circa sixteenth century). Riis wrote: "It is important to recognise from the outset that we rarely, if ever, see the medieval poor as they saw themselves" (Riis,

1979). Further, Riis interpretively describes the impression that the medieval poor may have left on those they encountered which included "pity, fear and disgust" (Riis, 1979). Riis wrote about poverty as a form of deprivation that flowed from structural issues like under and unemployment. The complexities and contradictions noted in the example of Robin Hood having to steal from persons with more to support persons with less poses larger philosophical, existential, and moral questions about unmet need, the human right to exist beyond surviving as survival is a low bar.

4.1   Fear-Based Narrative, Race, and Poverty

There has been a negatively constructed narrative and image of poverty; when negative constructs and images of poverty intersect with race, the impact is compounded toxicity. Bloeser and Williams confirm the implication that redistributive policies have traditionally been associated with negative racial stereotypes and Whites who are racially resentful will generally oppose such policies even when they might be of economic benefit to them (Bloeser & Williams, 2020). Bloeser and Williams examine the implications of the relationship between racial resentment and redistributive policies by employing American National Election study. In short, they revealed that the affiliation between racial resentment and opposition to redistributive policies was significantly higher in high-income Whites and weaker for lower-income Whites (Bloeser & Williams, 2020). Results suggest that in the context of racial antagonism, White opposition to redistributive policies is elevated especially when they will not directly benefit from the/a policy (Bloeser & Williams, 2020). Studies reveal that negative stereotypes about poverty are compounded when race is considered, namely, being Black and poor results in social constructs and narrative marked by fear, criminality, low intelligence, and subhumanness (Al-Khouja, Graham, Weinstein, & Zheng, 2020; Okeke, Howard, Kurtz-Costes, & Rowley, 2009; Priest et al., 2018; Taylor, Guy-Walls, Wilkerson, et al., 2019).

4.2   Economic Downturn and Poverty

It was amid significant national economic downturn and in the context of widespread deprivation and financial uncertainty, namely, after the Great Depression around 1933, that the concept of the welfare state became predominant in the United States. A welfare state is branded as a national contingency to socially support citizens, based on principles of equality and redistributive wealth (Bergqvist, Yngwe, & Lundberg, 2013). The welfare state, in the United States, may be considered as an anecdote/reaction to the Great Depression, characterized by a governmental response, under the leadership of Franklin D. Roosevelt (as part of the New Deal), constructed to equitably buoy and stabilize the economic conditions of society. Factually there have been many objections to the welfare state (Feldstein, 2005;

Jansson, 2015). Reagan expressed reservations to the social safety nets that President Johnson had prior established by associating the welfare state with big government (Bailey & Duquette, 2014), redistributive wealth, and a fiscal drain that threatened the core of democracy itself (Bailey & Duquette, 2014). Some economists and historians have highlighted philosophical reservations and fears regarding the welfare state to include the idea that making people pay for the social needs of others (via taxes) while gaining no benefit is unmotivating and infuriating (Wicksell, 1967). Moral objections include the thinking that social programs usurp the institution of the family and leads to social ills (Barnard, 2016; Feagin, 1972; Lindbeck, Nyberg, & Weibull, 1999; Niskanen, 1996). Political objections include the argument that civil society is threatened and debilitated with the influx of interest groups supporting welfare states (Murray, 1984). Fear of loss of status and redistribution of are some of the drivers in the underlying resistance to reducing poverty. Lianos writes about the hope and fear of the welfare state highlighting that in the case of recovering from a depressed economic state and/or depressed conditions, "that those who are more threatened fear the re-establishment of a new normality where their places will have been weakened or lost" (Lianos, 2020).

There are multiple working definitions of poverty. The United Nations defines poverty as structural and states that "its manifestations include hunger and malnutrition, limited access to education and other basic services, social discrimination and exclusion, as well as the lack of participation in decision-making" (United Nations, 2019). The World Bank's definition of poverty is based on an actual dollar amount per day they refer to as the poverty line. According to the World Bank, there are approximately 689 million people living on less than $1.90 per day. This is profound poverty (World Bank, 2021). The US Census Bureau defines poverty by establishing a minimum threshold based on the estimated cost of a nominally nutritious diet, estimated by the US Department of Agriculture (USDA), and multiplied by three (US Census Bureau, 2019).

According to US Census Bureau data, in 2019, 34 million Americans were living in poverty. According to US Census Bureau data on the distribution of poverty by age and race from 1959 to 2019, in 1959, 44% of children under the age of 18 and 14% of people 65 or over were living in poverty. In 2019, 30% of children under age 18 and 14% of people 65 or over were living in poverty. When this same data set is broken down by race (data goes back to 2002), 25% of Black children under the age of 18 and 10% of Black people 65 or over were living in poverty; in 2019, those numbers shifted to 24% and 8%, respectively (US Census Bureau, 2019; US Census Bureau, 1960 to 2020).

While there are various definitions of poverty, poverty has common impacts that traverse nutrition, learning, development, and behavioral and physical health. Living in poverty mostly guarantees living with inconsistent access to food, clean water, healthcare, secure housing, and income and being marginalized, ostracized, and subject to blame and shame (Braveman & Gottlieb, 2014; Worku & Woldesenbet, 2015). Uncertainty, exclusion, discrimination, and unmet basic needs are among the top contributors to chronic stress in the context of poverty (Braveman & Gottlieb, 2014). In the early 1940s, Abraham Maslow introduced a five-tiered pyramid hierarchy of human needs. The foundation of the pyramid included basic needs like food and water, above food and water is safety (financial, physical, spiritual), above safety is love and belonging, and above love and belonging is esteem (Kenrick, Griskevicius, Neuberg, & Schaller, 2010; Maslow, 1943). Maslow's model suggests that humans are less likely to reach the acme of the hierarchy which is self-actualization in the absence of base/basic needs being met. Poverty is the absence of basic needs being met and a denial of access to resources required for survival. There is a connection between unmet basic needs, trauma, the structural components of poverty, and the cascading effects of fear.

4.3 Poverty and Its Impact on Brain Development

Making the connection, the same areas of the brain that are involved in fear conditioning are impacted, developmentally, in the case of poverty. Poverty and its conditions pose a chronic physiologic and psychological stress on the body. It can leave individuals in survival mode and in a chronic state of fear. Several studies have confirmed an association between changes in prefrontal function, cognitive ability, and achievement with socioeconomic status (SES) (Blair & Raver, 2016; Bradley & Corwin, 2002; Hackman & Farah, 2009; Hackman, Farah, & Meaney, 2010; Kishiyama, Boyce, Jimenez, Perry, & Knight, 2009; Mezzacappa, 2004; Nicholas, Ahmed, Tang, Morrison, & Davis-Kean, 2021; Noble, Norman, & Farah, 2005; Stevens, Lauinger, & Neville, 2009). SES takes into consideration the social and environmental influences on development.

Moriguchi et al. investigated the relationship between low SES and functional brain development (Moriguchi & Shinohara, 2019). The study consisted of 93 preschool children with varied levels of SES exposed to cognitive shifting tasks with concomitant measurement of prefrontal activation by near-infrared spectroscopy (Moriguchi & Shinohara, 2019). The study revealed that children who were identified as low SES had limits in their lateral prefrontal region activation amid cognitive shifting tasks compared to children with mid- to higher-level SES which did show prefrontal activation during tasks. While there were no demonstrable differences in behavior in the various SES groups, this study did submit that low SES status may affect the functional development of the prefrontal cortex (Moriguchi & Shinohara, 2019), consistent with prior studies.

Innumerable studies have demonstrated the deleterious impact of low SES on hippocampal volume and structure (Farah et al., 2006; Hanson, Chandra, Wolfe, & Pollak, 2011; Hanson et al., 2015). The hippocampus plays an important role in memory and learning. Smaller hippocampal volumes have been noted in children with lower SES compared to children with higher SES (Farah et al., 2006; Hanson et al., 2011; Hanson et al., 2015; Olszewski-Kubilius & Corwith, 2018). This same phenomenon has been shown in animal models; the hippocampus is susceptible to stress (Alfarez, Joëls, & Krugers, 2003; McEwen, 1999).

The amygdala and SES are not as robustly studied as the prefrontal cortex; however, a study by Merz et al. investigated SES and amygdalar volume by age. The study found lower SES and parental education were pointedly associated with smaller amygdala volume in adolescence (13–21 years), but no significant association in younger children ages 3–12. Smaller amygdala volume was associated with higher rates of depression (Merz, Tottenham, & Noble, 2018). McEwen and Gianaros (2010) demonstrated a link to the stress of low SES and deleterious impact on the amygdala (fear center of the brain) (McEwen & Gianaros, 2010).

Low SES has a deleterious impact on brain development; this impact may be compounded when race-based discrimination and structural racism are considered (Assari, Boyce, & Bazargan, 2020a, 2020b; DeSantis et al., 2007; Dismukes et al., 2018; Hanson et al., 2015; Miller & Taylor, 2012). Chronic stress, economic disparity, and underemployment are higher in minority communities, amplifying the impacts of low SES (Miller & Taylor, 2012).

Judd and colleagues contend that genetic factors and socioeconomic status (SES) inequalities combined may play a large role in educational attainment and be associated with variations in brain structure and cognition (Judd et al., 2020). Conditions like poverty marked by deprivation, stress, and unmet need impact parts of the brain involved in fear conditioning to include the prefrontal cortex, hippocampus, and amygdala. Several studies have also highlighted the impacts of SES on declarative memory (a hippocampal function) and spatial cognition (hippocampal and medial temporal lobe function) (Farah et al., 2006; Herrmann & Guadagno, 1997; Levine, Vasilyeva, Lourenco, Newcombe, & Huttonlocher, 2005; Noble, McCandliss, & Farah, 2007).

4.4   Poverty and Nutrition

Trending data demonstrate that nutritional deficits can compromise healthy brain development in utero and beyond, influencing disease risks, cognitive capacity, and health outcomes (Mattei & Pietrobelli, 2019). Vitamin and minerals (also known as micronutrients) and fats, proteins, and carbohydrates (also known as macronutrients) are requisite for healthy human development, especially brain development (Carreiro et al., 2016; Chianese et al., 2018; Fogelholm, Anderssen, Gunnarsdottir, & Lahti-Koski, 2012; Wasantwisut, 1997). If a nutritional mandate is not met at a specific point in time during development, the trajectory for healthy development is negatively impacted (Cusick & Georgieff, 2012; Cusick & Georgieff, 2016; Rosales, Reznick, & Zeisel, 2009). Macro- and micronutrient requirements are critical for healthy brain development in the first 1000 days which includes conception to 3 years of age (Cusick & Georgieff, 2012; Cusick & Georgieff, 2016). Malnutrition deleteriously impacts the nervous system and brain activity (Guedes, Monteiro, & Teodósio, 1996). A nutritious diet robustly strengthens brain development in children with significant positive impacts on learning, behavior, and productivity (Prado & Dewey, 2014).

Well-studied micronutrients and macronutrients implicated in brain development and development globally include vitamin A (found in things like dairy, spinach, peppers squash, sweet potatoes, liver), vitamin D (found richly in foods like salmon, beef liver, cheese, tuna, and egg yolks), zinc (found richly in oysters, red meat, poultry, beans), folic acid (found in food like broccoli, Brussel sprouts, leafy green vegetables), and docosahexaenoic acid (DHA) found richly in fish and seafood. Vitamin A deficiency in animal studies has shown the relationship between deficiency and low cognition, compromised learning, neuronal growth, and survival (Olson & Mello, 2010). Vitamin D deficiency may play a role in neuronal development and a reduction of microglial inflammatory function contributing to increased brain infections with possible links to the development of diabetes mellitus and neurodevelopmental disorders (Anjum, Jaffery, Fayyaz, Samoo, & Anjum, 2018).

Zinc deficiency may negatively impact skills of perception, thinking, memory, learning, and attention (Bhatnagar & Taneja, 2001). Zinc has also been shown to be involved in brain development from the neonatal phase through the life span – it modulates gene expression, neuronal growth, reorganization, and signaling (Gower-Winter & Levenson, 2012). Folic acid plays a role in helping the neural tube (the blueprint for the brain, spinal cord, spine, and skull) to fold properly (Naninck, Stijger, & Brouwer-Brolsma, 2019). DHA is a fatty acid (found in fish oil, seafood, and breastmilk), and its deficiency has been linked with cognitive compromise, diminished behavioral performance, and deleterious impact on brain development globally (Innis, 2007). Undernutrition and deficiencies of iodine, iron, and folate impact the development of the brain and the emergent cognitive functions (Bryan et al., 2004). A review of British childhood nutrition inequity and poverty highlighted the pervasiveness of poverty and poor nutrition combined indicating that low income was associated with poor nutrition at all stages of life (Nelson, 2000). Poor nutrition related to high-fat and lower antioxidant-rich diets – this poor nutrition trend was linked with lower immunity, poor dental hygiene, shoddier learning cognitive capacity, and lower rates of breastfeeding (a natural source of fatty acids and nutrients critical for brain development) (Nelson, 2000). Nutrition (or the lack thereof) has epigenetic implications as it has been demonstrated to alter gene structure and expression with concomitant downstream effects on brain growth and development (Rosales et al., 2009). Poverty is structural and systemic; it is observed that individuals with lower SES are more likely to live in food deserts and have limited access to healthy food options which have downstream implications for mental and physical health (Engels, Tian, Govoni, Wynn, & Smith, 2018).

4.5   Poverty Is Structural

The effects of poverty are compounded (as it is structural) when you consider homelessness, lack of nutrition, underemployment, and unemployment increase the likelihood of chronic stress and physical and mental depravity. Homelessness is developing into a national and international crisis (Turnbull, Muckle, & Masters,

2007). According to a 2019 report from the Council of Economic Advisers on the state of homelessness in the America, in January of 2018, over half a million Americans were homeless in the United States. Of which one third were unsheltered and two thirds were sheltered. Overarching homeless population in the United States on a single night is 17 people per 10,000 in the population (The Council of Economic Advisors, 2019). According to the United Nations, globally, 1.6 billion people worldwide live in inadequate housing conditions (United Nations, 2020). Persons living in poverty are at greater risk of being homeless, underemployed, or unemployed, have poor education, are underinsured, and have a history of child-hood trauma (Nooe & Patterson, 2010). Persons living in poverty are also more likely to have experienced disruption in the family unit because of it (Shinn, Gibbons-Benton, & Brown, 2015; Turnbull, Muckle, & Masters, 2007).

4.6   Poverty + Environmental Injustice

Living in poverty also increases the risk of living in substandard housing conditions with poor sanitation, overcrowding, insufficient ventilation – all factors that increase and amplify the risk for chronic disease (Hirsch, 1998, 2000; Hood, 2005). Where you live is just as important as how you live; there are also neighborhood-level effects on overall health that include, but not limited to, exposure to violence, modu-lated by low SES (Sampson, Raudenbush, & Earls, 1997). There are differences in lead exposure stratified by race and SES, with greater exposure in racial minorities with low SES (Krieger & Higgins, 2002; Lynch & Meier, 2020). Persons with low SES and racial minority groups have higher incidences of living in conditions where air is polluted and suffer grave health conditions (Gochfeld & Burger, 2011; Hajat, Hsia, & O'Neill, 2015). Other factors linked with low SES and how and where individuals live include whether or not there is access to sidewalks, bike paths, run-ning trails, parks, and recreational centers (which help to increase the possibility of physical activity) combined with globally not feeling safe in a neighborhood sec-ondary to crime have deleterious implications for physical and behavioral health (Hood, 2005).

4.7   Poverty and Unemployment, Underemployment, Low Skills, and the Technological Divide

There is also the phenomenon of jobs being available, but individuals aren't skilled and/or educated enough to seize the opportunity of employment (Arulampalam, Booth, & Taylor, 2000; Dynarski & Sheffrin, 1990). This is further complicated by a technological divide – persons living in poverty are less likely to have access to high-speed Internet and reliable cell service and are more likely to be technologically illiterate (Chesser, Burke, Reyes, & Rohrberg, 2016; Hoang, Blank, & Quan-Haase, 2020; Ranchordas, 2020; Scheerder, van Deursen, & van Dijk, 2017). Not only can they not afford the technology and/or maintenance fees but end up being less savvy when it comes to the use of technology (Chesser et al., 2016; Hoang et al., 2020; Ranchordas, 2020; Scheerder et al., 2017). Overwhelmingly, more jobs mandate the ability to use computers and all its applications – inability to participate in the technological expectation translates into limited ability to participate in the larger global economy (Chesser et al., 2016; Hoang et al., 2020; Ranchordas, 2020; Scheerder et al., 2017). The cascading impacts of poverty run far, deep, and wide.

Fear is compounded in the case of poverty as there is the fear others hold for persons who are poor (negative stereotypes among others) and then there is the fear that persons in poverty live with scarcity and depravation conditions. Being subject to the stereotypes and negativity of others combined with being in survival mode from conditions of exceptional lack is a profound physiological, physical, and mental tax. Felitti and Anda's seminal 1998 study on adverse childhood experiences (ACEs) show the relationship between poverty and chronic toxic stress (Felitti, Anda, Williamson, et al., 1998). The study revealed that the higher the ACE, the higher the risk for chronic medical and behavioral conditions (Felitti et al., 1998). Spin-off studies further demonstrated that lower SES is associated with significant toxic stress (Braveman & Gottlieb, 2014; Francis, DePriest, Wilson, & Gross, 2018; Whiteside-Mansell, McKelvey, Saccente, & Selig, 2019) and greater risks of ACEs and maltreatment (Walsh, McCartney, Smith, & Armour, 2019).

4.8 Fear and Toxic Stress

There are certain conditions that turn on the stress response in humans like not knowing where the next meal is coming from, not having place to stay, and no secure means of paying bills and tending to healthcare needs. This constant state of worrying triggers those areas in the brain that are responsible for fear. Uncertainty and persistent lack = fear. Fear, as discussed in prior chapters, is meant to be a time and threat limited response. Fear is the body's mechanism for tapping into the body's stress response which is tied to the hypothalamic-pituitary-adrenal (HPA) axis. When the body is stressed, it releases several stress hormones to include cortisol. This fear-stress response helps humans to appropriately seek safety, and once safety is realized, this fear-stress response "should" turn off. In the literature, toxic stress is described as abnormal stress response characterized by instability of the stress response resulting in prolonged cortisol activation and a persistent inflammatory state, with failure of the body to normalize these changes after the stressor is absent (Franke, 2014; Johnson, Riley, Granger, & Riis, 2013; Wolf, Miller, & Chen, 2008). Early and prolonged exposure to chronic stress has implications later in life as it increases inflammation and lowers immunity, increasing risk of infection and chronic disease (high blood pressure, diabetes, cardiac disease) (Danese et al., 2012; Felitti et al., 1998; Juster et al., 2010; Rogosch, Dackis, & Cicchetti, 2011).

Childhood poverty deleteriously impacts physical and mental health in adulthood (Javanbakht et al., 2015). Javanbakht and colleagues used fMRI to investigate the link between childhood poverty and neural processing of social signals in adulthood. There were 52 participants with ages 23–25 with varying SES whose brains were imaged while completing the Emotional Faces Assessment Task (Javanbakht et al., 2015). Childhood poverty was associated with higher amygdala and medial prefrontal cortical responses to threat over happy faces and less connectivity between the left amygdala (which plays a role in the expression and processing of fear) and mPFC (Javanbakht et al., 2015). Adults with a history of childhood poverty were more susceptible to social threat cues and less to positive social cues (happy faces) (Javanbakht et al., 2015). This is significant because it demonstrates the impact deprivation conditions that result in chronic stress have on the fear-stress response – structurally it looks like loss of top-down control (the cortex has decreased control on the amygdala, which is what is seen in conditions like post-traumatic stress disorder). The threshold for a fear response is effectively lowered.

Poverty is structural. Poverty is attached to historical, political, and social fear, and it results in fear and stress in persons subject to it. Poverty represents a series of fear on fear responses – fear-based narratives contribute to fear-based people which contribute to fear-based systems which contribute to fear-based societies. Fear that doesn't quite turn off is trauma. Fear on top of fear and trauma on top of trauma – a vicious cycle that must be disrupted if society is to move toward healing and change.

References

Alfarez, D. N., Joëls, M., & Krugers, H. J. (2003). Chronic unpredictable stress impairs long-term potentiation in rat hippocampal CA1 area and dentate gyrus in vitro. *The European Journal of Neuroscience, 17*(9), 1928–1934. https://doi.org/10.1046/j.1460-9568.2003.02622.x. PMID: 12752792.

Al-Khouja, M., Graham, L., Weinstein, N., & Zheng, Y. (2020). How autonomy support and ethical value alignment influences attitudes towards diversity in English police. *Journal of Moral Education, 49*(3), 365–380.

Anjum, I., Jaffery, S. S., Fayyaz, M., Samoo, Z., & Anjum, S. (2018). The role of vitamin D in brain health: A mini literature review. *Cureus, 10*(7), e2960. https://doi.org/10.7759/cureus.2960.

Arulampalam, W., Booth, A. L., & Taylor, M. P. (2000). Unemployment persistence. *Oxford Economic Papers, 52*(1), 24–50.

Assari, S., Boyce, S., & Bazargan, M. (2020a). Subjective family socioeconomic status and adolescents' attention: Blacks' diminished returns. *Children, 7*(80), 1–14. https://doi.org/10.3390/children7080080.

Assari, S., Boyce, S., & Bazargan, M. (2020b). Subjective socioeconomic status and children's amygdala volume: Minorities' diminish returns. *Neuroscience, 1*(2), 59–74. https://doi.org/10.3390/neurosci1020006.

Bailey, M. J., & Duquette, N. J. (2014). How Johnson fought the war on poverty: The economics and politics of funding at the Office of Economic Opportunity. *The Journal of Economic History, 74*(2), 351–388. https://doi.org/10.1017/s0022050714000291.

Barnard, P. A. (2016). The causes of poverty: Is a biblical understanding reflected in the experiences of today's poor? *Missiology., 44*(4), 448–465. https://doi.org/10.1177/0091829616669181.

Bergqvist, K., Yngwe, M. Å., & Lundberg, O. (2013). Understanding the role of welfare state characteristics for health and inequalities – An analytical review. *BMC Public Health, 13*, 1234. https://doi.org/10.1186/1471-2458-13-1234.

Bhatnagar, S., & Taneja, S. (2001). Zinc and cognitive development. *The British Journal of Nutrition, 85*(Suppl 2), S139–S145. https://doi.org/10.1079/bjn2000306. PMID: 11509102.

Blair, C., & Raver, C. C. (2016). Poverty, stress, and brain development: New directions for prevention and intervention. *Academic Pediatrics, 16*(3 Suppl), S30–S36. https://doi.org/10.1016/j.acap.2016.01.010.

Bloeser, A. J., & Williams, T. (2020). The color of class politics: Economic position, racial resentment, and attitudes about redistribution. *Politics, Groups, and Identities*. https://doi.org/10.1080/21565503.2020.1773279.

Bradley, R. H., & Corwin, R. F. (2002). Socioeconomic status and child development. *Annual Review of Psychology, 53*, 371–399.

Braveman, P., & Gottlieb, L. (2014). The social determinants of health: It's time to consider the causes of the causes. *Public Health Reports (Washington, D.C.: 1974), 129*(Suppl 2), 19–31. https://doi.org/10.1177/00333549141291S206.

Bryan, J., Osendarp, S., Hughes, D., Calvaresi, E., Baghurst, K., & van Klinken, J. W. (2004). Nutrients for cognitive development in school-aged children. *Nutrition Reviews, 62*, 295–306.

Buraschi, D., Bustillos, A., & Huici, C. (2018). Attitudes toward immigrants, beliefs about causes of poverty and effects of perspective-taking. *The Spanish Journal of Psychology, 21*, E66. https://doi.org/10.1017/sjp.2018.65.

Carreiro, A. L., Dhillon, J., Gordon, S., Higgins, K. A., Jacobs, A. G., McArthur, B. M., Redan, B. W., Rivera, R. L., Schmidt, L. R., & Mattes, R. D. (2016). The macronutrients, appetite, and energy intake. *Annual Review of Nutrition, 36*, 73–103. https://doi.org/10.1146/annurev-nutr-121415-112624.

Chesser, A., Burke, A., Reyes, J., & Rohrberg, T. (2016). Navigating the digital divide: A systematic review of eHealth literacy in underserved populations in the United States. *Informatics for Health & Social Care, 41*(1), 1–19. https://doi.org/10.3109/17538157.2014.948171. Epub 2015 Feb 24. PMID: 25710808.

Chianese, R., Coccurello, R., Viggiano, A., Scafuro, M., Fiore, M., Coppola, G., Operto, F. F., Fasano, S., Laye, S., Pierantoni, R., & Meccariello, R. (2018). Impact of dietary fats on brain functions. *Current Neuropharmacology, 16*(7), 1059–1085. https://doi.org/10.2174/1570159X15666171017102547.

Cozzarelli, et al. (2001). Attitudes toward the poor and attributions for poverty. *Journal of Social Issues, 57*(2), 207–227.

Cusick, S. E., & Georgieff, M. K. (2012). Nutrient supplementation and neurodevelopment: Timing is the key. *Archives of Pediatrics & Adolescent Medicine, 155*, 481–482.

Cusick, S. E., & Georgieff, M. K. (2016). The role of nutrition in brain development: The Golden opportunity of the "first 1000 days". *The Journal of Pediatrics, 175*, 16–21. https://doi.org/10.1016/j.jpeds.2016.05.013.

Danese, et al. (2012). Adverse childhood experiences, allostasis, allostatic load, and age-related disease. *Physiology & Behavior, 106*(1), 29–39.

DeSantis, A. S., Adam, E. K., Doane, L. D., Mineka, S., Zinbarg, R. E., & Craske, M. G. (2007). Racial/ethnic differences in cortisol diurnal rhythms in a community sample of adolescents. *The Journal of Adolescent Health, 41*, 3–13. https://doi.org/10.1016/j.jadohealth.2007.03.006.

Dismukes, A., Shirtcliff, E., Jones, C. W., Zeanah, C., Theall, K., & Drury, S. (2018). The development of the cortisol response to dyadic stressors in black and white infants. *Development and Psychopathology, 30*, 1995–2008. https://doi.org/10.1017/S0954579418001232.

Durante, F., & Fiske, S. T. (2017). How social-class stereotypes maintain inequality. *Current Opinion in Psychology, 18*, 43–48. https://doi.org/10.1016/j.copsyc.2017.07.033.

Dynarski, M., & Sheffrin, S. M. (1990). The behavior of unemployment durations over the cycle. *Review of Economics and Statistics, 72*(2), 350–356.

Engels, L., Tian, X., Govoni, K., Wynn, M., & Smith, B. (2018). The effects of poor maternal nutrition on fetal brain development. *Journal of Animal Sciences, 96*, 80–102.

Farah, et al. (2006). Childhood poverty: Specific associations with neurocognitive development. *Brain Research, 1110*, 166–174.

Feagin, J. R. (1972). Poverty: We still believe that god help them who help themselves. *Psychology Today, 6*(6), 101–129.

Feldstein, M. (2005). Rethinking social insurance. *American Economic Review, 95*(1 March), 1–24.

Felitti, V. J., Anda, R. F., Williamson, D. F., et al. (1998). Relationship of childhood abuse and household dysfunction to many of the leading causes of death in adults. *American Journal of Preventive Medicine, 14*, 245–258.

Fogelholm, M., Anderssen, S., Gunnarsdottir, I., & Lahti-Koski, M. (2012). Dietary macronutrients and food consumption as determinants of long-term weight change in adult populations: A systematic literature review. *Food & Nutrition Research, 56*. https://doi.org/10.3402/fnr.v56i0.19103.

Francis, L., DePriest, K., Wilson, M., & Gross, D. (2018). Child poverty, toxic stress, and social determinants of health: Screening and care coordination. *Online Journal of Issues in Nursing, 23*(3), 2. https://doi.org/10.3912/OJIN.Vol23No03Man02.

Franke, H. A. (2014). Toxic stress: Effects, prevention and treatment. *Children (Basel, Switzerland), 1*(3), 390–402. https://doi.org/10.3390/children1030390.

Fritzsche, P. (1994). Vagabond in the Fugitive City: Hans Ostwald, Imperial Berlin and the Grossstodt-Dokumente. *Journal of Contemporary History, 29*(3), 385–402. https://doi.org/10.1177/002200949402900302.

Gochfeld, M., & Burger, J. (2011). Disproportionate exposures in environmental justice and other populations: the importance of outliers. *American Journal of Public Health, 101*(Suppl 1), S53–S63. https://doi.org/10.2105/AJPH.2011.300121. Age, poverty, and minority status place some groups at a disproportionately high risk for environmental disease.

Gower-Winter, S. D., & Levenson, C. W. (2012). Zinc in the central nervous system: From molecules to behavior. *BioFactors (Oxford, England), 38*(3), 186–193. https://doi.org/10.1002/biof.1012.

Guedes, R. C., Monteiro, J. S., & Teodósio, N. R. (1996). Malnutrition and brain function: Experimental studies using the phenomenon of cortical spreading depression. *Revista Brasileira de Biologia, 56*(Su 1 Pt 2), 293–301. PMID: 9394508.

Hackman, D. A., & Farah, M. J. (2009). Socioeconomic status and the developing brain. *Trends in Cognitive Sciences, 13*(2), 65–73.

Hackman, D. A., Farah, M. J., & Meaney, M. J. (2010). Socioeconomic status and the brain: Mechanistic insights from human and animal research. *Nature Reviews Neuroscience, 11*(9), 651–659. https://doi.org/10.1038/nrn2897.

Hajat, A., Hsia, C., & O'Neill, M. S. (2015). Socioeconomic disparities and air pollution exposure: A global review. *Current Environmental Health Reports, 2*(4), 440–450. https://doi.org/10.1007/s40572-015-0069-5.

Hanson, J. L., Chandra, A., Wolfe, B. L., & Pollak, S. D. (2011). Association between income and the hippocampus. *PLoS One, 6*(5), e18712. https://doi.org/10.1371/journal.pone.0018712. PMID: 21573231; PMCID: PMC3087752.

Hanson, J. L., Nacewicz, B. M., Sutterer, M. J., Cayo, A. A., Schaefer, S. M., Rudolph, K. D., Shirtcliff, E. A., Pollak, S. D., & Davidson, R. J. (2015). Behavioral problems after early life stress: Contributions of the hippocampus and amygdala. *Biological Psychiatry, 77*(4), 314–323. https://doi.org/10.1016/j.biopsych.2014.04.020. Epub 2014 May 23. PMID: 24993057; PMCID: PMC4241384.

Heider, F. (1958). *The psychology of interpersonal relations*. New York: Wiley.

Herrmann, D., & Guadagno, M. A. (1997). Memory performance and socioeconomic status. *Applied Cognitive Psychology, 11*, 113–120.

Hirsch, A. R. (1998). *Making the second ghetto: Race and housing in Chicago, 1940–1960.* (Original work published 1983). Chicago: University of Chicago Press.

Hirsch, A. R. (2000). Choosing segregation: Federal housing policy between Shelley and Brown. In J. F. Bauman, R. Biles, & K. M. Szylvian (Eds.), *From tenements to the Taylor Homes: In search of an urban housing policy in twentieth century America* (pp. 206–225). Pennsylvania: The Pennsylvania State University Press.

Hoang, L., Blank, G., & Quan-Haase, A. (2020). The winners and the losers of the platform economy: Who participates? *Information, Communication & Society*, 1–20. https://doi.org/10.108 0/1369118X.2020.1720771.

Hood, E. (2005). Dwelling disparities: How poor housing leads to poor health. *Environmental Health Perspectives, 113*(5), A310–A317. https://doi.org/10.1289/ehp.113-a310.

Innis, S. M. (2007). Dietary (n-3) fatty acids and brain development. *The Journal of Nutrition, 137*(4), 855–859. https://doi.org/10.1093/jn/137.4.855. PMID: 17374644.

Jansson, B. S. (2015). *The reluctant welfare state: Engaging history to advance social work practice in contemporary society.* Australia/Stamford: Cengage Learning.

Javanbakht, A., King, A. P., Evans, G. W., Swain, J. E., Angstadt, M., Phan, K. L., & Liberzon, I. (2015). Childhood poverty predicts adult amygdala and frontal activity and connectivity in response to emotional faces. *Frontiers in Behavioral Neuroscience, 9*, 154. https://doi. org/10.3389/fnbeh.2015.00154.

Johnson, S. B., Riley, A. W., Granger, D. A., & Riis, J. (2013). The science of early life toxic stress for pediatric practice and advocacy. *Pediatrics, 131*, 319–327. https://doi.org/10.1542/ peds.2012-0469.

Judd, N. et al. (2020, June 2). Cognitive and brain development is independently influenced by socioeconomic status and polygenic scores for educational attainment. *Proceedings of the National Academy of Sciences of the United States of America, 117*(22), 12411–12418; first published May 19, 2020. https://doi.org/10.1073/pnas.2001228117.

Juster, et al. (2010). Allostatic load biomarkers of chronic stress and impact on health and cognition. *Neuroscience and Biobehavioral Reviews, 35*(1), 2–16.

Kenrick, D. T., Griskevicius, V., Neuberg, S. L., & Schaller, M. (2010). Renovating the pyramid of needs: Contemporary extensions built upon ancient foundations. *Perspectives on Psychological Science, 5*(3), 292–314. https://doi.org/10.1177/1745691610369469.

Kishiyama, M. M., Boyce, W. T., Jimenez, A. M., Perry, L. M., & Knight, R. T. (2009). Socioeconomic disparities affect prefrontal function in children. *Journal of Cognitive Neuroscience, 21*, 1106–1115.

Krieger, J., & Higgins, D. L. (2002). Housing and health: Time again for public health action. *American Journal of Public Health, 92*(5), 758–768. https://doi.org/10.2105/ajph.92.5.758.

Lawrence, P. (2017). The Vagrancy Act (1824) and the Persistence of Pre-emptive Policing in England since 1750. *The British Journal of Criminology, 57*(3), 513–531. https://doi. org/10.1093/bjc/azw008.

Levine, S. C., Vasilyeva, M., Lourenco, S. F., Newcombe, N. S., & Huttonlocher, J. (2005). Socioeconomic status modifies the sex difference in spatial skill. *Psychological Science, 16*, 841–845.

Lianos, M. (2020). The welfare state: Where hope and fear meet. *European Societies, 22*(3), 291–292. https://doi.org/10.1080/14616696.2020.1771861.

Lindbeck, A., Nyberg, S., & Weibull, J. W. (1999). Social norms and economic incentives in the welfare state. *Quarterly Journal of Economics, 114*(1), 1–35.

Lindqvist, A., Björklund, F., & Bäckström, M. (2017). The perception of the poor: Capturing stereotype content with different measures. *Nordic Psychology, 69*(4), 231–247. https://doi.org/1 0.1080/19012276.2016.1270774.

Lynch, E. E., & Meier, H. C. S. (2020). The intersectional effect of poverty, home ownership, and racial/ethnic composition on mean childhood blood lead levels in Milwaukee County neighborhoods. *PLoS One, 15*(6), e0234995. https://doi.org/10.1371/journal.pone.0234995.

Malul, M. (2020). Poverty and social policy: Perceptions versus reality. *Poverty & Public Policy, 11*(4), 291–301. https://doi.org/10.1002/pop4.261dd.

Maslow, A. H. (1943). A theory of human motivation. *Psychological Review, 50*(4), 370–396.

Mattei, D., & Pietrobelli, A. (2019). Micronutrients and brain development. *Current Nutrition Reports, 8*, 99–107. https://doi.org/10.1007/s13668-019-0268-z.

McEwen, B. S. (1999). Stress and hippocampal plasticity. *Annual Review of Neuroscience, 22*, 105–122. https://doi.org/10.1146/annurev.neuro.22.1.105. PMID: 10202533.

McEwen, B. S., & Gianaros, P. J. (2010). Central role of the brain in stress and adaptation: Links to socioeconomic status, health, and disease. *Annals. New York Academy of Sciences, 1186*, 190–222. https://doi.org/10.1111/j.1749-6632.2009.05331.x.

McIntosh, M. K. (2005). Poverty, charity, and coercion in Elizabethan England. *Journal of Interdisciplinary History, 35*(3), 457–479. https://doi.org/10.1162/0022195052564234. S2CID144864528.

Merz, E. C., Tottenham, N., & Noble, K. G. (2018). Socioeconomic status, amygdala volume, and internalizing symptoms in children and adolescents. *Journal of Clinical Child and Adolescent Psychology, 47*(2), 312–323. https://doi.org/10.1080/15374416.2017.1326122.

Mezzacappa, E. (2004). Alerting, orienting, and executive attention: Developmental properties and sociodemographic correlates in an epidemiological sample of young, urban children. *Child Development, 75*, 1373–1386.

Miller, B., & Taylor, J. (2012). Racial and socioeconomic status differences in depressive symptoms among black and white youth: An examination of the mediating effects of family structure, stress and support. *Journal of Youth and Adolescence, 41*, 426–437. https://doi.org/10.1007/s10964-011-9672-4.

Moriguchi, Y., & Shinohara, I. (2019). Socioeconomic disparity in prefrontal development during early childhood. *Scientific Reports, 9*, 2585. https://doi.org/10.1038/s41598-019-39255-6.

Murray, C. A. (1984). *Losing ground: American social policy, 1950–1980.* New York: Basic Books.

Naninck, E., Stijger, P. C., & Brouwer-Brolsma, E. M. (2019). The importance of maternal folate status for brain development and function of offspring. *Advances in nutrition (Bethesda, Md.), 10*(3), 502–519. https://doi.org/10.1093/advances/nmy120.

Nelson, M. (2000). Childhood nutrition and poverty. *The Proceedings of the Nutrition Society, 59*(2), 307–315. https://doi.org/10.1017/s0029665100000343. PMID: 10946800.

Nicholas, E. W., Ahmed, S. F., Tang, S., Morrison, F. J., & Davis-Kean, P. E. (2021). Pathways from socioeconomic status to early academic achievement: The role of specific executive functions. *Early Childhood Research Quarterly, 54*, 321–331. https://doi.org/10.1016/j.ecresq.2020.09.008.

Niskanen, W. A. (1996). Welfare and culture of poverty. *Cato Journal, 16*(1), 1–15.

Noble, K. G., Norman, M. F., & Farah, M. J. (2005). Neurocognitive correlates of socioeconomic status in kindergarten children. *Developmental Science, 8*(1), 74–87. https://doi.org/10.1111/j.1467-7687.2005.00394.x. PMID: 15647068.

Noble, K. G., McCandliss, B. D., & Farah, M. J. (2007). Socioeconomic gradients predict individual differences in neurocognitive abilities. *Developmental Science, 10*, 464–480.

Nooe, R., & Patterson, D. (2010). The ecology of homelessness. *Journal of Human Behavior in the Social Environment, 20*(2), 105–152. https://doi.org/10.1080/10911350903269757.

Okeke, N. A., Howard, L. C., Kurtz-Costes, B., & Rowley, S. J. (2009). Academic race stereotypes, academic self-concept, and racial centrality in African American youth. *The Journal of Black Psychology, 35*(3), 366–387. https://doi.org/10.1177/0095798409333615.

Olson, C. R., & Mello, C. V. (2010). Significance of vitamin a to brain function, behavior and learning. *Molecular Nutrition & Food Research, 54*(4), 489–495. https://doi.org/10.1002/mnfr.200900246.

Olson, J. G., McFerran, B., Morales, A. C., & Dahl, D. W. (2020). How income shapes moral judgments of prosocial behavior. *International Journal of Research in Marketing*. https://doi.org/10.1016/j.ijresmar.2020.07.001.

Olszewski-Kubilius, P., & Corwith, S. (2018). Poverty, academic achievement, and giftedness: A literature review. *Gifted Child Quarterly, 62*(1), 37–55. https://doi.org/10.1177/0016986217738015.

Prado, E. L., & Dewey, K. G. (2014). Nutrition and brain development in early life. *Nutritional Reviews, 72*, 267–284.

Priest, et al. (2018). Stereotyping across intersections of race and age: Racial stereotyping among White adults working with children. *PLoS One, 13*(10), e0205614. https://doi.org/10.1371/journal.pone.0205614.

Pyle, H. (1883). *The merry adventures of Robin Hood*. Champaign: Project Gutenberg.

Ranchordas, S. (2020). Connected but still excluded? Digital exclusion beyond internet access. *SSRN Electronic Journal*. https://doi.org/10.2139/ssrn.3675360.

Reynolds, K., Watson, J., Densham, P., Lewis, R. B., Costner, K., Mastrantonio, M. E., Freeman, M., et al. (2003). *Robin Hood, prince of thieves*. Burbank: Warner Home Video.

Riis, T. (1979). Poverty in the middle ages, Scandinavian economic. *History Review, 27*(2), 174–176. https://doi.org/10.1080/03585522.1979.10415659.

Rodriguez-Bailon, R., Bratanova, B., Willis, G. B., Lopez-Rodriguez, L., Sturrock, A., & Loughnan, S. (2017). Social class and ideologies of inequality: How they uphold unequal societies. *Journal of Social Issues, 73*(1), 99–116. https://doi.org/10.1111/josi.12206.

Rogosch, F. A., Dackis, M. N., & Cicchetti, D. (2011). Child maltreatment and allostatic load: Consequences for physical and mental health in children from low-income families. *Development and Psychopathology, 23*(4), 1107–1124. https://doi.org/10.1017/S0954579411000587.

Rosales, F. J., Reznick, J. S., & Zeisel, S. H. (2009). Understanding the role of nutrition in the brain and behavioral development of toddlers and preschool children: Identifying and addressing methodological barriers. *Nutritional Neuroscience, 12*(5), 190–202. https://doi.org/10.1179/147683009X423454.

Rushton, N. S., & Sigle-Rushton, W. (2001). Monastic poor relief in sixteenth-century England. *Journal of Interdisciplinary History, 32*(2), 193–216. https://doi.org/10.1162/002219501750442378. PMID 19035026. S2CID 7272220.

Sampson, R. J., Raudenbush, S. W., & Earls, F. (1997). Neighborhoods and violent crime: A multilevel study of collective efficacy. *Science, 277*(5328), 918–924.

Scheerder, A., van Deursen, A., & van Dijk, J. (2017). Determinants of internet skills, uses and outcomes. A systematic review of the second- and third-level digital divide. *Telematics and Informatics, 34*(8), 1607–1624., ISSN 0736-5853. https://doi.org/10.1016/j.tele.2017.07.007.

Shakespeare, W. (2003). *Romeo and Juliet*. New York: SparkNotes.

Shakespeare, W., & Durband, A. (1985). *Romeo and Juliet*. Hauppage: Barron's.

Shinn, M., Gibbons-Benton, J., & Brown, S. R. (2015). Poverty, homelessness, and family breakup. *Child Welfare, 94*(1), 105–122.

Slack, P. (1988). *Poverty and policy in Tudor and Stuart England*. London: Longman. ISBN 0-582-48965-2.

Source: U.S. Census Bureau, Current Population Survey, 1960 to 2020 Annual Social and Economic Supplements (CPS ASEC).

Sources: How the US Census Measures Poverty, US Census Bureau; Income, Poverty, and Health Insurance Coverage in the United States: 2019, US Census Bureau (pp. 18–19).

Stevens, C., Lauinger, B., & Neville, H. (2009). Differences in the neural mechanisms of selective attention in children from different socioeconomic backgrounds: An event-related brain potential study. *Developmental Science, 12*, 634–646.

Taylor, E., Guy-Walls, P., Wilkerson, P., et al. (2019). The historical perspectives of stereotypes on African-American males. *Journal of Human Rights and Social Work, 4*, 213–225. https://doi.org/10.1007/s41134-019-00096-y.

The Council of Economic Advisors. (2019, September). *The Sate of Homelessness in America Report*. The White House. Retrieved from https://www.whitehouse.gov/wp-content/uploads/2019/09/The-State-of-Homelessness-in-America.pdf.

Turnbull, J., Muckle, W., & Masters, C. (2007). Homelessness and health. *Canadian Medical Association Journal = journal de l'Association medicale canadienne, 177*(9), 1065–1066. https://doi.org/10.1503/cmaj.071294.

United Nations. (2020, March). *First-ever United Nations resolution on homelessness.* Retrieved from https://www.un.org/development/desa/dspd/2020/03/resolution-homelessness/.

Walsh, D., McCartney, G., Smith, M., & Armour, G. (2019). Relationship between childhood socioeconomic position and adverse childhood experiences (ACEs): A systematic review. *Journal of Epidemiology and Community Health, 73*(12), 1087–1093. https://doi.org/10.1136/jech-2019-212738.

Wasantwisut, E. (1997). Nutrition and development: Other micronutrients' effect on growth and cognition. *The Southeast Asian Journal of Tropical Medicine and Public Health, 28*(Suppl 2), 78–82. PMID: 9561639.

Whiteside-Mansell, L., McKelvey, L., Saccente, J., & Selig, J. P. (2019). Adverse childhood experiences of urban and rural preschool children in poverty. *International Journal of Environmental Research and Public Health, 16*(14), 2623. https://doi.org/10.3390/ijerph16142623.

Wicksell, K. (1967). A new principle of just taxation. In R. A. Musgrave & A. T. Peacock (Eds.), *Classics in the theory of public finance*. London: Macmillan.

Wolf, J. M., Miller, G. E., & Chen, E. (2008). Parent psychological states predict changes in inflammatory markers in children with asthma and healthy children. *Brain, Behavior, and Immunity, 22*, 433–441. https://doi.org/10.1016/j.bbi.2007.10.016.

Worku, E. B., & Woldesenbet, S. A. (2015). Poverty and inequality – But of what – As social determinants of health in Africa? *African Health Sciences, 15*(4), 1330–1338. https://doi.org/10.4314/ahs.v15i4.36.

World Bank. (2021). *Poverty*. Retrieved from https://www.worldbank.org/en/topic/poverty. February 13, 2021.

Chapter 5
Education, Fear, and Trauma

In an article on the study of the history of education, Gillian Sutherland wrote: "The provision of education represents the most sustained and far reaching attempt of a society, or sections within it, to reproduce itself, to shape its future and it necessarily involves a degree of self-consciousness on the part of the providers about that society" (Sutherland, 1969).

5.1 History of Education, in Brief

Sutherland's summation on the history of education is compelling as it speaks to the supremacy of education to consciously and intentionally maintain legacy and sustain power – a passing down of culture, ideas, philosophy, and a way of being. Beneath this definition lie a significant truth and question – deservedness, who deserves education, power, status, and legacy. In Ancient civilizations (circa 3000 BC–AD 500), education was informal and used as a means of preserving culture, enriching society (Allen, 2016; Kaster, 1983), and sharpening and homing of skills to meet community and family needs like maintaining the farm. Education in the Middle Ages (from the fifth to eight century) included small schools that were established in churches and eventually monasteries, namely, benefiting young boys from wealthy families (Adamson, 1951; Thorndike, 1944; Weisphel, 1964). Colonial education (1607–1776 before the founding of the United States) was marked by social class and very gendered (male >>>> female) (Boorstin, 1958; Cremin, 1970; Reisner & Butts, 1936; Wright, 1957). Of note, in a book written by historian Doris Kearns-Goodwin *Leadership: In Turbulent Times*, President Lincoln was raised in the Midwest and was educated only to the level of what we call middle school (Goodwin, 2018). He had to drop out of education because his father needed and wanted him to learn how to take care of the farm. As history would tell it, Lincoln was an autodidact, not the result of a formal education, an example of education as

A. Moreland-Capuia, *The Trauma of Racism*,
https://doi.org/10.1007/978-3-030-73436-7_5

a means of utility. The Colonial and pre-Colonial period was shaped by the slave trade. It was not legal for slaves to read and/or write – these laws were held steady in place from the time of the Colonial period to well in the Reconstruction period (after the Civil War ended). There are several historical accounts of slaves being autodidactic, educating themselves, teaching themselves how to read, taking tattered bibles and newspapers, and learning to count. There are also accounts of wives of slave owners teaching slaves to read and write. There were anti-literacy laws in place that forbade any Black person, free and enslaved, to learn to read and/or write – it was a crime punishable by law (Rasmussen, 2010; Span, 2005; Williams, 2006). Of note, although anti-literacy laws were in place, there were a handful of schools in the North dedicated for the education of African-Americans. The Civil War was fought from 1861 to 1865, the confederacy lost, and anti-literacy laws were challenged near the end of the war. During the Reconstruction era (1863–1877, the period after the Civil War), slaves were mostly free, but illiteracy rates were incredibly high. African-Americans knew that genuine liberation would stem from education. To this end and with this conviction, many freed African-American slaves were compelled to form learning communities, much of the education efforts took place at Black churches (no coincidence that during the Jim Crow era churches were burned down as an act of racism and White supremacy) (Anderson, 2018; Tyack & Lowe, 1986). African-Americans were so eager to learn that they used what limited resources they had which according to some text included tattered spelling books. The political and social conditions did not support the freeing of slaves – structures were put in place to railroad efforts for quality education. State-funded education was growing in Northern states but stymied in Southern states. Southerners held the belief that education was a private matter and understood that education was power, a kind of power that many did not believe freed slaves should have access to. The Reconstruction era was shaped by the rise of Jim Crow segregation, discrimination, and anti-Black racism. The social construct of Whites-only became poignant and powerful. While Black Americans could be educated, they were not given the same resources as their White counterparts (Anderson, 1988; Barnard & Burner, 1975; Butchart, 2010; Goldin & Lawrence, 1999; Hudson, 2002; Jones, 2018; Pruitt, 1987; The Conversation, 2021).

5.2 Civil War, Reconstruction Era, and Civil Rights Act of 1964 and Its Impact on Education

Amid the Reconstruction era, in 1867, the Department of Education was born. While public education existed, it was limited and did not allow for African-Americans to participate. The establishment of the Department of Education was part of the effort to collect data on public schools to determine allocation of resources and a means of self-improvement. Free education was not a new concept; free public education for privileged, White boys had been available during the Colonial period since circa

1635; and when upon the United States was birthed, 1821 marked the first free public education for privileged White families. The Department of Education was established during a time where free public education was being mandated for African-Americans. Of historical significance, Howard University (a historically Black college and university) was chartered as a university by Congress in 1867 (Albritton, 2012; Roebuck & Murty, 1993; United States Commission on Civil Rights, 2010). While there were a few areas of progress on the education front for Black Americans after having been forbidden from reading and writing, there was significant opposition. Black Americans were not even constitutionally considered complete citizens until the ratification of the 14th amendment in 1868 (Hudson, 2002). The South established "Black codes" – the idea was that if laws were going to free Black Americans, practices and policies would not oblige (Cohen, 1976; Unger, 1966; Vaughn, 1946). Black codes in the South were designed to limit the kind of work that Black Americans could do, mostly relegating them to domestic workers with limited pay. The intensification of the Klu Klux Klan was concurrent with heightened violence toward Black citizens and Black institutions marked by the burning of churches and schools, and lynching. Racial segregation in education was deemed legal with the caveat that learning facilities and resources were equal, separate but equal – this was the ruling of the Supreme Court in Plessy v Ferguson in 1896.

Sheer terror of African-Americans continued; limited access to equal education remained unchanged until Brown versus the Board of Education. In 1954, the Supreme Court ruled that the separate but equal precedent that had been set by Plessy v Ferguson was unconstitutional – in a unanimous ruling, the Supreme Court decided that racial segregation in public education was not equal and would not stand. One of the more prominent integration experiments happened in Little Rock, Arkansas, in 1957 where nine Black students required the presence of nearly a thousand federal guards to facilitate their entry into Central High School. Integration was met by White violence, hatred, and fear. Southern states benefited greatly from slave labor; the southern economy was strengthened by it and because of it. The ending of slavery disrupted the economic engine and power of Southern Whites, and it also disrupted a socialized hierarchy. According to a thesis by Motycka, "schools became the marketplace for addressing how to preserve hierarchy" (Motycka, 2017). Threat to status undergirded violence and hate.

5.3   The Department of Education, Title 1, and No Child Left Behind (NCLB)

The Department of Education was compelled to reevaluate its policies and resource distribution in the context of this ruling. This ruling was one of the many sparks for the Civil Rights Movement which had many implications. Specifically, the Civil Rights Movement and President Lyndon B. Johnson's anti-poverty campaign in the 1960s brought equal access into focus for the Department of Education. In 1966, as mandated by Title VI of the Civil Rights Act of 1964, the Office for Civil Rights was established by the Congress – this prohibited public education discrimination based on race, color, and/or national origin. Of relevance is the establishment of Title I of the Elementary and Secondary Education Act of 1965. Title 1 tied federal funding for education to the expectation that all students would have access to quality education (Hallinan, 2001; Taylor & Piche, 1991). In theory, funding could only be received if education was equivalent to non-Title 1 schools. Title 1 has become synonymous with impoverished, under-resourced schools with predominantly students of color and students living below the federal poverty line.

From 1954 leading up to and after the Title VI, there were varying iterations and timelines of integration. The poor reception of Blacks integrating White schools was consistent throughout much of the country. Education in the twenty-first century still contains the trappings of education pre-Title VI. Sociologists that write extensively on inequities in education and education policy and practice have almost unanimously noted that the narrative for education equality does not match the practice and/or outcomes, hence the myriad studies and focus on reducing the achievement gap in minority students. Segregation and inequality are pervasive. Some studies suggest inherent inequities in the funding of school systems with relatively poor, urban schools receiving less instructional resources compared to their suburban counterparts (Carmichael, 1997; Kozol, 1991; Taylor & Piche, 1991).

In a 2001 publication on schooling and education inequality in the twenty-first century, Gamoran writes about how the more things change, they stay the same because "socioeconomic inequality is 'maximally maintained': Privileged groups protect their advantages until virtually all members reach a given status, at which point the axis of inequality shifts upward to another level of educational outcome" (Gamoran, 2001). This certainly held true in studies examining education disparities across class and race outlining Black-White inequality in reading and math in the K-12 system (Hallinan, 2001; Robinson, 2010), overrepresentation of Black and minority student suspensions (Eitle & Eitle, 2004; Gopalan & Nelson, 2019; McCarthy & Hoge, 1987; Wallace, Goodkind, Wallace, & Bachman, 2008; Wiggan, 2007), disproportionate overrepresentation of Black and minority students in special education (Artiles & Trent, 1994; Coutinho & Oswald, 2000; Kihle, 2019; Kreskow, 2013), and a wide and ever-widening achievement gap stratified by race (Eyler, Cook, & Ward, 1983; Lee & Smith, 1995; Logan, Minca, & Adar, 2012; Morris & Monroe, 2009; Vars & Bowen, 1998).

In the early 2000s, the controversial No Child Left Behind (NCLB) policy emerged. NCLB was understood as an upgrade to the 1965 Elementary and Secondary Education Act, intended to make federal involvement and enforcement of student outcomes more robust, holding educational institutions accountable for reducing the achievement gap in chronic marginalized minority communities (Whitney & Candelaria, 2017). Criticism was high as there was concern that prioritizing testing and test-taking skills over social-emotional learning would contribute to greater mental health concerns and not meet the goal of buoying communities educationally and socioeconomically (McMurrer, 2007; Whitney & Candelaria, 2017). The concern was highest for minority children who had prior been challenged by math, reading, and writing. The forced accountability of school systems was met with mixed results; the expectation conjured up fear that if schools didn't get students up to par in reading in math, they would either be restructured and/or closed – this fear-inducing expectation did help some schools perform better, while others could not operate under such pressure. Whether NCLB was effective or not will depend on who you ask. The greater point is that NCLB was a twenty-first-century intervention, less than 50 years outside of the Civil Rights Movement and, for even greater perspective, close to 136 years from anti-literacy laws. The achievement gap is historical, societal, political, and structural. How long does it take to change narrative and expectations over generations in the context of persistent struggle and resistance, at every level?

According to US Census Bureau data, in 2019, the poverty rate for Black Americans was 18.8% and represented a moderate decrease from the year prior (20.8% – 2018) (US Census Bureau, 1960–1920; US Census Bureau, 2020). The poverty rate for Hispanic Americans in 2019 was 15.7% and represented a moderate decrease from the year prior (20.8% – 2018) (US Census Bureau, 1960–1920; US Census Bureau, 2020). The rates are disproportionate and disparate; further analysis of the 2019 poverty rates reveals the following when compared to the general population (US Census Bureau, 1960–1920; US Census Bureau, 2020):

– The share of Black Americans in poverty was 1.8 times higher than their share in the general population – making up 13.2% of the population but representing ~24% of the population living in poverty.
– The share of Hispanic Americans in poverty was 1.5 times higher than their share in the general population – making up 18.7% of the population but representing 28% of the population living in poverty.
– Compared to non-Hispanic Whites who make up ~60% of the population but representing ~42% of the population living in poverty.
– Disparities are more profound in *children* and older adults (65 +).

In 2007, Ferguson et al. published an article on the impact of poverty and educational outcomes and reminded the reading public about the link between child school readiness and social determinants of health to include poverty and poverty-related factors (Ferguson, Bovaird, & Mueller, 2007). Poverty-related factors can change the trajectory of learning in children and include the incidence of poverty, how profound the poverty, how long a child has been living in poverty, the age a child first started living in poverty, and the community, neighborhood, and social networks (Ferguson et al., 2007). Several studies highlight the association of low SES and low academic achievement (Cedeño, Martinez-Arias, & Bueno, 2016; Reardon & Portilla, 2016).

According to US Department of Education data on Scholastic Aptitude Testing (SAT) scores for high school seniors broken down by sex and race, Black and American Indian/Alaska Native students scored the lowest. Average reading and writing score for Black students was 483 + math score of 463 for a total of 946. Average reading and writing score for Native Indian/Alaska Native students was 480 + math score of 469 for a total score of 949 – compared to total score for all students of 1068 with reading and writing score average of 536 and math average of 531 (US Department of Education, 2019).

5.4   Education as a Determinant of Health

Chapter 4 addressed the structural aspects of poverty to include nutrition and/or the lack thereof. There is a link between poverty, poor nutrition, hunger, and poor learning outcomes (brain development, cognition, and learning implications). The interplay of hunger/food insecurity/undernutrition and its impact on academic achievement and education is profound. Hunger is related to the fear and distress linked with lack of food and deprivation. Food insecurity is the unreliable and inconsistent access to affordable and healthy food. Undernutrition is related to eating but with insufficient calories from macro- and micronutrients; calories from fat and unhealthy sources are predominant. Malnutrition refers to not having a balanced diet that can include undernourishment, food insecurity, and hunger. In 2017, 12.5 million Americans lived in food-insecure households (Feeding America, 2019). In fiscal year 2018, 40.3 million people *per month* participated in the Supplemental Nutrition Assistance Program (SNAP) according to the US Department of Agriculture (USDA) (USDA, Food and Nutrition Service, 2018).

Not only are racial minority students more likely to be living below the federal poverty line, fearful of where their next meal will come from, and impacted by societies' perception of them, but they are also fearful of what educators may think of them when they are in class. Multiple studies point to the impact that stereotype threat and negative attitudes and perceptions have on student learning and link such threats and attitudes to an increase in achievement gap (Alexander, Entwisle, & Thompson, 1987; Dovidio, Kawakami, & Gaertner, 2002; Downey & Pribesh, 2004; Ehrenberg, Goldbaber, & Brewer, 1995; Kawakami, Young, & Dovidio, 2002; Morris, 2005; Rosenthal, 2003; Sbarra & Pianta, 2001; Smith & Hung, 2008; van den Bergh, Denessen, Hornstra, Voeten, & Holland, 2010). Stereotype threat involves members of a racial minority group being aware of the negative beliefs, constructs, and low expectations that exist about them, and they are fearful that they may acquiesce to the beliefs, constructs, and low expectation (Allen & Webber, 2019; Aronson, Fried, & Good, 2002; Aronson & Inzlicht, 2004; Gonzales, Blanton, & Williams, 2002; Johnson-Ahorlu, 2012, 2013; Owens & Massey, 2011; Steele & Aronson, 1995). Stereotype threat has been shown to deleteriously impact ethnically diverse groups because the stereotypes are so deeply negative and persistent (appreciate the history). This is appreciated in test performances in racial minorities and women who have been stereotyped to not be good learners, particularly in math and testing overall (Allen & Webber, 2019; Aronson et al., 2002; Aronson & Inzlicht, 2004; Gonzales et al., 2002; Johnson-Ahorlu, 2012, 2013; Owens & Massey, 2011; Steele & Aronson, 1995). Gonzales et al. (2002) articulate the impact of double-minority status, being a racial minority and a woman, and the impact of compounded negative stereotypes of intelligence and ability (in subjects like math) on academic performance (Gonzales et al., 2002).

The beginning of this chapter started with Gillian Sutherland who wrote: "The provision of education represents the most sustained and far reaching attempt of a society, or sections within it, to reproduce itself, to shape its future and it necessarily involves a degree of self-consciousness on the part of the providers about that society" (Sutherland, 1969).

If we consider the system of education, the history of racial/ethnic minorities in relation to education and combine it with the additional (structural) stressors of being more likely to be food insecure/undernourished or hungry, living in poverty, insufficiently housed, and subject to the negative stereotypes of people and systems they rely on for help. If the provision of education represents sustained and profound societal attempts to reproduce and shape the future, consciously, what is being reproduced? What is observed is the compounded structural impacts of fear-constructed narratives multiplied by fear-based system. A visual of fear is reproduced and amplified then we could appreciate the systematic, multiplicative, augmented impact of fear and trauma (see Fig. 5.1).

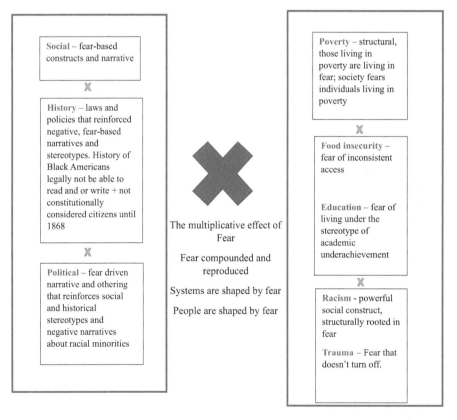

Fig. 5.1   The multiplicative effect of fear

References

Adamson, J. W. (1951). Education. In C. G. Crump & E. F. Jacob (Eds.), *The legacy of the middle ages*. Oxford: Clarendon Press.

Albritton, T. J. (2012). Educating our own: The historical legacy of HBCUs and their relevance for educating a new generation of leaders. *The Urban Review, 44*, 311–331. https://doi.org/10.1007/s11256-012-0202-9.

Alexander, K. L., Entwisle, D. R., & Thompson, M. S. (1987). School performance, status relations, and the structure of sentiment: Bringing the teacher Back in. *American Sociological Review, 52*, 665–682.

Allen, A. (2016). Out of weakness: The 'educational good' in late antiquity. *Pedagogy, Culture & Society, 24*(2), 239–254. https://doi.org/10.1080/14681366.2016.1149506.

Allen, J. M., & Webber, M. (2019). Stereotypes of minorities and education. In S. Ratuva (Ed.), *The Palgrave handbook of ethnicity*. Singapore: Palgrave Macmillan. https://doi.org/10.1007/978-981-13-0242-8_107-1.

Anderson, J. D. (1988). *The Education of Blacks in the South, 1860–1935*. Chapel Hill: University of North Carolina Press.

Anderson, J. D. (2018, December). Educational reconstruction: African American schools in the urban south, 1865–1890. *Journal of American History, 105*(3), 691–692. https://doi.org/10.1093/jahist/jay347.

Aronson, J., Fried, C., & Good, C. (2002). Reducing the effects of stereotype threat on African American college students by shaping theories of intelligence. *Journal of Experimental Social Psychology, 38*, 113–125.

Aronson, J., & Inzlicht, M. (2004). The ups and downs of attributional ambiguity: Stereotype vulnerability and the academic self-knowledge of African-American students. *Psychological Science, 15*, 829–836.

Artiles, A. J., & Trent, S. C. (1994). Overrepresentation of minority students in special education: A continuing debate. *The Journal of Special Education, 27*(4), 410–437. https://doi.org/10.1177/002246699402700404.

Barnard, J., & Burner, D. (1975). *The American Experience in Education*. New York: New Viewpoints, (a Division of Franklin Watts, Inc.).

Boorstin, D. (1958). *The Americans: The colonial experience* (pp. 10–14). New York: Random House, Vintage Books.

Butchart, R. E. (2010). *Schooling the freed people: Teaching, learning, and the struggle for black freedom, 1861–1876*. Chapel Hill: University of North Carolina.

Carmichael, P. (1997). Who receives Federal Title I Assistance? Examination of program funding by school poverty rate in New York state. *Educational Evaluation and Policy Analysis, 19*(4), 354–359. Retrieved January 17, 2021, from http://www.jstor.org/stable/1164449.

Cedeño, L. F., Martinez-Arias, R., & Bueno, J. A. (2016). Implications of socioeconomic status on academic competence: A perspective for teachers. *International Education Studies, 9*(4), 257–267. https://doi.org/10.5539/ies.v9n4p257.

Cohen, W. (1976). Negro involuntary servitude in the south, 1865-1940: A preliminary analysis. *The Journal of Southern History, 42*(1), 31–60. https://doi.org/10.2307/2205660.

Coutinho, M. J., & Oswald, D. P. (2000). Disproportionate representation in special education: A synthesis and recommendations. *Journal of Child and Family Studies, 9*, 135–156.

Cremin, L. A. (1970). *American education: The colonial experience, 1607–1789* (p. 40). New York: Evanston and London: Harper and Row.

Dovidio, J. F., Kawakami, K., & Gaertner, S. L. (2002). Implicit and explicit prejudice and interracial interaction. *Journal of Personality and Social Psychology, 82*, 62–68.

Downey, D., & Pribesh, S. (2004). When race matters: Teachers' evaluations of students' classroom behaviors. *Sociology of Education, 77*, 267–282.

Ehrenberg, R. G., Goldbaber, D. D., & Brewer, D. J. (1995). Do teachers' race, gender, and ethnicity matter? Evidence from the National Educational Longitudinal Study of 1988. *Industrial and Labor Relations Review, 48*, 547–561.

Eitle, T. M., & Eitle, D. J. (2004). Inequality, segregation, and the overrepresentation of African Americans in school suspensions. *Sociological Perspectives, 47*(3), 269–287. https://doi.org/10.1525/sop.2004.47.3.269.

Eyler, J., Cook, V. J., & Ward, L. E. (1983). Resegregation: Segregation within desegregated schools. In C. H. Rossell & W. D. Hawley (Eds.), *The consequences of school desegregation* (pp. 126–162). Philadelphia: Temple University Press.

Feeding America. (2019). *Map the meal gap 2019: A report on county and congressional district food insecurity and county food cost in the United States in 2017* (p. 35). Chicago: Feeding America. https://www.feedingamerica.org/sites/default/files/2019-05/2017-map-the-meal-gap-full.pdf.

Ferguson, H., Bovaird, S., & Mueller, M. (2007). The impact of poverty on educational outcomes for children. *Paediatrics & Child Health, 12*(8), 701–706. https://doi.org/10.1093/pch/12.8.701.

Gamoran, A. (2001). American schooling and educational inequality: A forecast for the 21st century. *Sociology of Education, 74*, 135–153. https://doi.org/10.2307/2673258.

Goldin, C., & Lawrence, F. K. (1999, Winter). The shaping of higher education: The formative years in the United States, 1890-1940. *Journal of Economic Perspectives, 13*, 37–62.

Gonzales, P. M., Blanton, H., & Williams, K. J. (2002). The effects of stereotype threat and double-minority status on the test performance of Latino women. *Personality & Social Psychology Bulletin, 28*, 659–670.

Goodwin, D. K. (2018). *Leadership in turbulent times*. New York: Simon & Schuster.

Gopalan, M., & Nelson, A. A. (2019, April). Understanding the racial discipline gap in schools. *AERA Open*. https://doi.org/10.1177/2332858419844613.

Hallinan, M. T. (2001). Sociological perspectives on black-white inequalities in American schooling. *Sociology of Education, 74*, 50–70.

Hudson, D. L. (2002). *The fourteenth amendment: Equal protection under the law*. Berkeley Heights: Enslow Publishers.

Johnson-Ahorlu, R. N. (2012). The academic opportunity gap: How racism and stereotypes disrupt the education of African American undergraduates. *Race Ethnicity and Education, 15*(5), 633–652. https://doi.org/10.1080/13613324.2011.645566.

Johnson-Ahorlu, R. N. (2013). "Our biggest challenge is stereotypes": Understanding stereotype threat and the academic experiences of African American undergraduates. *The Journal of Negro Education, 82*(4), 382–392. https://doi.org/10.7709/jnegroeducation.82.4.0382.

Jones, M. (2018). *Birthright Citizens: A History of Race and Rights in Antebellum America* (Studies in legal history). Cambridge: Cambridge University Press. https://doi.org/10.1017/9781316577165.

Kaster, R. (1983). Notes on "primary" and "secondary" schools in late antiquity. *Transactions of the American Philological Association (1974-), 113*, 323–346. https://doi.org/10.2307/284019.

Kawakami, K., Young, H., & Dovidio, J. F. (2002). Automatic stereotyping: Category, trait, and behavioral activations. *Personality and Social Psychology Bulletin, 28*, 3–15.

Kihle, K. (2019). The overrepresentation of African American students in special education. *Culminating Projects in Special Education*, 74. https://repository.stcloudstate.edu/sped_etds/74.

Kozol, J. (1991). *Savage inequalities*. New York: Crown.

Kreskow, K. (2013). *Overrepresentation of Minorities in Special Education*. Education Masters. Paper 257.

Lee, V. E., & Smith, J. B. (1995). Effects of school restructuring and size on gains in achievement and engagement for early secondary school students. *Sociology of Education, 68*, 241–270.

Logan, J. R., Minca, E., & Adar, S. (2012). The geography of inequality: Why separate means unequal in American public schools. *Sociology of Education, 85*(3), 287–301. https://doi.org/10.1177/0038040711431588.

McCarthy, J. D., & Hoge, D. R. (1987). The social construction of school punishment: Racial disadvantage out of universalistic process. *Social Forces, 65*, 1101–1120.

McMurrer, J. (2007). *Choices, changes, and challenges: Curriculum and instruction in the NCLB era*. Washington, DC: Center on Education Policy.

Morris, E. W. (2005). From 'middle class' to 'trailer trash': Teachers' perceptions of white students in a predominately minority school. *Sociology of Education, 78*, 99–121.

Morris, J. E., & Monroe, C. R. (2009). Why study the U.S. south? The Nexus of race and place in investigating black student achievement. *Educational Researcher, 38*(1), 21–36. https://doi.org/10.3102/0013189X08328876.

Motycka, A. E. (2017). White Southerners respond to Brown v. Board of Education: Why Crisis Erupted When Little Rock, Arkansas, Desegregated Central High School. *Honors Projects*, 82. https://digitalcommons.bowdoin.edu/honorsprojects/82.

Owens, J., & Massey, D. S. (2011). Stereotype threat and college academic performance: A latent variables approach. *Social Science Research, 40*(1), 150–166. https://doi.org/10.1016/j.ssresearch.2010.09.010.

Pruitt, A. S. (1987). *Pursuit of equality in Higher Education*. Dix Hills: The Southern Education Foundation, Inc./General Hall, Inc..

Rasmussen, B. (2010). "Attended with great inconveniences": Slave literacy and the 1740 South Carolina Negro Act. *PMLA, 125*(1), 201–203. Retrieved February 15, 2021, from http://www.jstor.org/stable/25614450.

Reardon, S. F., & Portilla, X. A. (2016). Recent trends in income, racial, and ethnic school readiness gaps at kindergarten entry. *AERA Open, 2*(3), 1–18. https://doi.org/10.1177/2332858416657343.

Reisner, E., & Butts, R. (1936). History of American education during the colonial period. *Review of Educational Research, 6*(4), 357–363. Retrieved February 15, 2021, from http://www.jstor.org/stable/1167454.

Robinson, K. (2010). Black-White inequality in Reading and math across K-12 schooling: A synthetic cohort perspective. *Review of Black Political Economy, 37*, 263–273. https://doi.org/10.1007/s12114-010-9074-y.

Roebuck, J. B., & Murty, K. S. (1993). *Historically black colleges and universities: Their place in American higher education*. Westport: Praeger.

Rosenthal, R. (2003). Covert communication in laboratories, classrooms and the truly real world. *Current Directions in Psychological Science, 12*, 151–154.

Sbarra, D., & Pianta, R. (2001). Teachers' ratings of African American and Caucasian children during the first two years of school. *Psychology in the Schools, 38*, 229–238.

Smith, C. S., & Hung, L. C. (2008). Stereotype threat: Effects on education. *Social Psychology of Education, 11*, 243–257. https://doi.org/10.1007/s11218-008-9053-3.

Span, C. (2005). Learning in spite of opposition: African Americans and their history of educational exclusion in antebellum America. *Counterpoints, 131*, 26–53. Retrieved February 15, 2021, from http://www.jstor.org/stable/42977282.

Steele, C. M., & Aronson, J. (1995). Stereotype threat and the intellectual test performance of African Americans. *Journal of Personality and Social Psychology, 69*(5), 797–811.

Sutherland, G. (1969, February). The study of the history of education. *The Journal of the Historical Association, 54*(180), 49–59. https://doi.org/10.1111/j.1468-229X.1969.tb01237.x.

Taylor, W. L., & Piche, D. M. (1991). *A report on shortchanging children: The impact of fiscal inequity on the education of students at risk* (Prepared for the committee on education and labor, U.S. House of representatives). Washington, DC: U.S. Government Printing Office.

The Conversation. (2021). *Exploiting Black Labor after the abolition of slavery*. Retrieved from https://theconversation.com/exploiting-black-labor-after-the-abolition-of-slavery-72482. February 15, 2021.

Thorndike, L. (1944). *University records and life in the middle ages*. New York: Columbia University Press.

Tyack, D., & Lowe, R. (1986). The constitutional moment: Reconstruction and black education in the south. *American Journal of Education, 94*(2), 236–256. Retrieved February 15, 2021, from http://www.jstor.org/stable/1084950.

U.S. Department of Agriculture, Food and Nutrition Service. (2018). *Supplemental nutrition assistance program.* Available at: https://www.ers.usda.gov/data-products/charts-of-note/charts-of-note/?topicId=734dae31-1bae-4db4-81d3-9a1cab76e1a3 on January 18, 2021.

U.S. Department of Education, National Center for Education Statistics. (2019). *Digest of Education Statistics, 2018* (NCES 2020–009), Table 226.10.

Unger, I. (1966). *The Florida Historical Quarterly, 45*(2), 183–185. Retrieved February 15, 2021, from http://www.jstor.org/stable/30147751.

United States Commission on Civil Rights. (2010). *The educational effectiveness of historically Black colleges and universities.* [briefing report]. Washington, DC: Author. Retrieved from http://www.usccr.gov/pubs/HBCU_webversion2.pdf.

US Census Bureau, Current Population Survey, Annual Social and Economic Supplement, 2020 (CPS ASEC).

US Census Bureau Population Survey, 1960 to 2020 Annual Social and Economic Supplement (CPS ASEC).

van den Bergh, L., Denessen, E., Hornstra, L., Voeten, M., & Holland, R. W. (2010). The implicit prejudiced attitudes of teachers: Relations to teacher expectations and the ethnic achievement gap. *American Educational Research Journal, 47*(2), 497–527. https://doi.org/10.3102/0002831209353594.

Vars, F., & Bowen, W. G. (1998). Scholastic aptitude test scores, race, and academic performance in selective universities. In C. Jenks & M. Phillips (Eds.), *The black-white test score gap.* Washington: Brookings Institution Press.

Vaughn, R. (1946). Black codes. *Negro History Bulletin, 10*(1), 17–19. Retrieved February 15, 2021, from http://www.jstor.org/stable/44174624.

Wallace, J. M., Goodkind, S., Wallace, C. M., & Bachman, J. G. (2008). Racial, ethnic, and gender differences in school discipline among U.S. High school students: 1991-2005. *The Negro Educational Review, 59*(1–2), 47–62.

Weisheipl, J. A., & O.P. (1964). Curriculum of the arts Faculty at Oxford in the early fourteenth century. *Mediaeval Studies, 26,* 143–165.

Whitney, C. R., & Candelaria, C. A. (2017, July). The effects of no child left behind on Children's socioemotional outcomes. *AERA Open.* https://doi.org/10.1177/2332858417726324.

Wiggan, G. (2007). Race, school achievement, and educational inequality: Toward a student-based inquiry perspective. *Review of Educational Research, 77*(3), 310–333. Retrieved January 17, 2021, from http://www.jstor.org/stable/4624901.

Williams, V. L.. (2006). *Reading, writing, and reparations: Systemic reform of public schools as a matter of justice,* 11 MICH. J. RACE & L. 419. Available at: https://repository.law.umich.edu/mjrl/vol11/iss2/4.

Wright, L. B. (1957). *The cultural life of the American colonies* (p. 108). New York: Harper and Row Pub., Inc.

Chapter 6
Law Enforcement/Policing and Fear

Consciously and subconsciously, humans are concerned about safety – feeling safe, being safe, and/or seeking safety. Safety (psychological, physical, spiritual) is a basic human need emphasized in Maslow's hierarchy (Maslow, 1943). Every human being has the right to be safe. Law enforcement and policing systems are designed to buoy and support the goal of public safety but have not consistently met this objective. The criminal justice system includes the court system, probation, and parole and policing, but this chapter will focus primarily on law enforcement in the form of policing. The historical subtext is that safety has not been a right extended to and secured by all. In the current day, there are disparities in how law enforcement maintains versus breaches safety – these disparities are notable in racial/ethnic minorities, persons with lower SES, immigrants, differently abled persons, and persons with mental illness (Alang, McAlpine, McCreedy, & Hardeman, 2017; Bor, Venkataramani, Williams, & Tsai, 2018; Edwards, Lee, & Esposito, 2019). The issue of safety and who deserves it and/or is worthy of it must be examined. What will not be ignored in this chapter is the harsh reality of twenty-first-century views on policing and the demand for reform (Tesler, 2020).

As a matter of public and recent record, on January 6, 2021, a group of armed, White extremists entered our nation's Capitol building with American and Confederate flags (Mogelson, 2021; Turner Lee, 2021; Wamsley, 2021). They broke windows; beat up Capitol State cops; burned certain Governor's in effigy; constructed a noose, ransacked legislative offices; started fires; carried signs that read: "the real threat is communism"; and proclaimed that America was their country and that the Capitol was theirs. Several were injured, one Capitol officer was beaten to death, multiple injuries happened, and there was a profound trauma witnessed and experienced by an entire nation/world. Legislators were utterly terrified, fearing for their lives – safety and security were breached. Insurgency at the Capitol represented the culmination of fear-based, hateful rhetoric and actions.

A. Moreland-Capuia, *The Trauma of Racism*,
https://doi.org/10.1007/978-3-030-73436-7_6

6.1   Hatred Undergirded by Fear Grows When Unchecked

April of 2020, at the height of the uncertainty and spread of COVID-19, hundreds of mostly White, mask-less, openly armed individuals stormed Michigan's Capitol building (Censky, 2020; BBC News – Armed Protesters, 2020a). They were let into the Capitol building by police while expressing exceptional anger for the Governor who they believed violated their constitutional rights with stay at home orders secondary to COVID-19 spread and uncertainty. Unforgettable are the images of these individuals who were given the benefit of being called "demonstrators" as they confronted police officers while yelling, spitting, cursing, threatening, and carrying weapons. Police officers demonstrated great restraint on this day. Some would contend that this April event gave rise to greater aggression in Michigan. October of 2020, six White men were arrested status post Federal Bureau of Investigation's discovery of a suspected scheme to apprehend the Governor of Michigan (Allen, 2020; Bogel-Burroughs, 2020). They were indicted by a federal grand jury for conspiring to harm the Governor of Michigan. The question is: What would motivate such behavior? Based on the investigation details, these men were angry about stay at home orders and felt like the governor was reaching beyond the scope of the constitution; they also held the conviction that a second civil war was imminent and feared that society was on edge of ruin. Their convictions were motivated by hate filled fear-based political narrative at the time.

August of 2017, amid heated debate around removing and replacing public Confederate statues and images, a group of mostly White men nationalists carrying Tiki torches gathered on the campus of the University of Virginia to protest and defend what they deemed to be their heritage (Politi, 2017; Wilson, 2017; BBC News -Charlottesville, 2017). There were specific discussions about removing a statue of Confederate Gen. Robert E. Lee (commander of the Confederate Army during the Civil War). This group of White men lit Tiki torches in hand and paraded around campus chanting racist and anti-Semitic sentiments. The narrative of these White men centered on who has a right to citizenship, who has a right to history and belonging, and a very real fear of being replaced. Most unfortunate is that this march escalated to significant violence that resulted in multiple injuries and death. Of note, when the President of the United States was asked to unequivocally condemn racism, xenophobia, and White supremacy, he was unwilling to do so. Also, of note, university police officers were criticized for intentionally remaining on the periphery, not de-escalating and allowing much of the violence and hate motivated by racial rage to unfold.

There are multiple instances where police and law enforcement have demonstrated great restraint and negotiated in what seems like unreasonable circumstances. One other poignant, twenty-first-century example is on January 2, 2016, when a heavily armed group of White extremists occupied the headquarters of the Malheur National Wildlife Refuge, located in Harney County, Oregon (Allen, 2018; Kennedy & Gonazales, 2021; Parks, 2016). The wildlife refuge is federal property – the occupation started the beginning of January, but the final arrests were made by law enforcement in the middle of February (almost 6 weeks from the start of the occupation). There were negotiations and a desire to preserve life and de-escalate. Law enforcement has the capacity to center safety even when there is a looming threat.

In late August 2020, a Black man named Jacob Blake in Kenosha, Wisconsin, was shot seven times in the back while walking away from police. Jacob was shot in front of his children (Bosman & Mervosh, 2020; BBC News-Kenosha shooting, 2020b). He is alive but paralyzed. Black Lives Matter demonstrations and calls for police reform amplified. On the approximately the third day of protests in Wisconsin, a 17-year-old White child came to the Wisconsin demonstrations for justice, in protest of the protests, openly bearing a military style semi-automatic rifle in front of law enforcement with limited consequence and/or questioning (Willis et al., 2020). This 17-year-old child was alleged to have been menacing to the crowd and subsequently killed two people and utterly incapacitated another. His actions were captured on video, and 1 day later (not same day immediately, but nearly 24 h elapsed), he was charged with one count of first-degree intentional homicide and one count of first-degree reckless homicide.

6.2 Disproportionality in Black Men and Women Killed by Police

The urgent question is who is deemed worthy of protecting and safeguarding? Who is worthy of being safe? To appreciate pattern, it is critical to juxtapose the twenty-first-century scenarios mentioned with the stark contrast observed between law enforcement and dominant culture and law enforcement versus racial minorities. The use of "and" and "versus" is intentional here. The names of Black citizens killed by police are too numerous to mention and so heartbreakingly unacceptable. A 2019 study by Edwards and colleagues on the risk of being killed by police use of force in the United States by age, race ethnicity, and sex employed data on police-involved deaths from 2013 to 2018 to demonstrate how being killed by police use of force in the United States differs across social groups (Edwards et al., 2019).

Edwards et al.'s (2019) study asserts:

- Police violence is the leading cause of death for young men in the United States.
- Black men and women and American Indian and Alaska Native women and men are significantly more likely compared to White women and men to be killed by police.
- Through the life course, approximately 1 in every 1000 Black men can expect be killed by police. Black men are *2.5 times* more likely to be killed by police over the life course compared to White men and women.
- When compared to White men and women's risk of being killed by police, Black women are 1.4 times more likely to be killed by police; American Indians are approximately 1.4 times more likely to be killed by police; American Indian and

Alaska Native women are approximately 1.6 times more likely; and Latino men are approximately 1.4 times more likely (Edwards et al., 2019).

There is also data that demonstrates high incidences of use of force by police in the case of persons with mental illness and/or differently abled (Alang et al., 2017; Bor et al., 2018).

The data pans out in real life as indicated by 2019–2020 shootings by police based on sex and race to include but not limited to:

1. George P. Floyd (the world watched the soul-shattering video of this Black man crying out for his mother and indicating that he could not breathe as his neck was being crushed by the knee of a White officer for 8 min and 46 s in Minnesota).
2. Dreasjon S. Reed was shot in Indiana by police.
3. Daniel T. Prude was asphyxiated by police in New York.
4. Breonna Taylor was shot and killed by police in her own home in Kentucky.
5. John E. Neville was hog-tied by police in North Carolina and suffered a heart attack and brain injury.
6. Atatiana K. Jefferson was shot and killed by police in Texas.
7. Elijah McClain who had a neurodevelopmental disorder (which means the lens from which he views the world is different, communication can be scary) – Elijah was only 23 years old, no record, a gifted musician, when he was accused of being suspicious and subsequently put in a chokehold, given two times too much of the sedative ketamine to subdue him, and died in Colorado. Elijah's untimely, preventable death operates on the intersection of so many stereotypes of Black emotion and Black pain as Black boys are quickly transitioned to and treated like men and lack of understanding of mental health and medical conditions – the contradictions and complexities are too numerous to mention, but they have been addressed in the entirety of this book.
8. Ronald Greene was stun gunned and subject to excessive use of force by police in Louisiana.
9. Javier Ambler was tasered by police in Texas and died.

The antithesis of safety is fear – fear-based actions observed in law enforcement as evidenced by expressed fear and a heightened sense of threat with concomitant disparate and unfortunate outcomes as it pertains to engagement with racial minorities and racial minorities whose safety has been chronically breached, who have been needlessly and excessively subject to trauma and re-traumatization and live in constant fear. There are real-time fear-on-fear interactions when it comes to law enforcement and racial minorities. To contextualize current-day happenings with law enforcement, it is critical to revisit the history of policing.

6.3   Slave Patrols

In the 1700s, before America was America, but colonies, policing was noted in the form of slave patrols. Slave patrols consisted of White volunteers who took it upon themselves to employ inhumane strategies to keep slaves bound by plantation rules (de Jong, 2002; Ralph, 2019).

If a slave escaped or attempted to escape and/or was caught trying to learn to read and write, they were punished by slave patrols. According to historians, one of the first slave patrols were in South Carolina, but eventually every colony had slave patrols (de Jong, 2002; Ralph, 2019). Keeping slaves in control was a means of controlling and maintaining the Southern economy. Law enforcement in colonial America was deemed a local obligation (Arnold, 1986; Blanchard, Bloembergen, & Lauro, 2017). According to Spitzer in "The Rationalization of Crime Control in Capitalist Society," policing in the United States mirrored the establishment of policing in England, and policing in the colonies was described as informal and collective (Spitzer, 1979).

6.4   Law Enforcement During the Reconstruction Era

History reveals that after the Civil War, amid the Reconstruction era, prior Confederate soldiers re-branded and emerged as law enforcement in the form of police officers and judges in the South predominantly (de Jong, 2001; Emsley, 1983; Ralph, 2019). By way of reminder, Confederate soldiers were in full support of maintaining slavery, maintaining anti-literacy laws; limiting Black Americans from becoming citizens; and maintaining a segregated education system to name a few – the sociopolitical philosophy helped to give birth to groups like the Klu Klux Klan (KKK). Former Confederate soldiers became the law and created significant barriers for new, free Black citizens to progress as they established and enforced what were called Black codes – a set of extremely restraining laws created to curtail Black freedom and economic upward mobility and progress (de Jong, 2001; Emsley, 1983; Ralph, 2019). It was also very difficult for Black Americans to proceed with and win court cases as the court system was literally stacked against them.

In 1829, the Metropolitan Police Act was passed by Parliament establishing the Metropolitan Police of London. This Act centralized policing, shifting the responsibility of law enforcement from communities and neighborhood watchmen and women to a centrally organized law enforcement system in the form of policing (Campion, 2005; Colquhoun, 1806). This transition in the early nineteenth century to centralized enforcement was also happening in the United States and was concomitant with population growth, industrialization, pushing of urban boundaries, and more robust immigration (Emsley, 1983; Lane, 1980). As the population diversified and grew, urban boundaries expanded, and urban spaces were concentrated, the incidences of poverty and lack of sanitation increased exponentially (Lundman,

1980; Oliver, 2006; Silver, 1967). These are some of the conditions that compelled the centralization and organization of law enforcement in the United States (Emsley, 1983; Lane, 1980; Walker, 1996).

6.5 Twentieth-Century Policing

Twentieth-century policing was shaped by an influx of ex-military members joining the force and police departments who assumed several military practices and techniques. The special weapons and tactics (SWAT) were established in the 1960s (ACLU, 2014; Lawson, 2018; Mummolo, 2018). With the introduction of military-inspired practices and approaches also came a demonstrable shift in police behavior. Incidences of police excessive use of force became more prominent and rose to significant levels in the twenty-first century (Meares, 2016; President's Task Force on 21st Century Policing, 2015). Excessive use of force disproportionately and deleteriously affected minority communities and persons with and in mental health crisis (Headley, D'Alessio, & Stolzenberg, 2017). The use of military-type force by the hands of the police contributed to significant erosion of community and public trust, more so in racial minority communities (ACLU, 2014; Lawson, 2018; Mummolo, 2018).

During the Reconstruction era, not only did former Confederate officers become the law in the form of police officers, judges, lawyers, and local authorities in Southern states initially, but the KKK was established around 1865 (Chalmers, 1987; Du Bois, 1926). The KKK was a formal-informal social structure that aided White southerners in their quest to maintain power over freed Black men and women. The social and political climate in the post-Civil War south did not support the idea of free Black men and women participating equally in society, being economically upwardly mobile or politically savvy – they didn't believe that Blacks should have any form of power (Chalmers, 1987; Du Bois, 1926). The KKK buoyed these unfortunate beliefs and reinforced them by terrorizing Blacks. The unfortunate reality was that law enforcement officials were members of the KKK, and if they weren't official members, they were less likely to oppose KKK actions and/or methods (i.e., KKK members were not likely to be prosecuted if they killed and/or injured Black members of or Black institutions in the community) (Chalmers, 1987; Du Bois, 1926).

The KKK would parade through streets threatening violence – their physical presence was violent; became known for burning crosses to intimidate and make Black men and women and/or Black sympathizers afraid; tried to prevent Blacks from being civically engaged by attempting to disrupt via fear tactics to stop Black voter registration; facilitated public lynching, killing, and beating to any group and/or person who did not acquiesce to their vision and definition of what it meant to be a citizen in America (Castle, 2020; Chalmers, 1987; Du Bois, 1926; Howell, 2018; Steinmetz, Schaefer, & Henderson, 2017). From about 1865 to around the Great Depression, the KKK successfully recruited several White members of society because of their socially constructed fear-based narrative which included that Blacks and immigrants were taking away economic and social opportunity from Whites – that their identity and birthright were being threatened and would continue to be threatened if they didn't intervene to stop it (Castle, 2020; Chalmers, 1987; Du Bois, 1926; Howell, 2018; Steinmetz et al., 2017). The economic crash in the 1920s didn't help temper the fear-based us or them narrative but only strengthened it. KKK presence, practices, and methods buoyed Jim Crowism during the Civil Rights movement. Police brutality and practices were disproportionately violent toward Black citizens in this era (Castle, 2020; Chalmers, 1987; Du Bois, 1926; Howell, 2018; Steinmetz et al., 2017). Unfortunately, in the twenty-first century, scholars contend that modern-day policing methods mirror pre-Civil War slave patrol-reconstruction-Jim Crow south methods and contribute to the persistence of economic, social, and racial inequality (Chalmers, 1987; Du Bois, 1926). Historically and as observed as recently as the insurrection on January 6, 2021, at the US Capitol, some members of law enforcement have demonstrated affiliation with White nationalist/extremist groups as members and/or sympathizers (Castle, 2020; Steinmetz et al., 2017).

6.6 Conditioned Fear, Perception of Threat/Extremism, and Behavior Modification

This brings the discussion back to fear as a driver for survivalist, un-rational behavior – not to serve as an excuse but perhaps an explanation for how and why humans would kill and destroy other humans. There is a connection between fear, extremism, and violence. Extremism is a form of terrorism – terrorism is the employment of threats or violence to produce fear. A study by Asad Ali Shah and colleagues assert that in the context of terrorism, fear is at the core of the deleterious impact on psychological well-being and that the persistence of fear must be addressed with regularity in order to preserve and protect well-being (Asad Ali Shah, Yezhuang, Muhammad Shah, Khan Durrani, & Jamal Shah, 2018). According to Asad Ali Shah and colleagues, terrorists' attacks like 9/11 and the Boston Marathon left many folks fearful and anticipatory anxiety heightened when considering the risk of future attacks. Anticipatory anxiety and fear can be shaped by persistent narrative (Elmas, 2020). One study contends that extremism has mostly been constructed as a security issue and that increases in the intensity of security construct exaggeratedly increase the public's worry of being subject to terrorism (Smith, Stohl, & Al-Gharbi, 2019). It is difficult not to consider extremism as a breach in safety (psychological, physical, spiritual). There is evidence that terroristic and extremists' leaders tap into fear and the irrational aspects of human beings – it is fear that motivates survivalist behavior (Harrington, 2013; Trip, Bora, Marian, Halmajan, & Drugas, 2019).

Extremism and supremacy are grounded in the perception held by dominant members that they matter more and most. A 2008 Amsterdam study on de-radicalization demonstrated that vicissitudes in behavior don't always mirror change in convictions and that radical behavior can be halted in absence of change in beliefs (Demant, Slootman, Buijs, & Tillie, 2008). Behavior can be modified by shifts in narrative and environment (Goddu, Raffel, & Peek, 2015; Steeves, Thompson, Bassett, Fitzhugh, & Raynor, 2012; Wasik, Senn, Welch, & Cooper, 1969; Wolraich, 1979).

Fear is a universal human response to threat, perceived or real, and is attached to human proclivity for survival and coping with uncertainty. Fear compels humans to seek safety. Fear is designed to be threat and time limited. Fear is linked to heightened stress response (increased cortisol, norepinephrine corresponding to increased heart rate, compromise in cognition) and survival behaviors (fleeing, fighting, freezing). Fear impacts the brain and modulates behavior. Anxiety is associated with activation in ventromedial prefrontal cortex and hippocampus, while fear is associated with activation in periaqueductal gray, with amygdala involved in processing aspects of both emotional responses (Rigoli, Ewbank, Dalgleish, & Calder, 2016; Steimer, 2002). Parts of the brain responsible for triggering the fear response include the amygdala and hippocampus and prefrontal cortex which modulate the behavioral aspects of fear and retrieve historical memories of what breached safety in the past and creating context (Rigoli et al., 2016; Fiddick 2011; Steimer, 2002). Some studies implicate the amygdala in the processing of immediate threats and the cingulate cortex (and insular) processing potential threats (Fiddick, 2011; Shechner, Hong, Britton, Pine, & Fox, 2014). Context is linked to memory and provides meaning – how and what humans recall is attached to an emotion. Context can be determined unconsciously or without awareness and inability to appropriately contextualize can have deleterious behavioral impact (Barrett & Kensinger, 2010; Davis & Whalen, 2001; Hartley & Phelps, 2010; Maren, Phan, & Liberzon, 2013). When a threat disappears, fear should subside. Underscore the word "should" because studies highlight a phenomenon called fear conditioning, and it is exactly as it sounds – learned fear. Prior chapters highlighted Pavlovian classical condition and/or learning via association.

6.7 Classical Conditioning and Fear Conditioning

Classical conditioning and fear conditioning involve parts of the brain that are responsible for the processing and interpretation of threat. As demonstrated first in animal models, classical conditioning (fear conditioning) is defined by attaching a formerly neutral cue (in the literature, this is referred to as a conditioned stimulus and can include a visual signal) with an exceptionally threatening stimulus (in the literature, this is referred to as the unconditioned stimulus and can include electric shocks, burning sensation, etc.) – the formerly neutral stimulus will invoke fear in the absence of the threatening stimulus (Maren et al., 2013; Steimer, 2002). This is learned fear, associative fear (Maren et al., 2013; Steimer, 2002). Fear conditioning and associative fear as neurobiological phenomena have very real social and behavioral implications.

Several studies confirm that threat perception and risks of violence are dangerously influenced by racial and gender bias (Blair, Judd, & Fallman, 2004; Correll, Park, Judd, & Wittenbrink, 2007; Cottrell & Neuberg, 2005; Cunningham et al., 2004; Duncan, 1976; Edwards, Esposito, & Lee, 2018; Lundberg, Neel, Lassetter, & Todd, 2018; Miller, Maner, & Becker, 2010; Sagar & Schofield, 1980; Thiem, Neel, Simpson, & Todd, 2019; Trawalter, Todd, Baird, & Richeson, 2008; Turner & Turner, 1992): Blacks perceived as more dangerous than Whites, men more dangerous than women (Thiem et al., 2019; Turner & Turner, 1992).

6.8 Attitudes Toward the Police and Fear

Multiple studies have illustrated differences in attitudes toward and perceptions about the police, and these differences do fall among racial lines (Huebner, Schafer, & Bynum, 2004; Kamalu, 2016; Miller & Davis, 2008; Reisig & Parks, 2000; Schafer, Huebner, & Bynum, 2003; Skogan & Frydyl, 2004; Schuck & Martin, 2013; Schuck & Rosenbaum, 2005; Schuck, Rosenbaum, & Hawkins, 2008; Wu, Sun, & Triplett, 2009). Blacks and other racial minority groups were less likely to perceive the police as positive and/or contributing to their overall safety compared to Whites who tended to have a more positive view (Huebner et al., 2004; Kamalu, 2016; Miller & Davis, 2008; Reisig & Parks, 2000; Schafer et al., 2003; Schuck et al., 2008; Schuck & Martin, 2013; Schuck & Rosenbaum, 2005; Wu et al., 2009). These differences in experiences were associated with more police stops and higher incidences of racial profiling and excessive use of force in racial minorities (Kamalu, 2016; Schafer et al., 2003; Schuck & Martin, 2013). Even when education and socioeconomic status were accounted for, racial minorities with education and higher socioeconomic status were less likely to be satisfied with the police (Wu et al., 2009).

One study distinguished between attitudes toward police behavior versus police work as a profession and found that there were differences in public-police attitudes between White and racial minority groups and that both White and minority racial groups showed positive perceptions toward police work (Mbuba, 2010). In general, the public can appreciate the importance of police and law enforcement to maintain public safety (and many officers by statue are deemed peace officers), but there are reservations with police behavior especially in racial minority communities, largely driven by disparate treatment and negative treatment.

Race as a steady prognosticator of attitudes toward police has been demonstrated in multiple studies (Mbuba, 2010). A study by Weitzer and Tuch (2004) considered the role of personal experience, mass media, neighborhood, and certain demographic variables and their influence on attitudes toward the police. The study employed data from a national survey over a 2-month period; a total of 1792 residents were surveyed who lived in Metropolitan areas. The study revealed that African-Americans and Hispanics are significantly more dissatisfied with the police than their White counterparts; and African-Americans hold more critical views of police based on their disproportionate antagonistic experiences with police and other external factors to include being subject to images of police brutality toward African-Americans and having negative encounters with police in neighborhoods like higher stop and frisks incidents that felt unwarranted (Weitzer & Tuch, 2004).

A study by Nadal et al. investigated the relationship between law enforcement and communities of color via examination of between-group differences of histori-cally/chronically marginalized racial groups. They did two studies, the first included over 1500 persons of diverse backgrounds who all completed the Perception of Police Scale (POPS). In study 1, there were no gender differences, but of note, Black participants were more likely than Whites and Latina/Latinos to view police negatively, and Black men were more likely to have negative perceptions of police compared to White and Asian men. Study 2 took a little over 200 participants from study 1 that had engaged with police officers upon being stopped – approximately one third of this group believed that they had been stopped unjustly (Nadal, Davidoff, & Allicock, 2017).

There is literature that questions whether police presence contributes to fear and/ or reduces it (Brown & Wycoff, 1987; Dietz, 1997; Gates & Rohe, 1987). Some stud-ies show that positive police presence can reduce fear of crime and upholds safety (Brown & Wycoff, 1987; Dietz, 1997; Gates & Rohe, 1987). The caveat though is that when there is positive police presence, fear is reduced. A study by Zhao et al. (2002) suggests that public satisfaction is strongly linked with the success of police fear reduction programs (Zhao et al. 2002). In other words, positive perceptions and attitudes toward police are linked with the reduction of fear. In the case of racial minorities, attitudes and perceptions of the police are less than favorable because interactions with law enforcement have been less than ideal and are more violent and less safe and police interactions with racial minorities are more likely to be informed by negative stereotypes.

This chapter began by outlining current law enforcement happenings, providing the history of the establishment of law enforcement, and juxtaposing this history with the neuroscience of fear, threat assessment, and behavior and how fear can be modulated by narrative and social constructs. The antithesis of safety is fear. From the beginning, Black citizens and immigrants have been constructed as dangerous threats to American civilization and socioeconomic status. Conditioned fear is a theme in law enforcement and does and will continue to result in disparate and harmful treatment and outcomes for racial/ethnic minorities and immigrants if the history of fear-based socially constructed negative narratives about immigrants and racial/ethnic minorities is not acknowledged and tempered. The fear-driven system that is law enforcement has contributed to the perpetuation of fear and trauma in communities of color. The real-life examples in 2020 alone of the disproportionate, inhumane, unacceptable killing of Black citizens in America has deep historical roots and should leave society asking this question, seriously: "What is the fear? Who deserves to be safe?" Law enforcement is a system that was built and is main-tained by fear, and it (law enforcement as a system) contributes to perpetual fear and trauma – this dynamic must change as healing of people, systems, and societies depends on it.

References

ACLU. (2014). *War comes home: The excessive militarization of policing*. New York: American Civil Liberties Union.

Alang, S., McAlpine, D., McCreedy, E., & Hardeman, R. (2017). Police brutality and black health: Setting the agenda for public health scholars. *American Journal of Public Health, 107,* 662–665.

Allen, J. (2018, July 10). *Trump pardons Oregon ranchers who inspired refuge standoff.* REUTERS. Retrieved from https://www.reuters.com/article/us-oregon-standoff-trump/trump-pardons-oregon-ranchers-who-inspired-refuge-standoff-idUSKBN1K021Q February 15, 2021.

Allen, J. (2020, December 17). *Grand jury indicts six men for Michigan governor kidnap plot.* REUTERS. Retrieved from https://www.reuters.com/article/michigan-whitmer/grand-jury-indicts-six-men-for-michigan-governor-kidnap-plot-idUSKBN28R2O5. February 15, 2021.

Arnold, D. (1986). *Police power and colonial rule: Madras 1859–1947.* Delhi: Oxford University Press.

Asad Ali Shah, S., Yezhuang, T., Muhammad Shah, A., Khan Durrani, D., & Jamal Shah, S. (2018). Fear of terror and psychological Well-being: The moderating role of emotional intelligence. *International Journal of Environmental Research and Public Health, 15*(11), 2554. https://doi.org/10.3390/ijerph15112554.

Barrett, L., & Kensinger, E. (2010). Context is routinely encoded during emotion perception. *Psychological Science, 21,* 599.

BBC News. (2017, August 14). *Charlottesville white nationalist marchers face backlash.* Retrieved from https://www.bbc.com/news/world-us-canada-40922698. February 15, 2021.

BBC News. (2020a, May 1). *Coronavirus: Armed protesters enter Michigan statehouse.* Retrieved from https://www.bbc.com/news/world-us-canada-52496514. February 15, 2021.

BBC News. (2020b, August 24). *Kenosha shooting: Protests erupt after US police shoot black man.* Retrieved from https://www.bbc.com/news/world-us-canada-53886070. February 15, 2021.

Blair, I. V., Judd, C. M., & Fallman, J. L. (2004). The automaticity of race and Afrocentric facial features in social judgments. *Journal of Personality and Social Psychology, 87,* 763–778. https://doi.org/10.1037/0022-3514.87.6.763.

Blanchard, E., Bloembergen, M., & Lauro, A. (Eds.). (2017). *Policing in colonial empires: Cases, connections, boundaries (1850–1970).* Bruxelles: Peter Lang.

Bogel-Burroughs, N. (2020, October 18). *What we know about the Alleged Plot to Kidnap Michigan's Governor: The group charged with planning the kidnapping met repeatedly for firearms training and combat drills, the F.B.I. said.* Retrieved from The New York Times. Retrieved from https://www.nytimes.com/2020/10/09/us/michigan-militia-whitmer.html. February 15, 2021.

Bor, J., Venkataramani, A. S., Williams, D. R., & Tsai, A. C. (2018). Police killings and their spill-over effects on the mental health of black Americans: A population-based, quasi-experimental study. *Lancet, 392,* 302–310.

Bosman, J., & Mervosh, S. (2020, August 26). *Justice Dept. to Open Investigation Into Kenosha Shooting.* The New York Times. Retrieved from https://www.nytimes.com/2020/08/26/us/kenosha-shooting-protests-jacob-blake.html. February 15, 2021.

Brown, L., & Wycoff, M. A. (1987). Policing Houston: Reducing fear and improving service. *Crime and Delinquency, 33,* 71–89.

Campion, D. A. (2005). 'Policing the peelers': Parliament, the public, and the metropolitan police, 1829–33. In M. Cragoe & A. Taylor (Eds.), *London politics, 1760–1914.* London: Palgrave Macmillan. https://doi.org/10.1057/9780230522794_3.

Castle, T. (2020). "Cops and the Klan": Police disavowal of risk and minimization of threat from the far-right. *Critical Criminology.* https://doi.org/10.1007/s10612-020-09493-6.

Censky, A (2020, May 14). *Heavily armed protesters gather again at Michigan capitol to decry stay-at-home order.* NPR. Retrieved from https://www.npr.org/2020/05/14/855918852/

heavily-armed-protesters-gather-again-at-michigans-capitol-denouncing-home-order. February 15, 2021.

Chalmers, D. J. (1987). *Hooded Americanism: The history of the Ku Klux Klan* (1st and 3rd edn.). Duke University Press. Project MUSE muse.jhu.edu/book/69315.

Colquhoun, P. (1806). *A treatise on the police of the Metropolis.* London: J. Mawman, Cadell and Davies.

Correll, J., Park, B., Judd, C. M., & Wittenbrink, B. (2007). The influence of stereotypes on decisions to shoot. *European Journal of Social Psychology, 37,* 1102–1117. https://doi.org/10.1002/ejsp.450.

Cottrell, C. A., & Neuberg, S. L. (2005). Different emotional reactions to different groups: A socio-functional threat-based approach to "prejudice". *Journal of Personality and Social Psychology, 88,* 770–789.

Cunningham, W. A., Johnson, M. K., Raye, C. L., Gatenby, J. C., Gore, J. C., & Banaji, M. R. (2004). Separable neural components in the processing of Black and White faces. *Psychological Science, 15,* 806–813.

Davis, M., & Whalen, P. (2001). The amygdala: Vigilance and emotion. *Molecular Psychiatry, 6,* 34.

de Jong, G. (2001). In S. E. Hadden (Ed.), *Slave Patrols: Law and violence in Virginia and the Carolinas.* Cambridge, MA: Harvard University Press.

de Jong, G. (2002, Fall). *Journal of Social History, 36*(1), 220–221. https://doi.org/10.1353/jsh.2002.0088.

Demant, F., Slootman, M., Buijs, F., & Tillie, J. (2008). *Decline and disengagement: An analysis of processes of de-radicalisation.* Amsterdam: Institute for Migration and Ethnic Studies (IMES).

Dietz, A. S. (1997). Evaluating community policing: Quality police service and fear of crime. *Policing: An International Journal of Police Strategy and Management, 20,* 83–100.

Du Bois, W. (1926). The shape of fear. *The North American Review, 223*(831), 291–304. Retrieved January 22, 2021, from http://www.jstor.org/stable/25110229.

Duncan, B. L. (1976). Differential social perception and attribution of intergroup violence: Testing the lower limits of stereotyping of blacks. *Journal of Personality and Social Psychology, 34,* 590–598.

Edwards, F., Esposito, M. H., & Lee, H. (2018). Risk of police-involved death by race/ethnicity and place, United States, 2012–2018. *American Journal of Public Health, 108,* 1241–1248.

Edwards, F., Lee, H., & Esposito, M. (2019). Risk of being killed by police use of force in the United States by age, race–ethnicity, and sex. *Proceedings of the National Academy of Sciences of the United States of America, 116*(34), 16793–16798. https://doi.org/10.1073/pnas.1821204116.

Elmas, M. S. (2020). Perceived risk of terrorism, indirect victimization, and individual-level determinants of fear of terrorism. *Security Journal.* https://doi.org/10.1057/s41284-020-00242-6.

Emsley, C. (1983). *Policing and its context, 1750–1870.* London: Macmillan.

Fiddick, L. (2011). There is more than the amygdala: Potential threat assessment in the cingulate cortex. *Neuroscience & Biobehavioral Reviews, 35*(4), 1007–1018. ISSN 0149-7634. https://doi.org/10.1016/j.neubiorev.2010.09.014.

Gates, L. B., & Rohe, W. M. (1987). Fear and reactions to crime: A revised model. *Urban Affairs Quarterly, 22,* 425–453.

Goddu, A. P., Raffel, K. E., & Peek, M. E. (2015, August). A story of change: The influence of narrative on African-Americans with diabetes. *Patient Education and Counseling, 98*(8), 1017–1024. https://doi.org/10.1016/j.pec.2015.03.022. Epub 2015 Apr 6. PMID: 25986500; PMCID: PMC4492448.

Harrington, N. (2013). Irrational beliefs and socio-political extremism. *Journal of Rational-Emotive and Cognitive-Behavior Therapy, 31,* 167–178. https://doi.org/10.1007/s10942-013-0168-x.

Hartley, C. A., & Phelps, E. A. (2010). Changing fear: The neurocircuitry of emotion regulation. *Neuropsychopharmacology, 35*(1), 136–146. https://doi.org/10.1038/npp.2009.121.

Headley, A. M., D'Alessio, S. J., & Stolzenberg, L. (2017). The effect of a complainant's race and ethnicity on dispositional outcome in police misconduct cases in Chicago. *Race and Justice, 10,* 43–61.

Howell, A. (2018). Forget 'militarization': Race, disability, and the 'martial politics' of the police and of the university. *International Feminist Journal of Politics, 20*(2), 117–136.

Huebner, B., Schafer, J., & Bynum, T. (2004). African American and white perceptions of police services: Within- and between-group variation. *Journal of Criminal Justice, 32*(2), 123.

Kamalu, N. C. (2016). African Americans and racial profiling by U.S. law enforcement: An analysis of police traffic stops and searches of motorists in Nebraska, 2002–2007. *African Journal of Criminology and Justice Studies, 9*(1), 187–206.

Kennedy, M., & Gonazales, R. (2021). *7 Defendants in Oregon wildlife refuge occupation found not guilty*. NPR. Retrieved from https://www.npr.org/sections/thetwo-way/2016/10/27/499668126/defendants-in-oregon-wildlife-refuge-occupation-found-not-guilty. February 15, 2021.

Lane, R. (1980). Urban police and crime in nineteenth-century America. In N. Morris & M. Tonry (Eds.), *Crime and justice*. Chicago: University of Chicago Press.

Lawson, E. (2018). Police militarization and the use of lethal force. *Political Research Quarterly, 72*(1), 177–189.

Lundberg, G., Neel, R., Lassetter, B., & Todd, A. R. (2018). Racial bias in implicit danger associations generalizes to older male targets. *PLoS One, 13*(6), e0197398. https://doi.org/10.1371/journal.pone.0197398.

Lundman. R. J. (1980). *Police and policing: An introduction*. New York: Holt, Rinehart & Winston.

Maren, S., Phan, K. L., & Liberzon, I. (2013). The contextual brain: Implications for fear conditioning, extinction and psychopathology. *Nature Reviews Neuroscience, 14*(6), 417–428. https://doi.org/10.1038/nrn3492.

Maslow, A. H. (1943). A theory of human motivation. *Psychological Review, 50*(4), 370–396.

Mbuba, J. M. (2010). Attitudes toward the police: The significance of race and other factors among college students. *Journal of Ethnicity in Criminal Justice, 8*(3), 201–215. https://doi.org/10.1080/15377938.2010.502846.

Meares, T. L. (2016). Policing in the 21st century: The importance of public security: Keynote address. *University of Chicago Legal Forum, 2016*, Article 2. Available at: http://chicagounbound.uchicago.edu/uclf/vol2016/iss1/2.

Miller, J., & Davis, R. (2008). Unpacking public attitudes to the police: Contrasting perceptions of misconduct with traditional measures of satisfaction. *International Journal of Police Science & Management, 10*, 9–22.

Miller, S. L., Maner, J. K., & Becker, D. V. (2010). Self-protective biases in group categorization: Threat cues shape the psychological boundary between "us" and "them". *Journal of Personality and Social Psychology, 99*, 62–77. https://doi.org/10.1037/a0018086.

Mogelson, L. (2021, January 15). *Among the Insurrectionists: The Capitol was breached by Trump supporters who had been declaring, at rally after rally, that they would go to violent lengths to keep the President in power. A chronicle of an attack foretold*. The New Yorker Magazine. Retrieved from https://www.newyorker.com/magazine/2021/01/25/among-the-insurrectionists. February 15, 2021.

Mummolo, J. (2018). Militarization fails to enhance police safety or reduce crime but may harm police reputation. *Proceedings. National Academy of Sciences. United States of America, 115*, 9181–9186.

Nadal, K. L., Davidoff, K. C., & Allicock, N. (2017). Perceptions of police, racial profiling, and psychological outcomes: A mixed methodological study. *Journal of Social Issues, 73*(4), 808–830. https://doi.org/10.1111/josi.12249.

Oliver, W. M. (2006). The fourth era of policing: Homeland security. *International Review of Law Computers & Technology, 20*(1–2), 49–62.

Parks, B. W. (2016, January 24). *Malheur occupation: A reference guide*. OPB. Retrieved from https://www.opb.org/news/series/burns-oregon-standoff-bundy-militia-news-updates/oregon-malheur-occupation-militia-bundy-ammon-ryan/. February 15, 2021.

Politi, D. (2017, August 12). *Torch-Bearing White Supremacists March at University of Virginia*. The Slate. Retrieved from https://slate.com/news-and-politics/2017/08/torch-bearing-white-supremacists-descend-on-uva-ahead-of-unite-the-right-rally.html. February 15, 2021.

President's Task Force on 21st Century Policing. (2015). *Final report of the President's task force on 21st century policing.* Washington, DC: Office of Community Oriented Policing Services.

Ralph, L. (2019). The logic of the slave patrol: The fantasy of black predatory violence and the use of force by the police. *Palgrave Communication, 5,* 130. https://doi.org/10.1057/s41599-019-0333-7.

Reisig, M. D., & Parks, R. B. (2000). Experience, quality of life, and neighborhood context: A hierarchical analysis of satisfaction with police. *Justice Quarterly, 17,* 607–630.

Rigoli, F., Ewbank, M., Dalgleish, T., & Calder, A. (2016). Threat visibility modulates the defensive brain circuit underlying fear and anxiety. *Neuroscience Letters, 612,* 7–13. https://doi.org/10.1016/j.neulet.2015.11.026.

Sagar, H. A., & Schofield, J. W. (1980). Racial and behavioral cues in black and white children's perceptions of ambiguously aggressive acts. *Journal of Personality and Social Psychology, 39,* 590–598. https://doi.org/10.1037/0022-3514.39.4.590.

Schafer, J., Huebner, B., & Bynum, T. (2003). Citizen perceptions of police services: Race, neighborhood context and community policing. *Police Quarterly, 6,* 440–468. https://doi.org/10.1177/109861102250459.

Schuck, A., & Martin, C. (2013). Residents' perceptions of procedural injustice during encounters with the police. *Journal of Ethnicity in Criminal Justice, 11*(4), 219–237. https://doi.org/10.1080/15377938.2012.762635.

Schuck, A., Rosenbaum, D., & Hawkins, D. (2008). The influence of race/ethnicity, social class, and neighborhood context on residents' attitudes toward the police. *Police Quarterly, 11,* 496–519.

Schuck, A. M., & Rosenbaum, D. P. (2005). Global and neighborhood attitudes toward the police: Differentiation by race, ethnicity and type of contact. *Journal of Quantitative Criminology, 21*(4), 391–418. Retrieved from https://doi.org/10.1007/s10940-005-7356-5.

Shechner, T., Hong, M., Britton, J. C., Pine, D. S., & Fox, N. A. (2014). Fear conditioning and extinction across development: Evidence from human studies and animal models. *Biological Psychology, 100,* 1–12. https://doi.org/10.1016/j.biopsycho.2014.04.001.

Silver, A. (1967). The demand for order in civil society: A review of some themes in the history of urban crime, police and riot. In D. Bordeau (Ed.), *The police: Six sociological essays.* New York: Wiley.

Skogan, W. G., & Frydl, K. (2004). *Fairness and effectiveness in policing: The evidence.* Washington, DC: National Academies Press.

Smith, B. K., Stohl, M., & Al-Gharbi, M. (2019). Discourses on countering violent extremism: The strategic interplay between fear and security after 9/11. *Critical Studies on Terrorism, 12*(1), 151–168. https://doi.org/10.1080/17539153.2018.1494793.

Spitzer, S. (1979). The rationalization of crime control in capitalist society. *Contemporary Crises, 3,* 187–206. https://doi.org/10.1007/BF00729229.

Steeves, J. A., Thompson, D. L., Bassett, D. R., Fitzhugh, E. C., & Raynor, H. A. (2012). A review of different behavior modification strategies designed to reduce sedentary screen behaviors in children. *Journal of Obesity, 2012,* Article ID 379215, 16. https://doi.org/10.1155/2012/379215.

Steimer, T. (2002). The biology of fear- and anxiety-related behaviors. *Dialogues in Clinical Neuroscience, 4*(3), 231–249. https://doi.org/10.31887/DCNS.2002.4.3/tsteimer.

Steinmetz, K. F., Schaefer, B. P., & Henderson, H. (2017). Wicked overseers: American policing and colonialism. *Sociology of Race and Ethnicity, 3*(1), 68–81.

Tesler, M. (2020). The Floyd protests have changed public opinion about race and policing. Here's the data. *The Washington Post,* June 9, 2020. Available at https://www.washingtonpost.com/politics/2020/06/09/floyd-protests-have-changed-public-opinion-about-race-policing-heres-data/.

Thiem, K. C., Neel, R., Simpson, A. J., & Todd, A. R. (2019). Are black women and girls associated with danger? Implicit racial Bias at the intersection of target age and gender. *Personality and Social Psychology Bulletin., 45*(10), 1427–1439. https://doi.org/10.1177/0146167219829182.

Trawalter, S., Todd, A. R., Baird, A. A., & Richeson, J. A. (2008). Attending to threat: Race-based patterns of selective attention. *Journal of Experimental Social Psychology, 44*(5), 1322–1327. https://doi.org/10.1016/j.jesp.2008.03.006.

Trip, S., Bora, C. H., Marian, M., Halmajan, A., & Drugas, M. I. (2019). Psychological mechanisms involved in radicalization and extremism. A rational emotive behavioral conceptualization. *Frontiers in Psychology, 10*, 437. https://doi.org/10.3389/fpsyg.2019.00437.

Turner, B. F., & Turner, C. B. (1992). Through a glass darkly: Gender stereotypes for men and women varying in age and race. In B. B. Hess & E. W. Markson (Eds.), *Growing old in America* (pp. 137–150). New Brunswick: Transaction Books.

Turner Lee, N. (2021, January 8). *The 'thugs' that stormed the Capitol just joined a long list of others.* Brookings. Retrieved from https://www.brookings.edu/blog/up-front/2021/01/08/the-thugs-that-stormed-the-capitol-just-joined-a-long-list-of-others/. February 15, 2021.

Walker, S. (1996). *The police in America: An introduction.* New York: McGraw-Hill.

Wamsley, L. (2021, January 15). *What we know so far: A timeline of security response at the capitol on Jan. 6.* NPR. Retrieved from https://www.npr.org/2021/01/15/956842958/what-we-know-so-far-a-timeline-of-security-at-the-capitol-on-january-6. February 15, 2021.

Wasik, B. H., Senn, K., Welch, R. H., & Cooper, B. R. (1969). Behavior modification with culturally deprived school children: Two case studies. *Journal of Applied Behavior Analysis, 2*(3), 181–194. https://doi.org/10.1901/jaba.1969.2-181.

Weitzer, R., & Tuch, S. (2004). *Rethinking minority attitudes toward the Police.* National Criminal Justice Reference Service. Retrieved from: http://www.ncjrs.gov/App/publications/abstract.aspx?ID=207145.

Willis, H., Xiao, M., Triebert, C., Koettl, C., Cooper, S., Botti, D., Ismay, J., & Tiefenthäler, A. (2020, August 27). *The New York Times.* Retrieved from https://www.nytimes.com/2020/08/27/us/kyle-rittenhouse-kenosha-shooting-video.html. February 15, 2021.

Wilson, J. (2017, August 12). *Charlottesville: Far-right crowd with torches encircles counter-protest group.* The Guardian. Retrieved from https://www.theguardian.com/world/2017/aug/12/charlottesville-far-right-crowd-with-torches-encircles-counter-protest-group. February 15, 2021.

Wolraich, M. L. (1979, September). Behavior modification therapy in hyperactive children. Research and clinical implications. *Clinical Pediatrics (Philadelphia), 18*(9), 563, 565–566, 568–570. https://doi.org/10.1177/000992287901800909. PMID: 466921

Wu, Y., Sun, I., & Triplett, R. (2009). Race, class or neighborhood context: Which matters more in measuring satisfaction with police? *Justice Quarterly, 26*, 125–156.

Zhao, J. S., Schneider, M., & Thurman, Q. (2002). The effect of police presence on public fear reduction and satisfaction: A review of the literature. *The Justice Professional, 15*(3), 273–299. https://doi.org/10.1080/0888431021000049471.

Chapter 7
Fear, Trauma, and Racism

There is a relationship between fear and trauma and fear and racism. This chapter will fully vet this relationship and discuss the trauma of racism. Let's begin with Fig. 7.1 that offers a visual storyboard that concisely tells the story about fear and trauma.

The story in short:

1. Fear is a shared human emotion – every human has been afraid.
2. Fear is a full brain and body response, and it stems from our human proclivity toward survival (to seek and require safety).
3. Fear involves multiple aspects of the brain to include the amygdala (where fear is processed, interpreted); hippocampus (fear memory is stored); frontal and temporal lobes (fear awareness); and hypothalamus (stress-related response of fear, increase in cortisol and other neurohormones that get the brain and body geared toward survival and seeking safety).
4. Fear is designed to be time- and threat-limited response (until it is not).
5. Fear that doesn't quite turn off – one way to think of the neurobiological under-pinnings of trauma. Imagine always feeling afraid, seeking safety.
6. Van der Kolk says #5 with more words: "Traumatization occurs when both internal and external resources are inadequate to cope with external threat" (van der Kolk & Ducey, 1989).

Racism as a powerful social construct has been demonstrated to have toxic impact on persons subject to it. There are multiple fears operating in the case of racism – there is the fear (constructed, perceived, and very real to them) of the perpetrator of racist views/ideologies/practice (fear of losing status, identity, position) and the fear (toxic stress, physical, psychological, and economic harm) of those subject to racism. In a study by Harrell (2000) on racism-related stress, racism was defined as "a system of dominance, power and privilege based on racial group designations….where members of the dominant group create or accept their societal privilege by maintaining structures, ideology, values, and behavior that

A. Moreland-Capuia, *The Trauma of Racism*,
https://doi.org/10.1007/978-3-030-73436-7_7

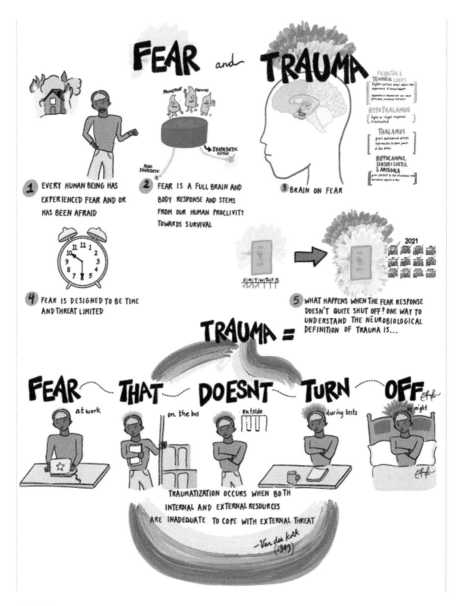

Fig. 7.1 Fear and trauma

have the intent or effect of leaving non-dominant group members relatively excluded from power, esteem, status and or equal access to societal resources" (Harrell, 2000). This definition demonstrates how pervasive, systemic, structural, and devastating racism is: an existence where basic needs are intentionally unmet – living in survivalist state.

As discussed in prior chapters, human existence centers around human need to be safe and feel safe. When safety is breached and/or compromised, fear is predominant. Imagine not feeling safe, daily. Imagine the stress that it has physically and psychologically. Racism experienced daily on a wide structural scale represents a persistent breach of safety, and individuals subject to racism daily live in fear, and living in fear daily (also known as trauma) has deleterious impact. Racism is a form of trauma (Polanco-Roman, Danies, & Anglin, 2016). If difficult to imagine, then let's consider the studies that link toxic stress to poor health and life outcomes.

7.1   Racism – Structural Impact (Employment, Economic, and Housing)

Where you live, what you eat, where you work, and what health insurance you have are all impacted by racism. Prior chapters addressed education, and subsequent chapters will address healthcare disparities specifically. This section will speak specifically to employment, housing, and economic disparities and their relationship to structural racism and discrimination. When the word structural is used to describe racism, it can sometimes be hard to fathom until it is matched with systems, data, and outcomes. Research point to the role that discrimination based on race can have on employment and opportunities for economic upward mobility. In the case of hiring discrimination, one study analyzed random-effects meta-analysis of callback data broken down by race/ethnicity over a 25-year window from 1989 to 2015 and found that Whites received 36% more callbacks than African-Americans and 24% more callbacks than Latinos (Quillian, Pager, Hexel, & Midtbøen, 2017). More disturbingly, the study found that discrimination in hiring and callbacks for African-Americans remained steady over the 25-year window (Quillian et al., 2017). Multiple studies highlight hiring discrimination and its deleterious impact on racial minorities and their ability to be economically upwardly mobile (Cancio, Evans, & Maume, 1996; Firebaugh & Davis, 1988; McConahay, 1983; Newman, 1978; Quillian et al., 2017).

Fekedulegn et al. (2019) produced national prevalence estimates of workplace discrimination from a community cohort of Black and White men and women 48 years of age or older – this cohort represented over 40 million US workers. Over a 2-year period, data was attained via computer-assisted telephone interviews; the interview consisted of yes and/or no responses to five questions that validly assess for discrimination. The analysis revealed that the prevalence of workplace discrimination is higher in Black women (up to 25%) and lower in White men (up to 11%); in terms of discrimination, Blacks reported 60% greater prevalence compared to Whites and women > men. There was correlation between mistreatment and discrimination (Fekedulegn et al., 2019).

7.2   Disparities in Wages

Not only is the work environment more challenging because of maltreatment and discrimination, but several studies demonstrate that there are significant racial and gender wage disparities, on average racial minorities earning less than their White counterparts and men earning more than women (Bollinger, 2003; Burtless, 1999; Card & Krueger, 1992; Kerwin & Jonathan, 2008; McCall, 2001; Western & Pettit, 2005). Wage disparities contribute to the phenomenon of being underemployed and compelling some to have to work multiple jobs to make ends meet. This level of stringing resources together places physical and psychological strain and stress on families and has even further downstream impacts (i.e., food options, living conditions, education for children, risks for abuse).

7.3   Housing Disparities

It is important to consider the fact that the Fair Housing Act became federal law in 1968 – (less than 52 years ago) its construction and passing was in response to intentional discrimination in the housing market. The Fair Housing Act bars discrimination based on race, religion, skin color, or gender in home buying, sales, rentals, and public or private financing to buy a home. While an important piece of federal legislation, it has not always been applied consistently as studies as early as 1968 and current as the early twenty-first century still demonstrate discrimination in housing practices and policies (Brown, 1995; Evans, Blount-Hill, & Cubellis, 2019; Galster, 1992; Galster & Carr, 1991; Heckman & Siegelman, 1993). One 2009 study highlighted the pervasive and profound impact of housing discrimination for African-American women and showed the role of various institutions/systems and people that potentiate the discrimination from insurers, real estate brokers, and financial institutions (Roscigno, Karafin, & Tester, 2009). For Blacks and Hispanics, discrimination in housing is still a common experience, and the relative cost of discrimination is profound as evidenced by inability to amass home equity and other forms of wealth (Yinger, 1998). A 2005 study found that while there was a notable decline in housing discrimination, disparities in discriminatory treatment in rental and owner-occupied housing markets persevere (Ross & Turner, 2005).

7.4   Adverse Childhood Experiences (ACEs)

Felitti and Anda's 1998 seminal ACEs study revealed that early and protracted exposure to trauma can increase the risk of chronic physical and behavioral health conditions by mechanism of what is understood as toxic stress (Centers for Disease Control and Prevention, 2021; Felitti et al., 1998). The demographics of the 1998 study matters because they were predominantly White, middle-class, educated, and insured individuals who indicated that they had at least one adverse childhood experience in their lifetime ranging from physical and sexual abuse to divorce to having a family member with a mental health challenge to a member of the family experiencing incarceration. The original group had several protective factors including access to insurance, a living wage, and education yet was still impacted by an adverse childhood experience (Centers for Disease Control and Prevention, 2021; Felitti et al., 1998). When the ACE lens is applied to chronically marginalized racial minorities, it is important to consider that they are more likely to be (based on structural and systemic discrimination and racism) underemployed, underhoused, underinsured, food insecure, to be entangled with or at risk of becoming entangled with the criminal justice system, and be subject to chronic discrimination and racism (which was not a component considered in the original ACE study). The chronic, toxic stress of discrimination and racism is physiologic and physical stress that can lead to increased inflammation in the body, lowered immunity, altered gene expression, and compromised brain development with implications for behavior and mood (Boullier & Blair, 2018; Guyon-Harris, Humphreys, & Zeanah, 2020; Sachs-Ericsson, Sheffler, Stanley, Piazza, & Preacher, 2017).

One study investigated the role of ACEs in premature death in adulthood. Over a 2-year (1995–1997) period, 17, 337 adults age 18 years or older were surveyed around health status and behavior and exposure to ACEs. During follow-up appointments in 2006, deaths were identified via mortality records from the National Death Index. Expected years of life lost and years of potential life lost were measured, and relative risk of death between ages 65 and 75 was estimated and matched with ACEs. Results revealed that in follow-up over 1539 people died; persons with an ACE score of six or more died nearly 20 years earlier compared to persons without ACEs; in the context of multivariable adjustment, persons with six ACEs or more were 2.4 times more likely to die before age 65 and 1.7 times more likely to die before 75 (Brown et al., 2009). ACEs accelerate death.

A 2011 study by Burke et al. studied ACEs prevalence and socio-behavioral and physical implications in a low-income, urban community via retrospective chart review of over 700 persons who received care from the Bayview Child Health Center in San Francisco. Over two thirds of persons had an ACE of 1 or more, and 12% had an ACE of 4 or more. The higher ACE scores were linked to increased risks for learning and behavior challenges and high instances of obesity (body mass index greater than 85% categorized as overweight and/or beyond overweight). Burke and colleagues concluded that ACE screens should be commonplace in urban areas and be used as a means of primary prevention and intervention (Burke, Hellman, Scott, Weems, & Carrion, 2011).

7.5 Philadelphia ACEs and Racism

The demographics of the 1998 ACE study were important to highlight because it demonstrates that trauma is ubiquitous and to point out that the original ACEs dealt with the trauma that happens within the context of a family system and centered around nearly 17,000 White, middle-class, educated, insured constituents. Upon seeing the results of the original ACE study, many were curious about the things that happen external to a family system that contribute to trauma. Around 2013, the Philadelphia ACE study was done including over 1700 participants who were assessed for adverse environmental experiences and exposures like racism, community violence, involvement in the foster care system, and other forms of trauma that might happen in institutions and systems external to the family system and home (The Philadelphia ACE Project, 2013). What is now referred to as the Philadelphia ACE, which enhanced the original ACE survey, found that over 80% of individuals surveyed had at least one ACE – when compared to the original ACE study, this is nearly 14% higher (The Philadelphia ACE Project, 2013). In a subsequent study by Cronholm, Forke, Wade, et al. (2015), further analysis was conducted in over 1700 participants of the Philadelphia ACE study as participants from Southeast Pennsylvania age 18 or older were petitioned to complete another survey by phone that measured ACEs (Cronholm et al., 2015). This additional survey was done over a 1-year period between 2012 and 2013. The study employed regression analysis to compare conventional ACE prevalence to Expanded ACE prevalence and revealed the following: close to 73% of the over 1700 participants had at least one Conventional ACE, 64% had at least one Expanded ACE, and 49% endorsed both Convention and Expanded (Cronholm et al., 2015). Cronholm et al. (2015) point out that the Expanded ACEs are prominent and would have gone largely unconsidered if it were not for intentional assessment as mandated by the Philadelphia ACE study (Cronholm et al., 2015).

Another study had 133 perinatal women (approximately 90 of the participants were White married/non-single women, and 43 were non-White) with a history of mental illness complete the ACE survey + the expanded six-question Philadelphia ACE study which includes antagonistic environmental experiences (Kim, Kuendig, Prasad, et al., 2020). They investigated the intersection between racial groups, ACE scores, mental health, and psychosocial components. On average, participants had an ACE of four or more, according to original ACEs. In the context of the expanded environmental ACEs, Black women reported higher rates of adverse environmental experiences to include racism and violence compared to White women (Kim et al., 2020). The study makes the connection between early and profound exposure to trauma postpartum and pregnant women with severe forms of mental illness and a more robust connection between trauma and severe mental illness when racism is accounted for (Kim et al., 2020). It is important to note that the adverse environmental component is in addition to the standard conventional ACEs – Black women were more likely to experience conventional ACEs + environmental adversities compounding the trauma (Kim et al., 2020). Other studies point to the racial disparities in birth outcomes (Dominguez, Dunkel-Schetter, Glynn, Hobel, & Sandman, 2008; Kelly, Becares, & Nazroo, 2013).

7.6 Culturally Informed Adverse Childhood Experiences – C-ACEs

Bernard and colleagues build on Philadelphia's Expanded ACE model and frame ACEs as a major public health concern and highlight the profound compounding effect of racism on ACEs and further point out the racial disparities in trauma exposure (Bernard, Calhoun, Banks, et al., 2020). The article contends that Black youth are disproportionately harmed and burdened by the combination of racism and ACEs – there is a double whammy as Black youth are more likely to experience trauma in the form of limited education, exposed to poverty, and be food and housing insecure which is compounded by the stress and lack of safety that racism establishes. In Black youth, trauma is structural and multifaceted and can be intergenerational (Bernard et al., 2020). This double whammy has toxic effect on the psyche of Black youth, and as such Bernard and colleagues have called on healers to extend the ACE lens to include the "c" standing for culturally informed, appreciating the role that racism plays in exacerbating and extenuating trauma in Black youth (Bernard et al., 2020).

7.7 Racism and Trauma

Williams, Metzger, Leins, and DeLapp (2018) evaluated racial trauma in the context of the *Diagnostic and Statistical Manual of Mental Disorders* fifth Edition (DSM-5) framework, calling attention to racism as form of trauma that may fit into the post-traumatic stress disorder (PTSD) category. The article contends that the psychological sequelae of racial trauma from conditions like work-related discrimination, police brutality, healthcare disparities, and economic disparities may warrant a diagnosis of PTSD in the presence of an identifiable form of trauma that contributes to re-experiencing, avoidance of trauma cues; negative mood/cognitions; and hyperarousal which represent Criterion A, B, C, D, and E respectively (Williams et al., 2018). The article asserts that racism (in the form of racial discrimination in various systems) is form of persistent trauma and in many ways represents "acute-on-chronic" trauma (Williams et al., 2018). While the connection between racism and PTSD may be controversial to some, it is worthwhile to consider a large portion of the population who are feeling unsafe daily and subject to systems that limit capacity for economic and social upward mobility contributing to economic uncertainty and insecurity which has further negative downstream cascading effects, which contributes to toxic stress (Williams, Lawrence, & Davis, 2019). This speaks to the structural and pervasive nature of racism as defined by Harrell (2000) earlier in this chapter.

Braveman, Cubbin, Egerter, Williams, and Pamuk (2010) demonstrate that even when you control for education and income, African-Americans have a lower life expectancy than Whites and Latinos. Digging deeper into the data, it is revealed that Blacks with a college degree or more education have a lower life expectancy than Whites and Latinos with a high school education (Braveman et al., 2010). Study after study confirms that ACEs are harmful to overall health and increase the risk for chronic physical and behavioral health conditions (Breslau, Davis, Andreski, & Peterson, 1991). Braveman et al.'s article presents an exceptionally harsh reality as the subtext is that even when Black citizens meet societal expectations, they are still subject to exceptional amounts of deleterious stress from having to manage environmental adversity that include racism and race-related discrimination (Hughes, Bellis, Hardcastle, et al., 2017; Williams & Williams-Morris, 2000). Most public health models that speak to improving overall community-population health speak to the critical nature of improving socioeconomic conditions as key (Bostic, Thornton, Rudd, & Sternthal, 2012; Braveman & Gottlieb, 2014; Institute of Medicine, 2002; Kivimäki et al., 2020). Improving socioeconomic conditions is critical, and managing and combatting racism must be parallel objectives to buoy the health of racial minorities, Black citizens in specific.

In Chap. 1 of this textbook, the ecosystem of fear in the predator-prey relationship was explored. By way of reminder, ecologists demonstrated that prey often demonstrated fear and displayed avoidance-type behaviors in the absence of a predator (a form of anticipatory fear and Pavlovian style associative learning at its finest). The term vicarious trauma was coined by Laurie Anne Pearlman, Karen W. Saakvitne, and I.L. McCann and is defined as trauma triggered by secondary and persistent exposure to the suffering of others. This secondary exposure can have PTSD impact on individuals who are in the helping profession (like educators, healthcare professionals, first responders) (Pearlman, 1990). Heard-Garris, Cale, Camaj, Hamati, and Dominguez (2018) highlight and amplify that the anticipatory fear and anxiety component observed in animal models can also be appreciated in humans – a Black child does not require direct exposure to racism in order to be negatively impacted by it (Heard-Garris et al., 2018). Indirect racism can contribute to vicarious traumatization. Racism has been shown to have negative toxic stress effects on Black, urban youth (Pachter, Lieberman, Bloom, et al., 2017).

A Black child does not even have to directly experience racism to be influenced (Heard-Garris et al., 2018) – vicarious racism (go back to prey and predator example, that prey behavior is changed by anticipatory and historical fear of predator). Literature by Carter (2007) suggest that a portion of racial and ethnic minorities may have been traumatically and psychologically impacted from racial discrimination resulting in a response that looks like PTSD (Carter, 2007). Subsequent studies on the perception of racial discrimination and PTSD support Carter's (2007) assertion (Flores, Tschann, Dimas, Pasch, & de Groat, 2010; Pascoe & Richman, 2009). Racism is a form of chronic stress and trauma; the literature has proven that chronic stress (in any form) is dangerous (Cohen, Kessler, & Gordon, 1995).

Helms, Nicolas, and Green (2012) consider racism and ethnoviolence as a reagent for PTSD and related symptoms and refers to racism and race-related discrimination as "life threatening" (Helms et al., 2012). Helms and colleagues refer to an acute (daily microaggressions and racial discriminatory) on top of chronic (historical trauma) trauma asserting that acute exposure is a trigger or historical trauma recall (Helms et al., 2012). The current literature is cited for ignoring the threat of racism in trauma assessments and interventions for African-Americans, Latina/Latino Americans, Asian/Pacific Islander Americans, Native Americans, and related immigrant groups when they show up with PTSD-like symptoms, arguing a systemic cultural responsivity gap (Alvarez, 2020; Bryant-Davis & Ocampo, 2005; Helms et al., 2012).

7.8 Making the Connection Between Trauma in Individuals, Organizations, and Society

Bryant-Davis and Ocampo (2005) contend that trauma can originate from individual and institutional racism (Bryant-Davis & Ocampo, 2005). In a 2006 article by Sandra Bloom entitled "Neither liberty nor safety," Bloom explains how pervasive and harmful the severe stress of trauma is individually, structurally, and societally. The article contends that stressed people contribute to stressed organizations that in turn contribute to stressed societies (Bloom, 2006). Statistics on community ACEs confirm Bloom's assertions; according to the Centers for Disease Control, approximately 61% of adults surveyed across 25 states reported that they had experienced at least one type of ACE, and nearly 1 in 6 reported they had experienced 4 or more types of ACEs. Trauma is widespread, far-reaching, and harmful. Bloom speaking to the universality of trauma should serve as a public health mandate to consider the role of trauma in individuals – tending to trauma in systems and society. Trauma can be prevented. Appreciating the data presented in this chapter on the effects of racism and racial discrimination on socioeconomic factors like employment and housing is an indicator of how structural and systemic it is. Racism is part organizational and societal trauma, and perhaps if it is viewed from this perspective, society would be more compelled to apply a public health approach to eradicate it (racism). Fear-based people contribute to fear-based organizations which contribute to a fear-based society. If society is to heal, then there must be focus on recognizing and managing fear in people and systems.

References

Alvarez, A. (2020). Seeing race in the research on youth trauma and education: A critical review. *Review of Educational Research, 90*(5), 583–626. https://doi.org/10.3102/0034654320938131.
Bernard, D. L., Calhoun, C. D., Banks, D. E., et al. (2020). Making the "C-ACE" for a culturally-informed adverse childhood experiences framework to understand the pervasive mental health impact of racism on black youth. *Journal of Child & Adolescent Trauma.* https://doi.org/10.1007/s40653-020-00319-9.

Bloom, S. L. (2006). Neither liberty nor safety: the impact of fear on individuals, institutions, and societies, part III. *Psychotherapy and Politics International, 3*(2), 96–111. https://doi.org/10.1002/ppi.23.

Bollinger, C. R. (2003). Measurement error in human capital and the black-white wage gap. *Review of Economics and Statistics, 85*(3), 578–585.

Bostic, R. W., Thornton, R. L., Rudd, E. C., & Sternthal, M. J. (2012). Health in all policies: The role of the U.S. Department of Housing and Urban Development and present and future challenges. *Health Affairs (Millwood), 31*, 2130–2137.

Boullier, M., & Blair, M. (2018). Adverse childhood experiences. *Paediatrics and Child Health, 28*(3), 132–137. ISSN 1751-7222. https://doi.org/10.1016/j.paed.2017.12.008.

Braveman, P., & Gottlieb, L. (2014). The social determinants of health: It's time to consider the causes of the causes. *Public Health Reports (Washington, DC: 1974), 129*(Suppl 2), 19–31. https://doi.org/10.1177/00333549141291S206.

Braveman, P. A., Cubbin, C., Egerter, S., Williams, D. R., & Pamuk, E. (2010). Socioeconomic disparities in health in the United States: What the patterns tell us. *American Journal of Public Health, 100*, S186–SS96.

Breslau, N., Davis, G. C., Andreski, P., & Peterson, E. (1991). Traumatic events and posttraumatic stress disorder in an urban population of young adults. *Archives of General Psychiatry, 48*, 216–222.

Brown, D. W., Anda, R. F., Tiemeier, H., Felitti, V. J., Edwards, V. J., Croft, J. B., & Giles, W. H. (2009). Adverse childhood experiences and the risk of premature mortality. *American Journal of Preventive Medicine., 37*(5), 389–396. ISSN 0749-3797. https://doi.org/10.1016/j.amepre.2009.06.021.

Brown, P. (1995). Race, class, and environmental health: A review and systematization of the literature. *Environmental Research, 69*, 15–30.

Bryant-Davis, T., & Ocampo, C. (2005). The trauma of racism: Implications for counseling, research, and education. *The Counseling Psychologist, 33*(4), 574–578. https://doi.org/10.1177/0011000005276581.

Burke, N. J., Hellman, J. L., Scott, B. G., Weems, C. F., & Carrion, V. G. (2011). The impact of adverse childhood experiences on an urban pediatric population. *Child Abuse & Neglect, 35*(6), 408–413. ISSN 0145-2134. https://doi.org/10.1016/j.chiabu.2011.02.006.

Burtless, G. (1999). Effects of growing wage disparities and changing family composition on the U.S. income distribution. *European Economic Review, 43*(4–6), 853–865., ISSN 0014-2921. https://doi.org/10.1016/S0014-2921(98)00099-3.

Cancio, A.-S., Evans, D., & Maume, D.-J. (1996). Reconsidering the declining significance of race: Racial differences in early career wages. *American Sociological Review, 61*, 541–556.

Card, D., & Krueger, A. (1992). School quality and black-white relative earnings: A direct assessment. *Quarterly Journal of Economics, 107*, 151–200.

Carter, R. T. (2007). Racism and psychological and emotional injury: Recognizing and assessing race-based traumatic stress. *The Counseling Psychologist, 35*(1), 13–105.

Centers for Disease Control and Prevention. (2021). *Preventing adverse childhood experiences.* Retrieved from https://www.cdc.gov/violenceprevention/aces/fastfact.html?CDC_AA_refVal=https%3A%2F%2Fwww.cdc.gov%2Fviolenceprevention%2Facestudy%2Ffastfact.html on January 28, 2021.

Cohen, S., Kessler, R. C., & Gordon, L. U. (1995). *Measuring stress: A guide for health and social scientists* (pp. 9–11). New York: Oxford University Press.

Cronholm, P. F., Forke, C. M., Wade, R., et al. (2015). Adverse childhood experiences: Expanding the concept of adversity. *American Journal of Preventive Medicine, 49*, 354–361. https://doi.org/10.1016/j.amepre.2015.02.001.

Dominguez, T. P., Dunkel-Schetter, C., Glynn, L. M., Hobel, C., & Sandman, C. A. (2008). Racial differences in birth outcomes: The role of general, pregnancy, and racism stress. *Health Psychology, 27*(2), 194–203. https://doi.org/10.1037/0278-6133.27.2.194.

Evans, D. N., Blount-Hill, K.-L., & Cubellis, M. A. (2019). Examining housing discrimination across race, gender and felony history. *Housing Studies, 34*(5), 761–778. https://doi.org/10.1080/02673037.2018.1478069.

Fekedulegn, D., Alterman, T., Charles, L. E., Kershaw, K. N., Safford, M. M., Howard, V. J., & MacDonald, L. A. (2019). Prevalence of workplace discrimination and mistreatment in a national sample of older U.S. workers: The REGARDS cohort study. *SSM – Population Health, 8*, 100444. https://doi.org/10.1016/j.ssmph.2019.100444.

Felitti, V. J., Anda, R. F., Nordenberg, D., Williamson, D. F., Spitz, A. M., Edwards, V., Koss, M. P., & Marks, J. S. (1998, May). Relationship of childhood abuse and household dysfunction to many of the leading causes of death in adults. The Adverse Childhood Experiences (ACE) Study. *American Journal of Preventive Medicine, 14*(4), 245–258. https://doi.org/10.1016/s0749-3797(98)00017-8. PMID: 9635069.

Firebaugh, G., & Davis, K.-E. (1988). Trends in antiblack prejudice, 1972–1984: Region and cohort effects. *The American Journal of Sociology, 94*, 251–272.

Flores, E., Tschann, J. M., Dimas, J. M., Pasch, L. A., & de Groat, C. L. (2010). Perceived racial/ethnic discrimination, posttraumatic stress symptoms, and health risk behaviors among Mexican American adolescents. *Journal of Counseling Psychology, 57*(3), 264.

Galster, G., & Carr, J. (1991). Housing discrimination and urban poverty of African-Americans. *Journal of Housing Research, 2*(2), 87–123. Retrieved January 27, 2021, from http://www.jstor.org/stable/24825920.

Galster, G. C. (1992). Research on discrimination in housing and mortgage markets: Assessment and future directions. *Housing Policy Debate, 3*(2), 637–683. https://doi.org/10.1080/10511482.1992.9521105.

Guyon-Harris, K. L., Humphreys, K. L., & Zeanah, C. H. (2020). Adverse caregiving in early life: The trauma and deprivation distinction in young children. *Infant Mental Health Journal, 42*(1), 87–95. https://doi.org/10.1002/imhj.21892.

Harrell, S. P. (2000). A multidimensional conceptualization of racism-related stress: Implications for the well-being of people of color. *American Journal of Orthopsychiatry, 70*, 42–57.

Heard-Garris, N. J., Cale, M., Camaj, L., Hamati, M. C., & Dominguez, T. P. (2018). Transmitting trauma: A systematic review of vicarious racism and child health. *Social Science & Medicine, 199*, 230–240. ISSN 0277-9536. https://doi.org/10.1016/j.socscimed.2017.04.018.

Heckman, J. J., & Siegelman, P. (1993). The Urban Institute audit studies: Their methods and findings. In M. Fix & R. J. Struyk (Eds.), *Clear and convincing evidence: Measurement of discrimination in America* (pp. 187–258). Washington, DC: Urban Institute Press.

Helms, J. E., Nicolas, G., & Green, C. E. (2012). Racism and Ethnoviolence as trauma: Enhancing professional and research training. *Traumatology, 18*(1), 65–74. https://doi.org/10.1177/1534765610396728.

Hughes, K., Bellis, M. A., Hardcastle, K. A., et al. (2017). The effect of multiple adverse childhood experiences on health: A systematic review and meta-analysis. *The Lancet Public Health, 2*, e356–e366. https://doi.org/10.1016/S2468-2667(17)30118-4.

Institute of Medicine (US) Committee on Assuring the Health of the Public in the 21st Century. The Future of the Public's Health in the 21st Century. Washington (DC): National Academies Press (US); 2002. 2, Understanding Population Health and Its Determinants. Available from: https://www.ncbi.nlm.nih.gov/books/NBK221225/.

Kelly, Y., Becares, L., & Nazroo, J. (2013). Associations between maternal experiences of racism and early child health and development: Findings from the UK Millennium Cohort Study. *Journal of Epidemiology and Community Health, 67*(1), 35–41. https://doi.org/10.1136/jech-2011-200814.

Kerwin, C., & Jonathan, G. (2008). Prejudice and wages: An empirical assessment of Becker's The Economics of Discrimination. *Journal of Political Economy, 116*(5), 773–809.

Kim, H. G., Kuendig, J., Prasad, K., et al. (2020). Exposure to racism and other adverse childhood experiences among perinatal women with moderate to severe mental illness. *Community Mental Health Journal, 56*, 867–874. https://doi.org/10.1007/s10597-020-00550-6.

Kivimäki, M., Batty, G. D., Pentti, J., Shipley, M. J., Sipilä, P. N., Nyberg, S. T., Suominen, S. B., Oksanen, T., Stenholm, S., Virtanen, M., Marmot, M. G., Singh-Manoux, A., Brunner, E. J., Lindbohm, J. V., Ferrie, J. E., & Vahtera, J. (2020). Association between socioeconomic status and the development of mental and physical health conditions in adulthood: A multi-cohort study. *The Lancet Public Health, 5*(3), e140–e149, ISSN 2468-2667. https://doi.org/10.1016/S2468-2667(19)30248-8.

McCall, L. (2001). Sources of racial wage inequality in metropolitan labor markets: Racial, ethnic, and gender differences. *American Sociological Review, 66*(4), 520–541. Retrieved January 27, 2021, from http://www.jstor.org/stable/3088921.

McConahay, J.-B. (1983). Modern racism and modern discrimination the effects of race, racial attitudes, and context on simulated hiring decisions. *Personality and Social Psychology Bulletin, 9,* 551–558.

Newman, J.-M. (1978). Discrimination in recruitment: An empirical analysis. *Industrial & Labor Relations Review, 32,* 15–23.

Pachter, L., Lieberman, L., Bloom, S., et al. (2017). Developing a communitywide initiative to address childhood adversity and toxic stress: A case study of the Philadelphia ACE Task Force. *Academic Pediatrics, 17,* S130–S135.

Pascoe, E. A., & Richman, L. S. (2009). Perceived discrimination and health: A meta-analytic review. *Psychological Bulletin, 135,* 531–554.

Pearlman, I. L. M. L. A. (1990). Vicarious traumatization: A framework for understanding the psychological effects of working with victims. *Journal of Traumatic Stress, 3*(1), 131–149.

Polanco-Roman, L., Danies, A., & Anglin, D. M. (2016). Racial discrimination as race-based trauma, coping strategies, and dissociative symptoms among emerging adults. *Psychological Trauma: Theory, Research, Practice and Policy, 8*(5), 609–617. https://doi.org/10.1037/tra0000125.

Quillian, L., Pager, D., Hexel, O., & Midtbøen, A. H. (2017). Meta-analysis of field experiments shows no change in racial discrimination in hiring over time. *Proceedings of the National Academy of Sciences of the United States of America.* first published September 12, 2017. https://doi.org/10.1073/pnas.1706255114.

Roscigno, V. J., Karafin, D. L., & Tester, G. (2009, February 1). The complexities and processes of racial housing discrimination. *Social Problems, 56*(1), 49–69. https://doi.org/10.1525/sp.2009.56.1.49.

Ross, S. L., Turner, M. A. (2005, May 1) Housing discrimination in metropolitan America: Explaining changes between 1989 and 2000. *Social Problems, 52*(2), 152–180. https://doi.org/10.1525/sp.2005.52.2.152.

Sachs-Ericsson, N. J., Sheffler, J. L., Stanley, I. H., Piazza, J. R., & Preacher, K. J. (2017). When emotional pain becomes physical: Adverse childhood experiences, pain, and the role of mood and anxiety disorders. *Journal of Clinical Psychology, 73*(10), 1403–1428. https://doi.org/10.1002/jclp.22444.

The Philadelphia ACE Project. (2013). *Philadelphia ACE survey*. Retrieved from https://www.philadelphiaaces.org/philadelphia-ace-survey on January 28, 2021.

van der Kolk, B. A., & Ducey, C. P. (1989). The psychological processing of traumatic experience: Rorschach patterns in PTSD. *Journal of Traumatic Stress, 2,* 259–274. https://doi.org/10.1007/BF00976231.

Western, B., & Pettit, B. (2005). Black-white wage inequality, employment rates, and incarceration. *American Journal of Sociology, 111*(2), 553–578. https://doi.org/10.1086/432780.

Williams, D. R., Lawrence, J. A., & Davis, B. A. (2019). Racism and health: Evidence and needed research. *Annual Review of Public Health, 40,* 105–125. https://doi.org/10.1146/annurev-publhealth-040218-043750.

Williams, D. R., & Williams-Morris, R. (2000). Racism and mental health: The African American experience. *Ethnicity and Health, 5,* 243–268. https://doi.org/10.1080/713667453.

Williams, M. T., Metzger, I. W., Leins, C., & DeLapp, C. (2018). Assessing racial trauma within a DSM–5 framework: The UConn racial/ethnic stress & trauma survey. *Practice Innovations, 3*(4), 242–260. https://doi.org/10.1037/pri0000076.

Yinger, J. (1998). Housing discrimination is still worth worrying about. *Housing Policy Debate, 9*(4), 893–927. https://doi.org/10.1080/10511482.1998.9521322.

Chapter 8
Healthcare, Fear, Discrimination, and Racism

8.1 The Relationship Between Fear, Discrimination, Racism, and Its Health Impact

Chapter 7 ended by making the connection between fear-based individuals contributing to fear-based systems which lead to fear-based societies. This chapter will address the healthcare system and highlight how fear has operated (and continues to operate) on so many levels within the system. Healthcare should be a basic human right as it is a critical element in the persistence and sustenance of any society, but it has not been equally accessible and/or helpful to all humans, and this has profound deleterious implications for the society. Fear, racism (undergirded by fear), and discrimination (also undergirded by fear) have shown up in the healthcare system in myriad ways and contributed to unequal access to quality care and unequal outcomes when care is sought. There is also the historical context of minority communities, specifically African-Americans who have a basic mistrust of the healthcare system because of intentional harms done to them to include things like the Tuskegee Syphilis Study – this will be addressed in greater detail in Chap. 9 of this book, but important to note here. Sociologists and scholars have long theorized that fear may be at the basis of racism and discrimination. The primary critique, however, is that fear should not be used as an excuse for racism and discrimination – a point well taken. Equally, it is critical to recognize the role of fear in racism and discrimination as a means of working to dismantle it. There is the fear of the perpetrator of racism and discrimination (addressed in prior chapters) and the respondent and persistent and profound fear and stress of persons subject to racism and discrimination. Several studies show that individuals subject to discrimination and racism experience a fear-stress response that has detrimental impact on overall health and well-being. One study showed that simply anticipating prejudice and/or discrimination triggered a physiologic stress response as evidenced by cardiovascular and psychological stress (Sawyer, Major, Casad, Townsend, & Mendes, 2012).

A. Moreland-Capuia, *The Trauma of Racism*,
https://doi.org/10.1007/978-3-030-73436-7_8

Racism and discrimination have been shown to consistently contribute to significant stress responses in racial minorities subject to it (Contrada & Ashmore, 2001; Dressler, 1990; Harrell, Hall, & Taliaferro, 2003).

McEwen has studied harmful changes to the hypothalamic-pituitary-adrenal axis (HPA axis) stress response when a person is under chronic stress – it is explained by what the neuroscientist calls changes in allostatic load (McEwen, 1998; McEwen, 2000; McEwen, 2002; McEwen, 2004; McEwen & Stellar, 1993). Being under chronic stress can change the mechanisms the body and brain normally employ to process and/or respond to stressful things, and this change can be dangerous leaving the body vulnerable to disease. Persistent subjection to discrimination and racism is a form of stress and trauma that can keep people of color in chronic fight, freeze, and/or flight mode and disrupt the HPA axis.

There are also studies that show differences in how fear is experienced and processed at the level of the amygdala when viewing Black and White faces and/or images (Cunningham et al., 2004; Lieberman, Hariri, Jarcho, Eisenberger, & Bookheimer, 2005; Phelps, Cannistraci, & Cunningham, 2003). Various studies that employed the use of Black and White faces while simultaneously investigating the activity of the amygdala have shown that Black and White participants had significantly higher spikes in amygdala brain activity (Cunningham et al., 2004; Lieberman et al., 2005; Phelps et al., 2003). Lieberman et al. (2005) contend that the increased activation in the amygdala is representative of social negative constructs applied to African-Americans (Lieberman et al., 2005). Unfortunately, these powerful social constructs not only impact other's views of perceived dangerousness of African--American citizens, but it has also negatively impacted African-American's perception of their level of dangerousness as perceived by others, a kind of stereotype threat (fear of becoming the constructed negative stereotype by society) at play. Multiple studies regarding health disparities speak to the roles of behavior, biology, genetics, and environment as contributors to disparities; however, it is critical to highlight the profound and pervasive impact of the environment on genetics (epigenetics), biology, and behavior.

Serena Williams is a superstar tennis player. She is well known, has economic means, is educated, speaks fluent French, and is family oriented. According to societal standards, Serena has checked off all the boxes required to be deemed a good citizen. Unfortunately, her fame, education, and good citizen standing did not help when she had a near-death medical emergency. The media covered Serena's story of how she almost died after giving birth. Of note, Serena recounted having trouble breathing after giving birth to her daughter. She was concerned about her prior history of pulmonary emboli and expressed concern to her care team that there may be a link between her history of blood clots in her lungs and her active trouble breathing. She quickly advocated for additional evaluation/intervention, and the growing blood clots in her abdomen and lungs were discovered. Serena pointed out that she was grateful to be able to advocate for herself and to have the resources to get the proper care, noting that this treatment is not afforded to all women, namely, women of color. Many birth-giving women have experienced less-than-ideal care in healthcare settings, and the literature highlights greater disparities in communities of color. According to the Centers for Disease Control and Prevention 2007–2016 data on pregnancy-related complications, approximately 700 women die annually in the United States from pregnancy and/or pregnancy-related complications, and American Indian/Alaska Natives and Black women are two to three times more likely to die from a pregnancy-related etiology compared to White women (CDC, 2007–2016).

A study by Rosenthal and Lobel (2011) addressed the role of intersectionality in increased rates of toxic stress experienced by Black pregnant women – the convergence of several identities that brush up against oppression (Rosenthal & Lobel, 2011). The study demonstrates a link between intersectionality-related maternal stress as a risk factor for less-than-ideal birth outcomes for Black women (Rosenthal & Lobel, 2011). A study by Dominquez et al. (2008) included 51 African-American and 73 non-Hispanic White pregnancy women who were prospectively assessed in the areas of maternal health and sociodemographic elements and stressors to include general stress/pregnancy stress and the stress of perceived racism. In specific, the study aimed at understanding the correlation between birth weight and gestational age at delivery and the factors mentioned above. The study employed regression analysis which revealed that perceived racism and general stress were strongly correlated with birth weight. Further, models within each race group demonstrated that perceived racism was a robust predictor of birth weight in African-Americans, but not in non-Hispanic Whites (Dominguez, Dunkel-Schetter, Glynn, Hobel, & Sandman, 2008). Several studies have shown strong correlates between perceived racism and/or discrimination and poor pregnancy and health outcomes for persons of color (Collins Jr, Herman, & David, 1997; Krieger, Smith, Naishadham, Hartman, & Barbeau, 2005).

A systematic review on racial discrimination and adverse birth outcomes exposed a vigorous relationship between racial discrimination and low birth weight, preterm birth, and small for gestational age (Alhusen, Bower, Epstein, & Sharps, 2016). The review also highlighted the role of institutional racism in adverse birth outcomes to include but not limited to social determinants of health, increased stress of racism and inflammation in the body, access to care, and quality of care (Alhusen et al., 2016). Structural racism and income inequality have also been linked to adverse birth outcomes (Wallace et al., 2015). Saftlas, Koonin, and Atrash (2000) assert that reproductive healthcare professions consider the high and low risk of pregnancy-related deaths in Black women in the construction of their care with the primary objective of reducing risks all together (Saftlas et al., 2000).

A study by Hardeman, Karbeah, Almanza, and Kozhimannil (2020) shows that systemic inequities compromise quality of care and deleteriously impact the lives of Black/African-Americans. They contend that culturally specific care is one means of reducing inequities and improving overall care for Blacks/African-Americans. The study enrolled over 280 families over a 4-year window who received culturally specific care (care was provided by a Black and/or African-American professional) and demonstrated that culturally specific care combined with close follow-up resulted in the complete prevention of preterm births (Hardeman et al., 2020). Extensive research has shown inferior patient outcomes for people of color – these less-than-ideal outcomes are related to many factors to include but not limited to lesser patient-provider interactions combined with limited and substandard provider communication and education, perception of patients of color not feeling like an equal partner in decision-making regarding their health, and perception of discrimination in healthcare encounters (Attanasio & Hardeman, 2019). Attanasio and colleagues show that the perception of discrimination was a powerful predictor for women who were more likely to decline procedures during birth (Attanasio & Hardeman, 2019). Discrimination significantly changed the trajectory of patient-provider relationship and birthing outcomes in women of color (Attanasio & Hardeman, 2019).

8.2 Disparities in Pain Management Due to Perception of Discrimination

The history of the negative and ill-informed perception of Black pain – that Blacks do not feel as much pain as Whites and/or any other group dating back to as early as the transatlantic slave trade – persists in the twenty-first century. Several studies show racial disparities in pain management in the healthcare setting. One study examined the racial disparities in pain management in primary care patients with chronic opioid therapy for chronic nonmalignant pain by analyzing data from 201 African-Americas and 691 Whites (Ezenwa & Fleming, 2012). The analysis showed robust distinctions between African-Americans and Whites on pain management and quality-of-life measures as African-Americans had notably worse quality-of-life measures and pain management comparatively (Ezenwa & Fleming, 2012). Perceived discrimination and hopelessness negatively impacted pain management (Ezenwa & Fleming, 2012). Other studies have confirmed the phenomenon of perceived discrimination negatively impacting pain management (Chen et al., 2005; Cintron & Morrison, 2006).

Another study examined whether racial bias in pain management in healthcare settings is associated with false narratives about biological differences between Blacks and Whites that included things like Blacks have thicker skin and therefore are less likely to feel pain (Hoffman, Trawalter, Axt, & Oliver, 2016). The study found that approximately half of White medical students and residents acquiesced to the belief that Blacks experienced less pain because of their physical features and medical trainees frequently rated Black pain considerably lower compared to Whites. Equally, these socially constructed false convictions negatively impacted medical judgment and treatment recommendations for pain management in Black patients, highlighting racial disparities in the treatment and assessment of pain (Hoffman et al., 2016). Racial bias and its deleterious impact on pain management have been well studied (Haider et al., 2011; Trawalter & Hoffman, 2015; Washington, 2006).

A study by Mossey (2011) highlighted racial disparities in reporting of pain intensity as a key factor in the substandard pain management for racial and ethnic minorities compared to Whites in the context of controlling for age, gender, and pain intensity. The study also noted physician lack of awareness of their biases, cultural beliefs, and stereotypes as it relates to pain in racial and ethnic minorities as a critical factor in disparate pain management (Mossey, 2011). Several studies have pointed out the unfortunate burden and cascading impact that racial discrimination and racism have not just on the treatment of pain to include but not limited to cardiovascular strain, increased stress and inflammation, lowered immunity, and lower productivity (ability to make a living secondary to undertreated pain) (Anderson, Green, & Payne, 2009; Dobscha et al., 2009; Green et al., 2003; Institute of Medicine, 2003; Kposowa & Tsunokai, 2002).

A review by Anderson et al. (2009) emphasized various studies that found African-American with low back pain often reported higher levels of disability and overall pain compared their White counterparts but were more likely to be rated as having less severe pain by their clinician (Anderson et al., 2009). This same analysis emphasized that African-Americans received lesser supply of nonsteroidal anti--inflammatory medication when compared to their White counterparts (Anderson et al., 2009).

Discrimination and racism in healthcare treatment and management has also been appreciated in the care of children. Goyal and colleagues evaluated racial differences in opioid analgesia administration in children who had been diagnosed with appendicitis (Goyal, Kuppermann, Cleary, Teach, & Chamberlain, 2015). Goyal et al. showed that Black children were less likely to receive pain medication for moderate pain and less likely to receive opioids for severe pain with the concern for the perception of higher and/or different pain thresholds in Black children (Goyal et al., 2015). Similar racial disparities in pain management in children have been observed in the management of blunt head trauma and hospitalization rates for specific medical conditions (Chamberlain, Joseph, Patel, & Pollack, 2007; Natale, et al., 2012).

8.3 Cardiovascular Health Disparities

Health disparities have been appreciated in cardiovascular disease as minority patients have a higher rate of and risk factors for coronary artery disease, less likely to have early detection and treatment, and more likely to have worse outcome characterized by higher morbidity and mortality (Graham, 2015; Mayberry, Boone, & Kaiser, 2002). Research on racial disparities in cardiovascular disease reveals, specifically, that minority patients with acute coronary syndrome (ACS) are at significantly higher risks for heart attack, being re-hospitalized, and death (Graham, 2015; Mayberry et al., 2002). By the time minority patients access care (secondary to multiple structural barriers which include but not limited to fear of the system, lack of insurance, etc.), the disease is more advanced and could have been prevented if care had been sought earlier (Graham, 2015; Mayberry et al., 2002). Advanced cardiovascular disease in minority patients is linked to higher rates of high cholesterol, hypertension, diabetes, and stress from structural environmental factors like racism, underemployment, and limited and/or lack of insurance (Graham, 2015; Mayberry et al., 2002). Additionally, minority patients are less likely to be offered and get beneficial treatments like angiography (Graham, 2015; Mayberry et al., 2002). These studies point out the connection between structural disparities (lack of insurance, racism, discrimination) and the impact on individual, community, and societal health.

In a review of cardiovascular disease burden by Mensah and Brown (2007), highlighted is the trend that African-Americans are two to three times more likely to die from cardiovascular disease at any given age compared to Whites. A systematic review on cardiovascular disparities confirms the increased risk of death and poor outcomes for minority patients (Davis, Vinci, Okwuosa, Chase, & Huang, 2007).

The role of perceived racism and discrimination in cardiovascular risk factors, treatment, and management cannot be understated and/or underestimated and demonstrated by Wyatt et al. (2003) study on racism and cardiovascular disease in African-Americans revealing that a major influential factor in increased cardiovascular disease risk was Black patients' perception of race-related stress (Wyatt et al., 2003).

Brewer et al. (2013) addressed the relationship between race consciousness (an individual's predominant and persistent consideration of their race), discrimination, and high blood pressure. The study revealed a directly proportional relationship between Black patients' contemplation of their race and high blood pressure (Brewer et al., 2013). Black patients were more likely and frequently to think about their race (the role of stereotype threat, e.g.), and this correlated with higher diastolic blood pressure (Brewer et al., 2013). The study encourages practitioners to consider higher incidences of race consciousness and its impact on cardiovascular health in minority patients (Brewer et al., 2013).

8.4 Disparities in Cancer Detection, Treatment, and Management

One review noted that while racial disparities in cancer detection, treatment, and management have been observed among most cancer types, the most common included invasive breast cancer, non-small cell lung cancer (NSCLC), and colorectal cancer. Age-adjusted breast cancer death rates were higher for African-American women compared to White women (Esnaola & Ford, 2012; Siegel, Ward, Brawley, & Jemal, 2011). Survival rates for Black women (while improved) have not improved fast and/or robustly enough (Brawley, 2002; Chevarley & White, 1997; Chu, Tarone, & Brawley, 1999; Esnaola & Ford, 2012). When lung and bronchus survival rates are considered, Black males are 1.5 times more likely to die compared to White males (Esnaola & Ford, 2012; Siegel et al., 2011). Equally, when it comes to colorectal cancer survival rates, Black men and women are 1.5 times more likely to die compared to White men and women (Esnaola & Ford, 2012; Siegel et al., 2011).

Gross, Smith, Wolf, and Andersen (2008) explored whether the disparities had decreased in cancer treatment from the early 1990s to the twenty-first century (Gross et al., 2008). The investigatory retrospective review included Medicare data spanning 10 years (1992–2002) from patients aged 66–85 who had a primary diagnosis of the following cancers: breast, lung, prostate, and colorectal. Of note, subjects selected for this analysis had a relationship with a physician in advance of their diagnosis (Gross et al., 2008). Regression analysis was employed. The retrospective review revealed racial disparities in therapy and treatment of specific cancers like in the case of lung cancer where early surgical resection in early stage was 64% for Black patients versus 78.5% for White patients; breast radiation after the removal of a breast lump was 77.8% for Black women compared to 85.8% for White women; colon cancer stage 3 therapy was 52.1% for Black patients compared to 64.1% for White patients; early stage treatment for prostate cancer was 72.4% for Black patients compared to 77.4% for White patients (Gross et al., 2008). This retrospective analysis not only highlighted the persistence of and slow change in racial disparities in cancer treatments, but it also demonstrated that they existed even when patients had an established relationship with a physician before their cancer diagnosis (Gross et al., 2008).

In a literature review, Shavers and Brown (2002) pointed out that African-Americans have a 33% higher risk of dying of cancer compared to Whites and that distinctions in incidence and stage of disease may contribute heavily to the disparities in cancer-related mortality (Shavers & Brown, 2002). Racial disparities were observed in the receipt of the following cancer therapies: primary, conservative, and adjuvant. Shavers and Brown (2002) assert that environmental and structural factors influence adverse outcomes in the health of minority patients to include but not limited frequent recurrence of disease, shorter disease-free survival, and higher death rates (Shavers & Brown, 2002).

Data from the National Cancer Institute provides the following data, updated as recent as November 2020:

- Death rates for most cancer types are highest in Blacks/African-Americans when compared to all other racial/ethnic groups.
- Regarding breast cancer deaths, Black/African-American women are more likely to die compared to White women.
- Colorectal, lung, and cervical cancer incidence rates are highest in rural Appalachia compared to regional urban areas.
- Of note, death rates from prostate cancer have declined in the last 10 years; Black/African-American men are still twice as likely to die when diagnosed compared to White men.
- In the case of cervical cancer, Hispanic/Latino and Black/African-American women have the highest rates compared to any other ethnic group. Black/African-American women still have the highest death rate.

8.5   Racial Disparities in Mental Health Diagnosis and Treatment

Racial disparities in mental health treatment and diagnosis is among the most unfortunate as this book has discussed the trauma impact of structural racism and discrimination on physical health and the psyche. Access to therapy and counselors is a major tool in mitigating negative mental health risks, which would really help minority communities and patients dealing with environmental stressors like racism and discrimination. The literature regarding mental health treatment and outcomes is like the data for all the other health conditions – the disparities are wide and have weighty implications. In a study on racial disparities in diagnosis and in an outpatient behavioral clinic by Gara et al., 2018, it was demonstrated that important diagnosis and treatment opportunities are missed in minority patients. They evaluated outpatient data via electronic medical records of over 1600 patients with the objective of determining the likelihood of African-Americans formerly diagnosed with schizophrenia and/or schizoaffective disorder screening positive for major depression compared to their White counterparts (Gara et al., 2018). The analysis found that African-American patients who had been diagnosed with schizophrenia were more likely to screen positive for major depression (Gara et al., 2018). Schizophrenia is socially deemed more severe than depression. This is important because of historical concern for under- and misdiagnosis of mental health disorders in Black/African-American patients (Gara et al., 2018). The study highlights an important question – how many Black/African-American patients were diagnosed with schizophrenia when the primary diagnosis may have been depression. The diagnosis, management, and treatment for depression are different than schizophrenia and come with a slew of physical health and quality-of-life implications.

Another study included a sample of over 900 persons who had been hospitalized for severe mental illness and followed them for 1 year after hospital discharge (Eack, Newhill, & Watson 2012). The study sought to better understand potential external-environmental influences on racial disparities observed in the management and treatment of minority patients living with severe mental illness (like schizophrenia and schizoaffective disorder). The study revealed that African-American persons with severe mental illness, post-hospitalization, were less likely to improve in overall functioning (maintaining housing, job, health) and impairing symptoms of the severe mental illness were persistent, pervasive, and more disruptive when compared to their White counterparts (Eack, Newhill, & Watson 2012). These findings are notable as the study adjusted for gender, socioeconomic status, and psychiatric diagnosis (Eack, Newhill, & Watson 2012).

Disparities in mental health diagnosis, management, and treatment are noted in literature. Statistics show that racial/ethnic minorities are more likely to suffer from a severe and persistent mental illness but are less likely to be able to access mental health treatment (Cook et al., 2019).

Stigmatization around getting mental health treatment is profound in racial/ethnic minorities. A meta-analytic review by Eylem, de Wit, van Straten, et al. (2020)

included over 2700 abstracts and 29 studies representing over 190,000 participants upon which over 35,000 of the over 190,000 represented racial minorities. Analysis revealed that when you compare mental health stigma rates between ethnic/racial minorities to White patients, mental illness stigma is significantly higher in ethnic/racial minorities (Eylem et al., 2020).

The implications and impact of mental illness stigma also differ along racial lines (Corrigan & Watson, 2007; Fox, Taverna, Earnshaw, & Vogt, 2018). Some research has shown that the perception persons with mental illness being a danger and/or threat was greatest in non-White participants compared to White participants (Corrigan & Watson, 2007; Fox et al., 2018). Again, if prior chapters in this book have been read, then the significance of this data may be appreciated – racial/ethnic minorities have historically been socially constructed as dangerous threats and will likely do all they can to avoid any additional perceptions of threat and danger, in this case, mental illness. This is cannot be understated and is a critical data point.

8.6   Structural Components to Health Disparities

Structural components to health disparities have been addressed in prior chapters of this book to include but not limited to lack of equal access to stable housing, adequate nutrition, employment, education, higher rates of poverty, and economic opportunity. It is important to reiterate this because these structural components also influence things like access to insurance. Many studies have shown that underinsurance and no insurance are high in racial and ethnic groups in the United States and contribute greatly to healthcare disparities (Kirby & Kaneda, 2010; Sohn, 2017). At all ages, African-American and people of Hispanic origin have lower insurance coverage rates when compared to non-Hispanic Whites (Sohn, 2017), and African-American and Latinos are more likely to be uninsured throughout adulthood compared to non-Hispanic persons (Kirby & Kaneda, 2010).

Economic downturns as witnessed in 2008 and 2019 to early 2021 with the COVID-19 pandemic, health insurance coverage decreases as job loss increases. Health and healthcare coverage are economic drivers. Racial/ethnic minorities, in the absence of an economic downturn, are more likely to be under- and uninsured, but this disparity is pronounced in the presence of economic hardship. Racial minorities are more likely to be living in poverty, more likely to qualify for Medicaid coverage, underemployed with no and/or limited health insurance benefits, and at greater risks of bankruptcy from medical bills if they had to access care. The Affordable Care Act (ACA) passed in 2010 was designed to improve healthcare coverage and access, improve affordability of healthcare, and improve healthcare outcomes (Blumenthal, Abrams, & Nuzum, 2015; Manchikanti, Helm Ii, Benyamin, & Hirsch, 2017; Reisman, 2015). Several states expanded Medicaid services and benefits under the ACA, while some states did not – this contributed to geographic disparities in coverage (Blumenthal et al., 2015; Manchikanti et al., 2017; Reisman, 2015). For states that did expand Medicaid benefits, some studies showed that the

ACA helped to increase healthcare coverage for millions of Americans with approximately three million African-Americans gaining coverage (Health Insurance Coverage in the United States, 2018, US Census Bureau), but coverage was still spotty and did not translate into improved affordability and/or improved healthcare outcomes (yet) (Blumenthal et al., 2015; Manchikanti et al., 2017; Reisman, 2015).

When persons with disabilities were surveyed, disparities in healthcare coverage and access were observed. One study pointed out that health insurance helped to reduce disparities in emergency room use in persons with disabilities but uninsured persons with lower SES and disabilities continued to experience (at high rates) delays in care, inability to obtain care, and overall access to care (Miller, Kirk, Kaiser, & Glos, 2014). There are studies that show that having health insurance has moderately assisted in reducing racial health disparities (Buchmueller, Levinson, Levy, & Wolfe, 2016; Chen, Vargas-Bustamante, Mortense, & Ortega, 2016; Lillie--Blanton & Hoffman, 2005; Sommers, Buchmueller, Decker, Carey, & Kronick, 2013).

8.7 Attitudes of Healthcare Providers and Clinicians

An important consideration in healthcare disparities is the attitudes of healthcare providers and clinicians as studies have shown that the presence of racial bias negatively impacts healthcare treatment, management, and outcomes for racial and ethnic minorities. A study by Sabin, Rivara, and Greenwald (2008) explored the relationship between implicit racial bias among pediatricians and its impact on quality of care (Sabin et al., 2008). A group of academic pediatricians who provide care in an urban setting completed a web-based Implicit Association Test (IAT) survey that measured implicit racial attitudes and stereotypes, case studies were employed to ascertain quality of care, and explicit attitudes were measured by self--report (Sabin et al., 2008). The study revealed what they called an implicit preference for European American compared to African-Americans; an implicit association that European Americans were more compliant as patients relative to African-Americans; medical care differences by patient race was only revealed in one of the four cases presented to the group of pediatricians; and there was no significant relationship found between implicit and explicit measures (Sabin et al., 2008).

A review by FitzGerald and Hurst (2017) included over 42 articles examining the role of conscious bias and its impact in patient care and revealed that healthcare professionals exhibit the same levels of implicit bias as the wider population (FitzGerald & Hurst, 2017). A review by Hall et al. (2015) concluded that most healthcare providers appeared to have implicit bias that included negative attitudes toward people of color and positive attitudes toward Whites (Hall et al., 2015).

A study by Chapman, Kaatz, & Carnes, 2013, in examining implicit bias among physicians concluded that health disparities would decline significantly if implicit bias in healthcare providers were acknowledged and changed. Further, Chapman and colleagues make the argument that one way to also decrease disparity is by making culturally specific care more robust through increasing the number of African-American/Black physicians (Chapman et al., 2013).

This chapter began by addressing how individuals influence systems and systems impact societies. The healthcare system is not immune to the influences of fear-based narratives and social constructs, discrimination, and stereotype threat. What is worthy of amplification is the point that these narratives, constructs, stereotypes, and discrimination can and do impact behavior and actions which have downstream cascading impacts of poor health management, treatment, and outcomes for racial/ ethnic minorities. Perhaps by considering the history and neuroscience of fear and trauma, systemic trauma perpetuated on racial/ethnic minorities subject to constructs, narrative, discrimination, and stereotypes combined with a reminder that healers have a responsibility to reduce and eliminate needless suffering will motivate a re-evaluation of individual behavior and the system overall.

References

Alhusen, J. L., Bower, K. M., Epstein, E., & Sharps, P. (2016). Racial discrimination and adverse birth outcomes: An integrative review. *Journal of Midwifery & Women's Health, 61*(6), 707–720. https://doi.org/10.1111/jmwh.12490.

Anderson, K. O., Green, C. R., & Payne, R. (2009). Racial and ethnic disparities in pain: Causes and consequences of unequal care. *The Journal of Pain, 10*(12), 1187–1204.

Attanasio, L. B., & Hardeman, R. R. (2019). Declined care and discrimination during the childbirth hospitalization. *Social Science & Medicine, 232*, 270–277., ISSN 0277-9536. https://doi.org/10.1016/j.socscimed.2019.05.008.

Blumenthal, D., Abrams, M., & Nuzum, R. (2015). The affordable care act at 5 years. *The New England Journal of Medicine, 372*(25), 2451–2458.

Brawley, O. W. (2002). Disaggregating the effects of race and poverty on breast cancer outcomes. *Journal of the National Cancer Institute, 94*(7), 471–473.

Brewer, L. P. C., Carson, K. A., Williams, D. R., Allen, A., Jones, C. P., & Cooper, L. A. (2013). Association of Race Consciousness with the patient–physician relationship, medication adherence, and blood pressure in urban primary care patients. *American Journal of Hypertension, 26*(11), 1346–1352. https://doi.org/10.1093/ajh/hpt116.

Buchmueller, T. C., Levinson, Z. M., Levy, H. G., & Wolfe, B. L. (2016). Effect of the affordable care act on racial and ethnic disparities in health insurance coverage. *American Journal of Public Health, 106*(8), 1416–1421. https://doi.org/10.2105/AJPH.2016.303155.

Centers for Disease Control and Prevention. *Infographic: Racial/Ethnic Disparities in Pregnancy-Related Deaths — United States, 2007–2016*. Retrieved from https://www.cdc.gov/reproductivehealth/maternal-mortality/disparities-pregnancy-related-deaths/infographic.html on January 28, 2021.

Chamberlain, J. M., Joseph, J. G., Patel, K. M., & Pollack, M. M. (2007). Differences in severity-adjusted pediatric hospitalization rates are associated with race/ethnicity. *Pediatrics, 119*(6), e1319–e1324.

Chapman, E. N., Kaatz, A., & Carnes, M. (2013). Physicians and implicit bias: How doctors may unwittingly perpetuate health care disparities. *Journal of General Internal Medicine, 28*(11), 1504–1510. https://doi.org/10.1007/s11606-013-2441-1.

Chen, I., Kurz, J., Pasanen, M., Faselis, C., Panda, M., Staton, L. J., & Cykert, S. (2005). Racial differences in opioid use for chronic nonmalignant pain. *Journal of General Internal Medicine, 20*(7), 593–598.

Chen, J., Vargas-Bustamante, A., Mortense, K., & Ortega, A. N. (2016). Racial and ethnic disparities in health care access and utilization under the affordable care act. *Medical Care, 54*(2),
140–146. https://doi.org/10.1097/MLR.0000000000000467.

Chevarley, F., & White, E. (1997). Recent trends in breast cancer mortality among white and black
US women. *American Journal of Public Health, 87*(5), 775–781.

Chu, K. C., Tarone, R. E., & Brawley, O. W. (1999). Breast cancer trends of black women compared with white women. *Archives of Family Medicine, 8*(6), 521–528.

Cintron, A., & Morrison, R. S. (2006). Pain and ethnicity in the United States: A systematic review.
Journal of Palliative Medicine, 9(6), 1454–1473.

Collins, J. W., Jr., Herman, A. A., & David, R. J. (1997). Very low birthweight infants and income
incongruity among African American and White parents in Chicago. *American Journal of
Public Health, 87*, 414–417.

Contrada, R. J., & Ashmore, R. D. (2001). Gary MLet al. Measures of ethnicity-related stress:
Psychometric properties, ethnic group differences, and associations with well-being. *Journal
of Applied Social Psychology, 31*(9), 1775–1820.

Cook, B. L., Hou, S. S.-Y., Lee-Tauler, S. Y., Progovac, A. M., Samson, F., & Sanchez, M. J. (2019).
A review of mental health and mental health care disparities research: 2011-2014. *Medical
Care Research and Review, 76*(6), 683–710. https://doi.org/10.1177/1077558718780592.

Corrigan, P. W., & Watson, A. C. (2007). The stigma of psychiatric disorders and the gender, ethnicity, and education of the perceiver. *Community Mental Health Journal, 43*, 439–458.

Cunningham, W. A., Johnson, M. K., Rave, C. L., Gatenby, J., Gore, J. C., & Banaji, M. R. (2004).
Separable neural components in the processing of black and white faces. *Psychological
Science, 12*, 806–813.

Davis, A. M., Vinci, L. M., Okwuosa, T. M., Chase, A. R., & Huang, E. S. (2007). Cardiovascular
health disparities: A systematic review of health care interventions. *Medical Care Research
and Review: MCRR, 64*(5 Suppl), 29S–100S. https://doi.org/10.1177/1077558707305416.

Dobscha, S. K., Soleck, G. D., Dickinson, K. C., Burgess, D. J., Lasarev, M. R., Lee, E. S., &
McFarland, B. H. (2009). Associations between race and ethnicity and treatment for chronic pain
in the VA. *The Journal of Pain, 10*, 1078–1087. https://doi.org/10.1016/j.jpain.2009.04.018.

Dominguez, T. P., Dunkel-Schetter, C., Glynn, L. M., Hobel, C., & Sandman, C. A. (2008).
Racial differences in birth outcomes: The role of general, pregnancy, and racism stress. *Health
Psychology: Official Journal of the Division of Health Psychology, American Psychological
Association, 27*(2), 194–203. https://doi.org/10.1037/0278-6133.27.2.194.

Dressler, W. W. (1990). Lifestyle, stress, and blood pressure in a southern black community.
Psychosomatic Medicine, 52(2), 182–198.

Eack, S. M., & Newhill, C. E. (2012). Racial disparities in mental health outcomes after psychiatric hospital discharge among individuals with severe mental illness. *Social Work Research,
36*(1), 41–52. https://doi.org/10.1093/swr/svs014.

Eack, S., Newhill, C., & Watson, A. (2012). Effects Of Severe Mental Illness Education on MSW
Student Attitudes about Schizophrenia. *Journal of Social Work Education, 48*(3), 425–438.
Retrieved May 13, 2021, from http://www.jstor.org/stable/41705876.

Esnaola, N. F., & Ford, M. E. (2012). Racial differences and disparities in cancer care and outcomes: where's the rub? *Surgical Oncology Clinics of North America, 21*(3), 417–viii. https://
doi.org/10.1016/j.soc.2012.03.012.

Eylem, O., de Wit, L., van Straten, A., et al. (2020). Stigma for common mental disorders in racial
minorities and majorities a systematic review and meta-analysis. *BMC Public Health, 20*, 879.
https://doi.org/10.1186/s12889-020-08964-3.

Ezenwa, M. O., & Fleming, M. F. (2012). Racial disparities in pain Management in Primary Care.
Journal of Health Disparities Research and Practice, 5(3), 12–26.

FitzGerald, C., & Hurst, S. (2017). Implicit bias in healthcare professionals: A systematic review.
BMC Medical Ethics, 18(1), 19. https://doi.org/10.1186/s12910-017-0179-8.

Fox, A. B., Taverna, A. C., Earnshaw, V. A., & Vogt, D. (2018). Conceptualizing and measuring mental illness stigma: The mental illness stigma framework and critical review of measures. *Stigma Health, 3*, 348–376.

Gara et al., (2018). *A naturalistic study of racial disparities in diagnoses at an outpatient behavioral health clinic.* Psychiatric Services, 10 Dec 2018. https://doi.org/10.1176/appi.ps.201800223.

Goyal, M. K., Kuppermann, N., Cleary, S. D., Teach, S. J., & Chamberlain, J. M. (2015). Racial disparities in pain Management of Children with Appendicitis in emergency departments. *JAMA Pediatrics, 169*(11), 996–1002. https://doi.org/10.1001/jamapediatrics.2015.1915.

Graham, G. (2015). Disparities in cardiovascular disease risk in the United States. *Current Cardiology Reviews, 11*(3), 238–245. https://doi.org/10.2174/1573403x11666141122220003.

Green, C. R., Anderson, K. O., Baker, T. A., Campbell, L. C., Decker, S., Fillingim, R. B., Kalauokalani, D. A., Lasch, K. E., Myers, C., Tait, R. C., Todd, K. H., & Vallerand, A. H. (2003). The unequal burden of pain: Confronting racial and ethnic disparities in pain. *Pain Medicine, 4*, 277–294. https://doi.org/10.1046/j.1526-4637.2003.03034.x.

Gross, C. P., Smith, B. D., Wolf, E., & Andersen, M. (2008). Racial disparities in cancer therapy: Did the gap narrow between 1992 and 2002? *Cancer, 112*(4), 900–908. https://doi.org/10.1002/cncr.23228.

Haider, A. H., et al. (2011). Association of unconscious race and social class bias with vignette-based clinical assessments by medical students. *Journal of the American Medical Association, 306*(9), 942–951.

Hall, W. J., Chapman, M. V., Lee, K. M., Merino, Y. M., Thomas, T. W., Payne, B. K., Eng, E., Day, S. H., & Coyne-Beasley, T. (2015). Implicit racial/ethnic Bias among health care professionals and its influence on health care outcomes: A systematic review. *American Journal of Public Health, 105*(12), e60–e76. https://doi.org/10.2105/AJPH.2015.302903.

Hardeman, R. R., Karbeah, J.'. M., Almanza, J., & Kozhimannil, K. B. (2020). Roots community birth center: A culturally-centered care model for improving value and equity in childbirth. *Healthcare, 8*(1), 100367., ISSN 2213-0764. https://doi.org/10.1016/j.hjdsi.2019.100367.

Harrell, J. P., Hall, S., & Taliaferro, J. (2003). Physiological responses to racism and discrimination: An assessment of the evidence. *American Journal of Public Health, 93*(2), 243–248.

Health Insurance Coverage in the United States: 2018, U.S. Census Bureau, November 2019., https://www.census.gov/content/dam/Census/library/publications/2019/demo/p60-267.pdf.

Hoffman, K. M., Trawalter, S., Axt, J. R., & Oliver, M. N. (2016). Racial bias in pain assessment and treatment recommendations, and false beliefs about biological differences between blacks and whites. *Proceedings of the National Academy of Sciences of the United States of America, 113*(16), 4296–4301. https://doi.org/10.1073/pnas.1516047113.

Institute of Medicine, Smedley, B. D., Stith, A. Y., & Nelson, A. R. (2003). *Unequal treatments: Confronting racial and ethnic disparities in health care.* Washington, DC: The National Academies Press.

Kirby, J. B., & Kaneda, T. (2010). Unhealthy and uninsured: Exploring racial differences in health and health insurance coverage using a life table approach. *Demography, 47*, 1035–1051.

Kposowa, A. J., & Tsunokai, G. T. (2002). Searching for relief: Racial differences in treatment of patients with back pain. *Race and Society, 5*, 193–223. https://doi.org/10.1016/j.racsoc.2004.01.004.

Krieger, N., Smith, K., Naishadham, D., Hartman, C., & Barbeau, E. M. (2005). Experiences of discrimination: Validity and reliability of a self-report measure for population health research on racism and health. *Social Science and Medicine, 61*, 1576–1596.

Lieberman, M. D., Hariri, A., Jarcho, J. M., Eisenberger, N. I., & Bookheimer, S. Y. (2005). An fMRI investigation of race-related amygdala activity in African-American and Caucasian-American individuals. *Nature Neuroscience, 6*, 720–722.

Lillie-Blanton, M., & Hoffman, C. (2005). The role of health insurance coverage in reducing racial/ethnic disparities in health care. *Health Aff (Millwood), 24*(2), 398–408.

Manchikanti, L., Helm Ii, S., Benyamin, R. M., & Hirsch, J. A. (2017). A critical analysis of Obamacare: Affordable care or insurance for many and coverage for few? *Pain Physician, 20*(3), 111–138. PMID: 28339427.

Mayberry, R., Boone, L., Kaiser, H. J. (2002). *Racial/Ethnic Differences in Cardiac Care: The Weight of the Evidence*. Family Foundation.

McEwen, B. S. (1998). Protective and damaging effects of stress mediators. *The New England Journal of Medicine, 338*, 171–179.

McEwen, B. S. (2000). Allostasis and allostatic load: Implications for neuropsychopharmacology. *Neuropsychopharmacology, 22*, 108–124.

McEwen, B. S. (2002). Protective and damaging effects of stress mediators: The good and bad sides of the response to stress. *Metabolism, 51*(6 Suppl. 1), 2–4.

McEwen, B. S. (2004). Protection and damage from acute and chronic stress, allostasis and allostatic load overload and relevance to the pathophysiology of psychiatric disorders. *Annals of the New York Academy of Sciences, 1032*, 1–7.

McEwen, B. S., & Stellar, E. (1993). Stress and the individual: Mechanisms leading to disease. *Archives of Internal Medicine, 153*, 2093–2101.

Mensah, G. A., & Brown, D. W. (2007). An overview of cardiovascular disease burden in the United States. *Health Affairs (Millwood), 26*(1), 38–48.

Miller, N. A., Kirk, A., Kaiser, M. J., & Glos, L. (2014). The relation between health insurance and health care disparities among adults with disabilities. *American Journal of Public Health, 104*(3), e85–e93. https://doi.org/10.2105/AJPH.2013.301478.

Mossey, J. M. (2011). Defining racial and ethnic disparities in pain management. *Clinical Orthopaedics and Related Research, 469*(7), 1859–1870. https://doi.org/10.1007/s11999-011-1770-9.

Natale, J. E., Joseph, J. G., Rogers, A. J., et al. (2012). PECARN (Pediatric Emergency Care Applied Research Network). Cranial computed tomography use among children with minor blunt head trauma: Association with race/ethnicity. *Archives of Pediatrics & Adolescent Medicine, 166*(8), 732–737.

National Cancer Institute, NIH. Cancer Stat Facts: Cancer of Any Site. Retrieved from https://seer.cancer.gov/statfacts/html/all.html on January 30, 2021. Last updated on November 17, 2020.

Phelps, E. A., Cannistraci, C. J., & Cunningham, W. A. (2003). Intact performance on an indirect measure of race bias following amygdala damage. *Neuropsychologia, 41*, 203–208.

Reisman, M. (2015). The affordable care act, five years later: Policies, Progress, and politics. *P & T : A Peer-Reviewed Journal for Formulary Management, 40*(9), 575–600.

Rosenthal, L., & Lobel, M. (2011). Explaining racial disparities in adverse birth outcomes: Unique sources of stress for black American women. *Social Science & Medicine, 72*(6), 977–983. ISSN 0277-9536. https://doi.org/10.1016/j.socscimed.2011.01.013.

Sabin JA, Rivara FP, Greenwald AG. Physician implicit attitudes and stereotypes about race and quality of medical care. Medical Care 2008;46(7):678–685. doi:https://doi.org/10.1097/MLR.0b013e3181653d58.

Saftlas, A. F., Koonin, L. M., & Atrash, H. K. (2000). Racial disparity in pregnancy-related mortality associated with livebirth: Can established risk factors explain it? *American Journal of Epidemiology, 152*(5), 413–419. https://doi.org/10.1093/aje/152.5.413.

Sawyer, P. J., Major, B., Casad, B. J., Townsend, S. S., & Mendes, W. B. (2012). Discrimination and the stress response: Psychological and physiological consequences of anticipating prejudice in interethnic interactions. *American Journal of Public Health, 102*(5), 1020–1026. https://doi.org/10.2105/AJPH.2011.300620.

Shavers, V. L., & Brown, M. L. (2002). Racial and ethnic disparities in the receipt of Cancer treatment. *JNCI: Journal of the National Cancer Institute, 94*(5), 334–357. https://doi.org/10.1093/jnci/94.5.334.

Siegel, R., Ward, E., Brawley, O., & Jemal, A. (2011). Cancer statistics, 2011: The impact of eliminating socioeconomic and racial disparities on premature cancer deaths. *CA: a Cancer Journal for Clinicians, 61*(4), 212–236.

Sohn, H. (2017). Racial and ethnic disparities in health insurance coverage: Dynamics of gaining and losing coverage over the life-course. *Population Research and Policy Review, 36*(2), 181–201. https://doi.org/10.1007/s11113-016-9416-y.

Sommers, B. D., Buchmueller, T., Decker, S. L., Carey, C., & Kronick, R. (2013). The affordable care act has led to significant gains in health insurance and access to care for young adults. *Health Aff (Millwood), 32*(1), 165–174.

Trawalter, S., & Hoffman, K. M. (2015). Got pain? Racial bias in perceptions of pain. *Social and Personality Psychology Compass, 9*(3), 146–157.

Wallace, M. E., et al. (2015). Joint effects of structural racism and income inequality on small-for-gestational-age birth. *American Journal Public Health.*

Washington, H. A. (2006). *Medical apartheid: The dark history of medical experimentation on black Americans from colonial times to the present.* New York: Doubleday.

Wyatt, S. B., Williams, D. R., Calvin, R., Henderson, F. C., Walker, E. R., & Winters, K. (2003). Racism and cardiovascular disease in African Americans. *The American Journal of the Medical Sciences, 325*(6), 315–331.

Chapter 9
Historical and Structural Fear Compounded

The discussion around COVID-19 cannot be had absent strong consideration of the historical, philosophical, social, and anthropological conversation on "othering." At the height of collective fear and uncertainty, malicious othering was centered as a means of amplifying and cementing greater fear on various levels. The literature on othering is extensive and clear. Brons (2015) defines othering as a construction of identification of the in-group (self) and the out-group (other) in mutual, unequal opposition by attributing relative inferiority and/or radical alienness to the other/ out-group (Brons, 2015). Othering is part of the human condition and need to categorize for simplicity, as a means of attempting to understand and for safety/survival. Other is bore out of the human desire for interdependence (not independence and/or co-dependence); a mandate for survival is connection and belonging. Other is a double-edged sword and a human function that does tap into survival mechanisms for protection and persistence which has been hijacked socially and politically to perpetuate fear, division, and hate.

Georg Hegel, a nineteenth-century philosopher, highlighted the interplay between multiple forms of self-consciousness through what he termed the "master-slave" dialectic – which could be understood as the philosophical and evolutionary argument for interdependence and belonging. The "master-slave" dialectic represented the tension between and clashing of two identities and is understood as a serious scuffle between living and surviving. It is also a recognition that "self" has blind spots that only "other" can help it (self) realize.

The idea that "self" evolves and is powerfully shaped by "other" is significant – the shaping of "self" is dependent on what "other" it has access to as a means of judging, assessing, accepting, denying, and/or modifying. Cole (2004) expounds on Hegel's "master-slave dialectic" by addressing critical questions about how humans find meaning and their place in the world; explores how human existence is validated and dignified; and wrestles with whether a human can truly be in a process of self-discovery absent of "others" concluding that Hegel's introduction of

A. Moreland-Capuia, *The Trauma of Racism*,
https://doi.org/10.1007/978-3-030-73436-7_9

self-consciousness as a working theme is heavily influenced by society and culture (Cole, 2004).

An article by Jensen (2011) asserts that "othering" can be appreciated through the historical lens of symbolic conditioning like identity formation and consideration of hierarchies in the form of power structures (Jensen, 2011). Erik Erikson, a twentieth-century psychologist and psychoanalyst, established a theory of psychosocial development which includes identity formation as a developmental stage (Jensen, 2011; Sollberger, 2013). According to Erikson's theory, identity starts at birth and continues throughout the lifespan (as identity shifts with time, exposures, and new understanding). Identify formation is most robust during the adolescent years marked by significant hormonal and physical changes and social expectations for improved responsibility. Identity formation mandates a consolidation of prior learning into an evolved, sophisticated emerging – responsible human (Erikson, 1950, 1968). There is a phase of identity crisis, understood as temporary misperception, as described by Erikson, marked by exceptional uncertainty as new growth is happening and new choices are being explored (Erikson, 1950, 1968). As a means of tempering this developmentally anticipated stage of uncertainty/identity crisis, many adolescents move toward interdependence in the form of forging close circles of friends and/or pursuing love interests while concomitantly excluding "others" who may not share similarities based on a need for protection, stability, and safety (Erikson, 1950, 1968). Understanding this phenomenon of interdependence as a means of the human condition is critical.

Psychoanalytic theorist, Jacques Lacan, established the developmental theory of the mirror stage, which happens around the age of 6–18 months as infants are aware of and begin to appreciate their own reflection (Lacan, 1988). Lacan asserts that this emerging awareness of a self-image is representative of a self-governing ego in the presence of the parent – with self in this case, being the extension or outgrowth as it is engaging with the outside world (Lacan, 1988). Lacan's theories were heavily influenced by Sigmund Freud's conceptualization of the self through conscious and unconscious exploration of the id, ego, and superego (Freud, 1921, 1930).

Albert Bandura, a twentieth-century psychologist, expounded on the social cognitive theory (SCT) making a connection between the impact of the external environment and actions of others on human behavior and experiences (Bandura, 1977, 1981). Human behavior is modulated by society and social conditions (Bandura, 1977, 1981). Several studies by van Dijk expanded on the SCT and emphasized the construction of ideologies and their respective impact on human behavior (van Dijk, 2001, 2004).

Simone de Beauvoir expanded the early developmental concepts of self, other, and identity formation by introducing otherness as means of investigating the construction of minority and majority identities (Beauvoir, 2005). Canales (2000) further explains othering as exclusionary and/or inclusionary processes with exclusionary othering employing the power intra relationships for control and subservience and inclusionary othering employing power intra relationship to be transformational in building coalitions (Canales, 2000). A study by Johnson et al. (2004)

demonstrates how individual behavior/narratives and institutional narratives contribute to establishing the conditions for othering (Johnson et al., 2004).

Some scholars have advanced the understanding of othering as part of the conceptualization of postcolonial theory (a framework to attempt to understand the deleterious impact of European colonial rule around the world) (van Dyk, 2016), the subtext for politicization and instability (Boyce & Chunnu, 2019), and stereotyping and racialization. Othering as a fear-based practice is explored in several studies and has been described as a form of marginalization (Boyce & Chunnu, 2019; Rohleder, 2014), a driver of tenacious inequality, and a bastardization (as opposed to appreciation) of human differences based on group identities (Boyce & Chunnu, 2019; Rohleder, 2014).

Malicious othering hijacks the human condition and need for interdependence by perverting the process of categorizing people to better understand the world, where one belongs, and how to act in the world and derive meaning from it. Chapter 9 begins by highlighting the powerful manipulation of human behavior (need to be safe; proclivity toward categorizing and excluding as a means of understanding the world/environment, simplifying, and deriving meaning) observed on a global scale as the narrative of how the disease entered the United States, who was likely to have it, and who and what was to be avoided was unfolding. The narrative around COVID-19 became a dominant public discourse in the US media near the end of January 2020, but most didn't pay close attention to it until there was a death related to it – understanding COVID-19 as a serious life-threatening condition became salient (Holshue et al., 2020). The narrative around the virus was that it originated in Wuhan, China, and the 45th President of the United States and some of his colleagues referred to the virus as "the China virus." This labeling resulted in an extreme form of racialized othering that had detrimental consequences. The combination of uncertainty (most Americans not understanding what the virus was and its objective impact) and fear that they might contract it and get severely ill and/or die was enough to modify the behavior of some. There were reports of significant ostracizing of Chinese-American citizens and their businesses as evidenced by increased rates of racialized violence, bullying, and hatred toward them. The level of fear and hate heavily impacted businesses owned by Chinese-Americans – some businesses who had faithfully and honorably served the community for years had to close their doors in the context of marked hatred and bigotry. Hatred and bigotry driven by irresponsible narrative that manipulated natural fear of uncertainty elevating it to levels of irrationality.

9.1   A Novel Virus, Absene of Leadership and Fear Intensified

Fear, worry and panic intensified as more information about SARS-CoV-2 virus (which causes the disease COVID-19) emerged to include that it sticks and stays on surfaces, it was spread by close contacts, more likely to spread in poorly ventilated spaces, could traverse over 6 feet to infect a person, proper handwashing with soap and hot water could neutralize the virus, masks are effective in reducing the spread, persons with pre-existing conditions and older adults were at increased risk of morbidity and mortality, ravaged through several nursing home facilities, the narrative from Federal leadership that it would go away was not matching the harsh reality that nearly 3,000 Americans were dead by the end of March 2020 (Carver & Phillips, 2020; Lechien et al., 2020; WHO, 2021) and healthcare professionals on the frontlines were afraid of what they were observing real-time (Carver & Phillips, 2020; Lechien et al., 2020; WHO, 2021). In the presence of the lack of a federal response and leadership, states were left to determine how to navigate this very scary COVID-19 space. As a matter of fact, states were uncoordinated in their response to COVID-19 as some issued "shelter in place" orders, requiring folks to remain at home and only go out for essentials (food, water, medication, take care of loved ones, brief exercise outside), and businesses were asked to re-imagine operations to include work from home options, use of e-options, and restaurants moving to a takeout model. Stay at home orders contributed to an unfortunate frenzy and survivalist state as the crisis within the crisis became lack of toilet paper, kale, potatoes, hand sanitizer, and sanitizing wipes. Selfishness and rugged individualism were on full display amid the crisis – the universe was put on pause, economy slowed, and the universal experience of survivalist behavior was witnessed. Hoarding behaviors were noted. A study by Mobbs, Hagan, Dalgleish, Silston, and Prévost (2015) on the ecology of human fear reminds of the following regarding primitive survival mechanisms: "One of the most pervasive ecological demands is predatory avoidance. The relentless pressure to outwit predators while balancing homeostatic threats, such as resource depletion, has produced a nervous system that optimizes survival actions" (Mobbs et al., 2015). Research on survivalist behavior assert that in the case of emergency (perceived or real) all implicit social agreements are abandoned and every man and woman doggedly attempt to save his or her own life at whatever expense to others (Brown, 1965; Dow, 1975; Sansom, Lind, & Cresswell, 2009). Fear is primitive, and it will make humans do whatever they must to survive to include hoarding toilet tissue and buying all the kale, hand sanitizer, and bottled water.

The use of the word "shelter in place" was triggering for some and did not sufficiently describe what citizens were being asked to do (Brooks et al., 2020). Narrative matters. Shelter in place in its historical context was associated with Cold War conditions of staying in a bunker until death and dying subsided; it has also been associated with mass shootings and natural disasters like hurricanes (Götz, Gvirtz, Galinsky, & Jachimowicz, 2021). While the overarching goal was to warn folks that there was and still is an emerging, ill-understood threat out there and the goal was prevention, the shelter in place order was interpreted as war-like conditions and negatively impacted mental health (Brooks et al., 2020; Shigemura, Ursano, Morganstein, Kurosawa, & Benedek, 2020). This misinterpretation potentiated pre-existing fear. With gentle nudging and education, shelter in place transitioned to stay at home. Folks were being asked to socially distance, which contributed to a greater sense of isolation. With gentle education and re-direction, social distancing transitioned to physical distancing with the recognition that there were multiple ways to stay socially connected while physically distanced.

As stay at home orders persisted, physical connection felt constrained, and a significant toll on mental health was observed. As the pandemic lingered with no clear end in sight, structural disparities intensified as individuals and communities were being asked to stay home, work from home, quarantine if exposed, obtain and use technology with enough savvy to do on-line learning/shopping, etc. – the only challenge is that these requirements assumed that everyone had the resources or could tap into resources that would allow them to function and survive. The reality is that there was an entire cohort of the nation that are deemed essential to include grocery store workers, healthcare providers, transportation operators, farmers, meat packing plants, janitorial services, and food service members. According to several studies, racial/ethnic minorities are more likely to have compounded and deleterious impact on social determinants of health in the following ways (CDC, 2020; Sharma et al., 2020; Yancy, 2020; Ajilore & Thames, 2020; Singu, Acharya, Challagundla, & Byrareddy, 2020; Abrams & Szefler, 2020; Federico, McFarlane 2nd, Szefler, & Abrams, 2020; Ahmed, Ahmed, Pissarides, & Stiglitz, 2020; Sharma et al., 2016):

- Working while still living below the federal poverty line
- More likely to be from a racial-ethnic minority background
- More likely to live in multigenerational homes because of affordability
- More likely to be underinsured or uninsured
- More likely to have limited access to personal protective equipment like masks
- More likely to be exposed to COVID-19 and have higher rates of morbidity and mortality
- More likely to be housing and food insecure (CDC, 2020; Sharma et al., 2020; Yancy, 2020; Ajilore & Thames, 2020; Singu et al., 2020; Abrams & Szefler, 2020; Federico et al., 2020; Ahmed et al., 2020; Sharma et al., 2016)
- More likely to have limited access to broadband (Beaunoyer, Dupéré, & Guitton, 2020)

COVID-19 has contributed to economic recession-like conditions. Margerison-Zilko and colleagues did a comprehensive literature review exploring the impact of the Great Recession on mental and physical health in developed nations and highlighted the negative effects on mental health and social functioning (Margerison-Zilko, Goldman-Mellor, Falconi, & Downing, 2016). Many studies show detrimental impacts of economic recession on health, particularly mental health. Not only did individuals experiencing job loss, financial strain, and housing distress exhibit increased risk of psychological distress, but psychological distress, diagnosed disorder, and suicide all appeared to increase at the population level (Burgard, Ailshire, & Kalousova, 2013; Fligstein & Goldstein, 2011; Hoynes, Miller, & Schaller, 2012; Margerison-Zilko et al., 2016). Several studies demonstrated increased intimate partner and domestic violence during the COVID-19 pandemic (Bright, Burton, & Kosky, 2020; Evans et al., 2020; Menon & Padhy, 2020; Sharma & Borah, 2020; Shigemura et al., 2020). The perfect storm of financial stressors, persistent uncertainty, and stay at home orders are cited as some of the contributors to the upward trend. COVID-19 represented the confluence of pre-existing, persistent, structural racial disparities in education, employment, healthcare, poverty, and housing – all of which have been addressed in prior chapters in this book. The point is that human behavior and systems efficiency are best understood when examined in the context of crisis. It didn't have to be this way. It does not have to be this way in the future.

9.2   Argument Over the Economy Versus Health and Safety

Political and ideological differences came to surface as some Americans felt that stay at home orders were a violation of their constitutional rights. The argument around violation of constitutional rights became more robust when businesses began to close and job loss intensified. Folks were fearful of not being able to take care of their families and in weighing taking chances on a dangerous virus and dying versus dying from lack of finances and food – many chose their basic needs. The argument of prioritizing the economy over health was politicized to the point of ridiculous violence. As discussed in multiple chapters in this book, when humans get into sur-vival/flight/freeze/fight and fear mode, the possibilities of poor decision making, violence, and danger are increased. The top, rational part of the brain is not working as well when humans are in the survivalist/stress state – expectations for rationality in the face of perceived and real fear may not be plausible for everyone. The real question is how to temper the fear, and a real important first step is acknowledging it. Again, no excuses, a very real physiologic phenomenon and explanation for some behavior.

9.3   Disparities Rise to the Top amid Crisis: 1918

The Spanish flu of 1918 (H1N1 influenza A virus) started in the spring while World War I was still happening (and didn't end until November of 1918). US 28th President Woodrow Wilson did not engage America in World War I until 1917, a year before it ended in 1918. This is worth noting as the country was under stressed conditions prior to the flu pandemic ravaging the nation. Crisis most usually accom-panies stress, and stress typically creates the conditions for greater mortality and morbidity. The Spanish flu of 1918 impacted nearly 500 million humans, which accounted for approximately one third of the world's population at the time. The Spanish flu started near the tail end of World War I in 1918 and stuck around viru-lently and violently, in multiple phases, for almost 2 years (ending in the spring of 1920) (Brundage & Shanks, 2007; Morens & Fauci, 2007). It took the lives of just under 1 million Americans and approximately 50 million worldwide. According to retrospective data review and analysis surrounding 1918 pandemic deaths, it was determined that poor hygiene, poor nutrition, overcrowding in hospitals and medical camps, overcrowding in communities, and stressed conditions imposed by World War I (intra, inter, and post) contributed to the heightened mortality as patients who died were more likely to have died from bacterial superinfection versus the flu virus itself (Brundage & Shanks, 2007; Morens & Fauci, 2007). There are so many lessons that might be gleaned from the 1918 flu pandemic, but of note here is the fact that external psychosocial conditions/social determinants of health (unattended) contributed to greater morbidity and mortality. This has implications for how COVID-19 is managed moving forward – there is evidence that improving structural and social disparities will decrease morbidity and mortality.

9.4 Historical Fear: Tuskegee Experiment and Other Experiments on Black People

In 1932, less than 100 years ago, nearly 600 African-American men who had limited familiarity with the healthcare system were recruited by physicians from the US Public Health Service (PHS) under the guise and commitment of free medical care. These Black men were from Macon County, Alabama, and, namely, worked as sharecroppers. The PHS was studying the acute and long-term manifestations of syphilis. 399 men had latent syphilis, and 201 men were without syphilis (the control) (Paul & Brookes, 2015; Scharff et al., 2010). At the beginning of the study, there was no known treatment for syphilis, but almost 15 years into the study, it was discovered that penicillin was a useful medication and recommended to treat it. Researchers in this study did not provide standard-of-care treatment, even with the knowledge that it existed; instead, they let men die and suffer irreversible consequences of the disease that were both psychiatric and neurologic in nature (Paul & Brookes, 2015; Scharff et al., 2010). It wasn't until 1960 that an investigator with the PHS determined that the unwillingness of researchers in this study to treat was unethical, and despite the concern lifted, the study continued until the media and public caught wind of the atrociousness of this study in the early 1970s; the study wasn't stopped until 1972. The unfortunate nature of this is that by the time the study had been shut down, tremendous damage had been done, the deleterious cascading impact of not treating these men is that spouses and children were infected needlessly. This was a study sponsored by the government that allowed for intentional harm to be done to chronically marginalized Black men, and 1972 was not that long ago (Paul & Brookes, 2015; Scharff et al., 2010).

The other notable reality is that of Henrietta Lacks. Henrietta Lacks was a Black woman who unfortunately had cervical cancer in the 1950s; treatment was lacking, but even more so for a Black woman. She died at the age of 31; however, without knowledge and/or consent, physicians maintained some of her tissues and distributed them to other researchers (Alsan & Wanamaker, 2018). It was discovered that her cells could survive and replicate – her cells (HeLa cells) are the foundation of basic biological research having helped advancing medicine in the areas of cancer and infectious diseases (Skloot, 2010). A Black woman died, and without consent and/or knowledge, her cells were used – this was less than 70 years ago in US history, not that long ago (Alsan & Wanamaker, 2018).

Black Americans have legitimate reservations with medicine and research. There has been no profound acknowledgement of how the Tuskegee experiment and Henrietta Lacks experience continue to traumatize Black citizens and compromise any sense of safety. The COVID-19 vaccination hesitancy among the Black community and other racial/ethnic minority communities is valid given the historical backdrop. In order to make progress in supporting communities in moving toward vaccination, safety must be created, and truth acknowledged. As of January of 2021, the US National Institutes of Health (NIH) had put out a notice of special interest for strategies that might help mitigate vaccine hesitancy in communities that experience health disparities – this is a start.

9.5 Regions Hit Harder Than Others: Real-Life Examples of the Disproportionate Impact of COVID-19

The data bore out that individuals disproportionately impacted by COVID-19 were racial and ethnic minorities. The nation bore witness to nearly 400,000 American deaths – all preventable – accentuating a history of unequal exposure and treatment of racial/ethnic minorities. In particular, the coronavirus pandemic has been unremitting and has hit some geographical regions harder than others. One such example is Los Angeles County where poverty is high and the persons who have been hurt the most by the virus in Los Angeles County is the Latino and Black community, disproportionately so. According to a 2020 *Los Angeles Times* article penned by Rong-Gong Lin II and Luke Money, the most impoverished persons who reside in Los Angeles County were averaging 36 deaths a day per 100,000 residents when compared to wealthier areas at 10 deaths a day per 100,000 residents (Lin II & Money, 2021). According the two different *Los Angeles Times* reports, Latino residents in L.A. County were dying eight times the rate they were before COVID (from 3.5 deaths per 100,000 to 28 deaths per 100,000) (Lin II & Money, 2021). The COVID mortality of Black residents peaked from 1 death a day per 100,000 to 15 deaths a day per 100,000; Asian residents grew from 1 death a day per 100,000 to 12 deaths a day per 100,000 – and it was noted that White residents have the lowest death rate compared to other groups at 10 deaths a day per 100,000 residents (Lin II & Money, 2021).

There is no secret behind the conditions that render COVID-19 more deadly in Black and Latino communities; the issues are structural to include poverty, toxic stress, racism, environmental racism, crowded housing conditions, more likely to be living intergenerationally, and more likely to be frontline essential workers with greater and unequal exposure and underinsured and/or uninsured. A 2012 study by Hoynes and colleagues highlighted the demographics of communities that suffer the greatest during a recession – their work demonstrated that the suffering was greater for Black and Hispanic laborers, young laborers, persons with less education, and men (Hoynes et al., 2012).

9.6 Los Angeles Health Workers, EMTs, and Vicarious Trauma

Vicarious trauma also known as occupational-related dysphoria is a form of trauma that comes from persons who are chronically subject to the suffering (fear, pain, illness, death, trauma) of others (Branson, 2019). The literature on vicarious trauma shows humans in the helping profession (social workers, healthcare workers, educators) are at greater risks of being traumatized vicariously (Jenkins & Baird, 2002). Globally, vicarious trauma has increased as the entire world has been subject to the suffering, dying, and death of millions of humans at the hand of COVID-19 around the world (Vagni, Maiorano, Giostra, & Pajardi, 2020; Benfante, Di Tella, Romeo, & Castelli, 2020; Cacchione, 2020; Conversano, Marchi, & Miniati, 2020; Li et al., 2020; Menon & Padhy, 2020; Pappa et al., 2020; Williamson, Murphy, & Greenberg, 2020; Jenkins & Baird, 2002).

Symptoms of vicarious trauma (also known as secondary trauma) can look like those in PTSD – avoidance, re-experiencing, negative thoughts and emotions, sleep disruption, and low threshold for irritability (Pappa et al., 2020). Vicarious trauma can lead to compassion fatigue or limited empathy marked by symptoms like sleep disturbance, headache, chronic fatigue, and impaired decision-making. Healthcare workers and EMTs, prior to COVID-19, were more likely to experience some form of vicarious and/or secondary trauma, but COVID-19 increased the incidences of it (Pappa et al., 2020).

The death rates from COVID were so high in Los Angeles that ICU beds and ventilator use were at capacity, healthcare workers were physically and emotionally exhausted (as their colleagues continued to be exposed requiring quarantine and effectively limiting the call pool, translating into long hours for already tired workers at the height of heavy death and sadness) (Rainey, Karlamangla, & Dolan, 2021), and ethics committees were consulted as hospitals were compelled to turn folks away and asking EMTs to not bring persons to the hospital who were not able to be rescuscitated in the field (Menon & Padhy, 2020; Rainey et al., 2021). The level of vicarious trauma at every level was pronounced as a system was asked to literally determine who lives and dies based on exceptionally limited resources. The impact of this reality will reside for years to come (Vagni et al., 2020; Benfante et al., 2020; Cacchione, 2020; Conversano et al., 2020; Li et al., 2020; Menon & Padhy, 2020; Pappa et al., 2020; Williamson et al., 2020; Jenkins & Baird, 2002).

9.7   Vaccination Disparities Well Before COVID

Vaccination disparities are not new. A study by Lu et al. (2015) assessed adult vaccination stratified by race/ethnicity in the United States through the analysis of 2012 National Health Interview Survey results (Lu et al., 2015). The analysis included assessment of six routine vaccines to include influenza, tetanus, pneumococcal, human papillomavirus, and zoster vaccines. Analysis revealed the following: vaccination rates were lower for non-Hispanic Blacks, Hispanics, and non-Hispanic Asians compared to non-Hispanic Whites (Lu et al., 2015). Lu and colleagues concluded that even when socioeconomic factors are adjusted for, vaccination disparities among racial and ethnic groups are slightly improved, but still low (Lu et al., 2015).

Vaccination fears and disparities aren't eliminated among healthcare workers (with working medical knowledge) who are racial/ethnic minorities. Ojha et al. (2015) investigated concerns about lack of safety of vaccines and how these concerns impacted racial/ethnic minority vaccine disparities among healthcare workers (Ojha et al., 2015). Via a web-based survey, the study assessed apprehensions surrounding the influenza vaccination and revealed that non-Hispanic Blacks had lower vaccination rates compared to non-Hispanic Whites and this difference was mostly mediated by vaccination fears and concerns about safety (Ojha et al., 2015). Longitudinal analysis by Østbye, Taylor, Lee, Greenberg, and van Scoyoc (2003) highlighted pronounced disparities in influenza vaccinations in racial/ethnic minorities (Østbye et al., 2003), and other analyses demonstrate grave disparities in influenza vaccination rates in adolescents in racial/ethnic minority groups (Webb, Dowd-Arrow, Taylor, & Burdette, 2018).

The flu vaccination has been around for almost 70 years, and yet there is documented high hesitancy and fear which contributes to vaccination disparities in racial/ethnic minorities. These fears have not been completely tempered because in part of the justified historical mistrust of the healthcare and research system. There should be no surprise that the trend of hesitancy, fear, and vaccination disparities would exist in the case of the COVID-19 vaccination. This concern was highlighted in a 2020 analysis of 6,735 Medicare-certified facilities who provided care for persons with end-stage kidney disease requiring dialysis (Danziger, Weinhandl, Friedman, & Mukamal, 2020). This analysis found that over a 3-year window (2014–2017), Medicare facilities that served majority racial/ethnic minorities had low rates of influenza vaccination and the gap continues to grow forecasting that the COVID vaccination may follow suit with the influenza trend which could contribute to greater disparities, morbidity, and mortality (Danziger et al., 2020).

According to the policy watch organization KFF who has been analyzing federal data and trends regarding COVID-19 vaccinations, as of January 19, 2021, over 12 million COVID-19 vaccinations had been administered nationwide; 17 states were publicly reporting vaccination data by race/ethnicity; according to vaccinations with known race/ethnicity, "the share of vaccinations among Black people is smaller than their share of cases in all 16 reporting states and smaller than their share of deaths in 15 states" (Ndugga, Pham, Follow, Artiga, & Mengistu, 2021). The

COVID-19 vaccination disparity is unfortunate especially in the setting of dispro-portionately heightened morbidity and mortality from COVID-19 among racial/ethnic minorities (Webb Hooper, Nápoles, & Pérez-Stable, 2020).

A study by Tsai and Wilson (2020) accentuated the fact that poverty, race and ethnicity, and homelessness, for example, have significant impact on COVID-19 outcomes as homeless families are at an elevated risk for viral transmission second-ary to overcrowding and lower contact with healthcare facilities (Tsai & Wilson, 2020).

Sharma et al. (2020) conducted a cross-sectional quantitative and qualitative analysis (with an open-ended question about family's greatest concerns) via survey among low-income households with children assessing for social needs, COVID-19-related concerns, and diet-related behaviors (Sharma et al., 2020). Surveys com-pleted by over 1,000 families revealed the following: over 80% of respondents were concerned about getting infected with COVID-19; close to 76% were worried about financial instability; close to 43% expressed worry around employment; close to 69% were worried about access to food; 31% were concerned about the stability of their housing situation; close to 36% had worries about access to healthcare; and nearly 94% reported food insecurity (Sharma et al., 2020). This study highlights the aggravating impact of the COVID-19 pandemic on social determinants of health.

9.8 COVID-19 Pandemic, Structural Disparities and Fear Compounded

The COVID-19 pandemic has been hard hitting – an international coalition travers-ing class, race, education level, ideological and religious diversity collaborated to construct a vaccine in under a year to temper the deadly impacts of the virus. In under 1 year, a coalition worked collaboratively to construct a preventative measure as COVID-19 is a global public health crisis. Systemic racism and discrimination as a persistent pandemic rage on and continue to take the lives of hundreds daily and needlessly. Racism poses a clear and present danger, globally. A public health lens should be applied to treating, containing, and eliminating it. Angela Davis was known for famously saying: "I am no longer accepting the things I cannot change, I am changing the things I cannot accept." Healers, community members, families, individuals, and businesses all have a responsibility to eliminate needless human suffering wherever it is observed. The urgent challenge for all is to work collectively to change unacceptable things – racism is unacceptable. The world has demonstrated that it can solve really hard things and produce life-saving measures when there is concerted effort and will. There are no more excuses. Starting with the following questions might prove useful in the effort to tear down the strong walls of racism:

- What is the fear?
- Why the fear?
- Where is the fear?
- What is the need?

References

Abrams, E. M., & Szefler, S. J. (2020). COVID-19 and the impact of social determinants of health. *The Lancet Respiratory Medicine, 8*(7), 659–661. https://doi.org/10.1016/S2213-2600(20)30234-4.

Ahmed, F., Ahmed, N., Pissarides, C., & Stiglitz, J. (2020). *Why inequality could spread COVID-19*. Lancet Public Health. https://doi.org/10.1016/S2468-2667(20)30085-2. published online May 5.

Ajilore, O., & Thames, A. D. (2020). The fire this time: The stress of racism, inflammation and COVID-19. *Brain, Behavior, and Immunity, 88*, 66–67. https://doi.org/10.1016/j.bbi.2020.06.003. Epub 2020 Jun 4. PMID: 32505712; PMCID: PMC7272146.

Alsan, M., & Wanamaker, M. (2018). Tuskegee and the health of black men. *The Quarterly Journal of Economics, 133*(1), 407–455. https://doi.org/10.1093/qje/qjx029.

Bandura, A. (1977). Self-efficacy: Toward a unifying theory of behavioral change. *Psychological Review, 84*, 191–215.

Bandura, A. (1981). Self-referent thought: A developmental analysis of self-efficacy. In J. H. Flavell & L. Ross (Eds.), *Social cognitive development: Frontiers and possible futures* (pp. 200–239). Cambridge: Cambridge University Press.

Beaunoyer, E., Dupéré, S., & Guitton, M. J. (2020). COVID-19 and digital inequalities: Reciprocal impacts and mitigation strategies. *Computers in Human Behavior, 111*, 106424. https://doi.org/10.1016/j.chb.2020.106424.

Beauvoir's Time/Our Time: The Renaissance in Simone de Beauvoir Studies. *Feminist Studies*, 31 (2005), 286–89 (p. 306).

Benfante, A., Di Tella, M., Romeo, A., & Castelli, L. (2020). Traumatic Stress in Healthcare Workers During COVID-19 Pandemic: A Review of the Immediate Impact. *Frontiers in Psychology, 11*, 569935. https://doi.org/10.3389/fpsyg.2020.569935.

Boyce, T., & Chunnu, W. (Eds.). (2019). *Historicizing Fear: Ignorance, Vilification, and Othering.* Louisville: University Press of Colorado. https://doi.org/10.2307/j.ctvwh8d12.

Branson, D. C. (2019). Vicarious trauma, themes in research, and terminology: A review of literature. *Traumatology, 25*(1), 2–10. https://doi.org/10.1037/trm0000161.

Bright, C. F., Burton, C., & Kosky, M. (2020). Considerations of the impacts of COVID-19 on domestic violence in the United States. *Social Sciences & Humanities Open, 2*(1), 100069. https://doi.org/10.1016/j.ssaho.2020.100069.

Brons, L. (2015). Othering, an analysis. *Transcience, A Journal of Global Studies, 6*(1), 69–90.

Brooks, S. K., Webster, R. K., Smith, L. E., Woodland, L., Wessely, S., Greenberg, N., et al. (2020). The psychological impact of quarantine and how to reduce it: rapid review of the evidence. *Lancet, 395*, 912–920. https://doi.org/10.1016/S0140-6736(20)30460-8.

Brown, R. (*1965*). *Social Psychology*. New York: Free Press.

Brundage, J. F., Shanks, G. D. (2007). What really happened during the 1918 influenza pandemic? The importance of bacterial secondary infections. *The Journal of Infectious Diseases* **196** (11): 1717–1718, author reply 1718–19. https://doi.org/10.1086/522355. PMID 18008258.

Burgard, S. A., Ailshire, J. A., & Kalousova, L. (2013). The Great Recession and Health: People, Populations, and Disparities. *The Annals of the American Academy of Political and Social Science, 650*(1), 194–213.

Cacchione, P. Z. (2020). Moral distress in the midst of the COVID-19 pandemic. *Clinical Nursing Research, 29*, 215–216. https://doi.org/10.1177/1054773820920385.

Canales, M. K. (2000). *Othering: Toward an Understanding of Difference. Advances in Nursing Science, 22*(4), 16–31.

Carver, P. E., & Phillips, J. (2020). Novel coronavirus (COVID-19): what you need to know. *Workplace Health Saf, 68*, 250–250. https://doi.org/10.1177/2165079920914947.

CDC, 2020; Sharma et al., 2020; Yancy, 2020; Ajilore and Thames, 2020; Singu et al, 2020; Abrams and Szefler, 2020; Frederico et al., 2020; Ahmed et al., 2020; Sharma et al., 2016

Centers for Disease Control and Prevention. Health equity considerations and racial and ethnic minority groups. https://www.cdc.gov/coronavirus/2019-ncov/need-extra-precautions/racial-ethnic-minorities.html. Updated July 24, 2020. Accessed 27 Augu 2020.

Cole, A. (2004). What Hegel's Master/Slave Dialectic Really Means. *Journal of Medieval and Early Modern Studies, 34*(3), 577–610. https://www.muse.jhu.edu/article/174870.

Conversano, C., Marchi, L., & Miniati, M. (2020). Psychological distress among healthcare professionals involved in the Covid-19 emergency: vulnerability and resilience factors. *Clinical Neuropsychiatry, 17*, 94–96. https://doi.org/10.36131/CN20200212.

Danziger, J., Weinhandl, E., Friedman, D., & Mukamal, K. J. (2020). Racial and Ethnic Disparities in Seasonal Influenza Vaccination among Dialysis Facilities in the United States. *JASN, 31*(9), 2117–2121. https://doi.org/10.1681/ASN.2020040483.

Dow, P. (1975). MACOS: The Study of Human Behavior as One Road to Survival. *The Phi Delta Kappan, 57*(2), 79–81. Retrieved February 4, 2021, from http://www.jstor.org/stable/20298151.

Erikson, E. H. (1950). *Childhood and society*. New York: Norton.

Erikson, E. H. (1968). *Identity: Youth and crisis*. New York: W W Norton & Company.

Evans, M. L., Lindauer, M., & Farrell, M. E. (2020). A Pandemic within a Pandemic — Intimate Partner Violence during Covid-19. *The New England Journal of Medicine, 383*, 2302–2304. https://doi.org/10.1056/NEJMp2024046.

Federico, M. J., McFarlane, A. E., 2nd, Szefler, S. J., & Abrams, E. M. (2020). The impact of social determinants of health on children with asthma. *Journal of Allergy and Clinical Immunology: In Practice*. https://doi.org/10.1016/j.jaip.2020.03.028. published online April 12.

Fligstein, N., & Goldstein, A. (2011). The Roots of the Great Recession. In D. B. Grusky, B. Western, & C. Wimer (Eds.), *The Great Recession*. New York: Russell Sage Foundation.

Freud, S. (1921). *Group Psychology and the Analysis of the Ego* (Standard ed.). London: Hogarth Press.

Freud, S. (1930). Civilization and Its Discontents. In S. Freud (Ed.), *Freud: Civilization, Society and Religion* (Vol. 12). Harmondsworth, UK: Penguin.

Götz, F. M., Gvirtz, A., Galinsky, A. D., & Jachimowicz, J. M. (2021). How Personality and Policy Predict Pandemic Behavior: Understanding Sheltering-in-Place in 55 Countries at the Onset of COVID-19. *American Psychologist, 76*(1), 39–49.

Holshue, M. L., DeBolt, C., Lindquist, S., Lofy, K. H., Wiesman, J., Bruce, H., Spitters, C., et al. (2020). First case of 2019 novel coronavirus in the United States. *New England Journal of Medicine, 382*, 929–936.

Hoynes, H., Miller, D. L., & Schaller, J. (2012). Who Suffers during Recessions? *Journal of Economic Perspectives, 26*(3), 27–48.

Jenkins, S. R., & Baird, S. (2002). Secondary traumatic stress and vicarious trauma: a validational study. *Journal of Traumatic Stress, 15*(5), 423–432. https://doi.org/10.1023/A:1020193526843. PMID: 12392231.

Jensen, S. (2011). Othering, identity formation and agency. *Qualitative Studies, 2*(2), 63–78. https://doi.org/10.7146/qs.v2i2.5510.

Johnson, J. L., Bottorff, J. L., Browne, A. J., Sukhdev, G., Ann Hilton, B., & Clarke, H. (2004). Othering and Being Othered in the Context of Health Care Services. *Health Communication, 16*(2), 255–271. https://doi.org/10.1207/S15327027HC1602_7.

Lacan, J. (1988). *The Seminar of Jacques Lacan. Book 2. The ego in Freud's theory and in the technique of psychoanalysis, 1954-1955*. New York: W.W. Norton.

Lechien, J. R., Chiesa-Estomba, C. M., Place, S., Van Laethem, Y., Cabaraux, P., Mat, Q., et al. (2020). Clinical and epidemiological characteristics of 1,420 European patients with mild-to-moderate Coronavirus Disease 2019. *Journal of Internal Medicine, 288*, 335–344. https://doi.org/10.1111/joim.13089. PMID.

Li, Z., Ge, J., Yang, M., Feng, J., Qiao, M., Jiang, R., et al. (2020). Vicarious traumatization in the general public, members, and non-members of medical teams aiding in COVID-19 control. *Brain, Behavior, and Immunity, 88*, 916–919. https://doi.org/10.1016/j.bbi.2020.03.007.

Lin II RG, Money L. Deaths among Latinos in L.A. County from COVID-19 rising at astonishing levels. Los Angeles Times, 2020, retrieved online from COVID-19 deaths among L.A. Latinos rising at alarming levels - Los Angeles Times (latimes.com) on February 1, 2021.

Lu, P. J., O'Halloran, A., Williams, W. W., Lindley, M. C., Farrall, S., & Bridges, C. B. (2015). Racial and Ethnic Disparities in Vaccination Coverage Among Adult Populations in the U.S. *American Journal of Preventive Medicine, 49*(6 Suppl 4), S412–S425. https://doi.org/10.1016/j.amepre.2015.03.005.

Margerison-Zilko, C., Goldman-Mellor, S., Falconi, A., & Downing, J. (2016). Health Impacts of the Great Recession: A Critical Review. *Current Epidemiology Reports, 3*(1), 81–91. https://doi.org/10.1007/s40471-016-0068-6.

Menon, V., & Padhy, S. K. (2020). Ethical dilemmas faced by health care workers during COVID-19 pandemic: issues, implications and suggestions. *Asian Journal of Psychiatry, 51*, 102116. https://doi.org/10.1016/j.ajp.2020.102116.

Mobbs, D., Hagan, C. C., Dalgleish, T., Silston, B., & Prévost, C. (2015). The ecology of human fear: survival optimization and the nervous system. *Frontiers in Neuroscience, 9*, 55. https://doi.org/10.3389/fnins.2015.00055.

Morens, D. M., & Fauci, A. S. (2007). The 1918 influenza pandemic: insights for the 21st century. *The Journal of Infectious Diseases, 195*(7), 1018–1028. https://doi.org/10.1086/511989. PMID 17330793.

Nambi Ndugga, Olivia Pham, Latoya Hill Follow, Samantha Artiga and Salem Mengistu (2021) *Early State Vaccination Data Raise Warning Flags for Racial Equity*. Retrieved from https://www.kff.org/policy-watch/early-state-vaccination-data-raise-warning-flags-racial-equity/ on February 6, 2021.

Ojha, R. P., Stallings-Smith, S., Flynn, P. M., Adderson, E. E., Offutt-Powell, T. N., & Gaur, A. H. (2015). The Impact of Vaccine Concerns on Racial/Ethnic Disparities in Influenza Vaccine Uptake Among Health Care Workers. *American Journal of Public Health, 105*(9), e35–e41. https://doi.org/10.2105/AJPH.2015.302736.

Østbye, T., Taylor, D. H., Lee, A. M., Greenberg, G., & van Scoyoc, L. (2003). Racial differences in influenza vaccination among older Americans 1996–2000: longitudinal analysis of the Health and Retirement Study (HRS) and the Asset and Health Dynamics Among the Oldest Old (AHEAD) survey. *BMC Public Health, 3*(1), 41.

Pappa, S., Ntella, V., Giannakas, T., Giannakoulis, V. G., Papoutsi, E., & Katsaounou, P. (2020). Prevalence of depression, anxiety, and insomnia among healthcare workers during the COVID-19 pandemic: a systematic review and meta-analysis. *Brain, Behavior, and Immunity, 88*, 901–907. https://doi.org/10.1016/j.bbi.2020.05.026.

Paul, C., & Brookes, B. (2015). The Rationalization of Unethical Research: Revisionist Accounts of the Tuskegee Syphilis Study and the New Zealand "Unfortunate Experiment". *American Journal of Public Health, 105*(10), e12–e19. https://doi.org/10.2105/AJPH.2015.302720.

James Rainey, Soumya Karlamangla, Jack Dolan. (2021). Triage officers' would decide who gets care and who doesn't if COVID-19 crushes L.A. hospitals. Los Angeles Times, 2020. Retrieved from Amid COVID surge, 'triage officers' may decide who gets care - Los Angeles Times (latimes.com) on February 1, 2021.

Rohleder, P. (2014). Othering. In T. Teo (Ed.), *Encyclopedia of Critical Psychology*. New York: Springer. https://doi.org/10.1007/978-1-4614-5583-7_414.

Sansom, A., Lind, J., & Cresswell, W. (2009). Individual behavior and survival: the roles of predator avoidance, foraging success, and vigilance. *Behavioral Ecology, 20*(6), 1168–1174. https://doi.org/10.1093/beheco/arp110.

Scharff, D. P., Mathews, K. J., Jackson, P., Hoffsuemmer, J., Martin, E., & Edwards, D. (2010). More than Tuskegee: understanding mistrust about research participation. *Journal of Health care for the Poor and Underserved, 21*(3), 879–897. https://doi.org/10.1353/hpu.0.0323.

Sharma, A., & Borah, S. B. (2020). Covid-19 and Domestic Violence: an Indirect Path to Social and Economic Crisis. *Journal of Family Violence*, 1–7. Advance online publication. https://doi.org/10.1007/s10896-020-00188-8.

Sharma, S. V., Chuang, R., Rushing, M., Naylor, B., Ranjit, N., Pomeroy, M., et al. (2020). Social Determinants of Health–Related Needs During COVID-19 Among Low-Income Households With Children. *Preventing Chronic Disease, 17*, 200322. https://doi.org/10.5888/pcd17.200322external.icon.

Sharma, S. V., Markham, C., Chow, J., Ranjit, N., Pomeroy, M., & Raber, M. (2016). Evaluating a school-based fruit and vegetable co-op in low-income children: a quasi-experimental study. *Preventive Medicine, 91*, 8–17.

Shigemura, J., Ursano, R. J., Morganstein, J. C., Kurosawa, M., & Benedek, D. M. (2020). Public responses to the novel 2019 coronavirus (2019-nCoV) in Japan: Mental health consequences and target populations. *Psychiatry and Clinical Neurosciences, 74*(4), 281–282. https://doi.org/10.1111/pcn.12988.

Singu, S., Acharya, A., Challagundla, K., & Byrareddy, S. N. (2020). Impact of Social Determinants of Health on the Emerging COVID-19 Pandemic in the United States. *Frontiers in Public Health, 8*, 406. https://doi.org/10.3389/fpubh.2020.00406.

Skloot, R. (2010). *The immortal life of Henrietta Lacks*. New York: Crown Publishers.

Sollberger, D. (2013). On identity: from a philosophical point of view. *Child and Adolescent Psychiatry and Mental Health, 7*(1), 29. https://doi.org/10.1186/1753-2000-7-29.

Tsai, J., & Wilson, M. (2020). COVID-19: a potential public health problem for homeless populations. *Lancet Public Health, 5*, e186–e187.

Vagni, M., Maiorano, T., Giostra, V., & Pajardi, D. (2020). Coping With COVID-19: Emergency Stress, Secondary Trauma and Self-Efficacy in Healthcare and Emergency Workers in Italy. *Frontiers in Psychology, 11*, 566912. https://doi.org/10.3389/fpsyg.2020.566912.

van Dijk, T. A. (2001). Opinions and ideologies in the press. In A. Bell & P. Garrett (Eds.), *Approaches to media discourse* (pp. 21–63). Oxford, UK: Blackwell.

van Dijk, T. A. (2004). Principles of critical discourse analysis. In M. Wetherell, S. Taylor, & S. J. Yates (Eds.), *Discourse theory and practice* (pp. 300–317). London: SAGE.

van Dyk, S. (2016). The othering of old age: Insights from Postcolonial Studies. *Journal of Aging Studies, 39*, 109–120. https://doi.org/10.1016/j.jaging.2016.06.005. Epub 2016 Jul 3. PMID: 27912849.

Webb Hooper, M., Nápoles, A. M., & Pérez-Stable, E. J. (2020). COVID-19 and racial/ethnic disparities. *JAMA, 323*(24), 2466.

Webb, N. S., Dowd-Arrow, B., Taylor, M. G., & Burdette, A. M. (2018). Racial/Ethnic Disparities in Influenza Vaccination Coverage Among US Adolescents, 2010-2016. *Public Health Reports, 133*(6), 667–676. https://doi.org/10.1177/0033354918805720.

WHO (2021). *Coronavirus disease 2019 (COVID-19)*. Available online at: https://www.who.int/emergencies/diseases/novel-coronavirus-2019 Accessed: 21Jan 2021.

Williamson, V., Murphy, D., & Greenberg, N. (2020). COVID-19 and experiences of moral injury in front-line key workers. *Occupational Medicine, 70*, 317–319. https://doi.org/10.1093/occmed/kqaa052.

Yancy, C. W. (2020). COVID-19 and African Americans. *JAMA, 323*(19), 1891–1892. https://doi.org/10.1001/jama.2020.6548. PMID: 32293639.

Chapter 10
The Trauma of Colonialism, European Supremacy, Truth, and Reconciliation

The role that fear has played in shaping individuals, systems, and societies cannot be underestimated. Colonialism is the intentional subjugation and domination of one group by another for economic, social, and political power. Colonialism has long and deep roots dating back to approximately the early fifteenth century marked by European expeditions near Africa's southern coast. Many have debated whether the various subtypes of colonialism should be specified to more accurately describe the depth and width of domination and thievery. This chapter will deal specifically with what is understood as modern colonialism circa the fifteenth century involving European entities that included the Portuguese and Spanish exploring faraway lands, forcibly possessing land and resources, and settling along the southern shores of Africa.

10.1 The Scramble for Africa

From about 1488 (when the first Portuguese and Spanish settlers brushed against African shores) to about the early seventeenth century, other European nations including England and France initiated their forceable seizure of African territories. When describing colonialism, history books employ words like "exploration" and "discovery." A good example is Sir Henry Morton Stanley, the Welsh-American journalist turned explorer (Driver, 1991; Stanley, 1989). Under the payroll of King Leopold II of Belgium, Stanley led a mapping study, to probe the source of the Nile. His knowledge of the region was instrumental in King Leopold II's eventual annexation of Congo as a Belgian colony. Colonialism involved hostile takeovers, and words like exploration and discovery are at best misleading, inaccurate terms as the underlying assumption is that nothing and no one existed prior to the arrival of Europeans in Africa. Of course, intentional subjugation of one group by others dates

© The Author(s), under exclusive license to Springer Nature Switzerland AG 2021   151
A. Moreland-Capuia, *The Trauma of Racism*,
https://doi.org/10.1007/978-3-030-73436-7_10

back Before Christ (BC). Understanding the true motivation, the rationale, and the intentional subjugation of Africans and the seizure of many parts of the African continent by European colonial forces as well as the generational impact is a worthy endeavor. Chapter 1 covered ecosystems and the prey-predator phenomenon – outlining animal nature and the hierarchical mandates within an ecosystem for the sake of survival and persistence of certain species. Some scholars frame Europe's exploration, seizure, and forceable possession of land that did not belong to them as an act of survival and as a matter of necessity (Bernhard, Reenock, & Nordstrom, 2004; Lawrence, 1980; Wolfe, 2006). Other historians frame colonialism as a power grab, indeed, a quest for resources and religious infiltration (as many European colonizers identified as Christian and held the conviction that Christianity was foundational to civilization) (Akeredolu-Ale, 1975; Beidelman, 2012; Bond, 2006; Odukoya, 2018; Rodney, 1972).

The partition of Africa, often referred to as the "Scramble for Africa," began aggressively in the last decades of the eighteenth century (Frankema, Williamson, & Woljer, 2015; Michalpoulos and Papaioannou, 2014, 2016; Wesseling, 1996. At stake was the deteriorating relationship between European nations and business conglomerates that intended to have a business hold on the resource-rich continent. European expansionism into Africa was accentuating political and diplomatic rivalries among European nations. There was an urgent need to curtail conflict that was simmering in major European capitals. Belgian King Leopold II had a lot to lose from the infighting and together with Portugal, a major colonial entity at the time, decided to convince Otto von Bismarck, the Germany chancellor, to host the important gathering of nations with territorial claims in Africa and elsewhere, to map out a trade-free zone that would encompass the Congo Basin and surrounding territorial lands (Bueno de Mesquita, 2007; Ewans, 2002; Gondola, 2002; Jewsiewicki, 1977; Viaene, 2008). They reasoned that the existence of such multilateral trade agreement would help quell disputes among European nations.

The Berlin Conference, held from November 1884 through February 1985, hosted 15 nations (Aghie, 2004; Chamberlain, 1999; Craven, 2015; Katzenellenbogen, 1996). The Great European Powers of that era – Germany, Great Britain, France, and Portugal – entertained second-tier European nations such as Austria-Hungary, Sweden-Norway, Belgium, Denmark, Spain, the Netherlands, Italy, Sweden, Norway, and Russia. The United States and Ottoman Empire attended the Berlin Conference as Observer Nations. The Berlin Conference was the meeting place for the "Scramble for Africa." The Conference consisted of planning the demarcation and the arbitrary setting of territorial borders of Africa. The "spoils system" adopted at the Berlin Conference bought great disarray to well-established African systems of governance. Until then, in pre-colonial Africa, both centralized and decentralized political entities had been prevalent. African societies that were often led by kings, rulers, and/or military leaders, before the arrival of European invaders, were left in shambles.

It is against this precarious background that the coercive, open-ended decision by European nations to divide and appropriate what was not theirs had deleterious political, economic, social, and cultural implications for the entire continent of Africa. This intentional breakup of a huge geographical territory today considered the cradle of humanity, by means of partitioning of a spoils system by colonial powers, exacerbated culture-political tensions within African territories, then and now, and has contributed significantly to unnecessary trauma, loss, and disruption of sacred beliefs and practices. Those ongoing existing tensions grew and persisted until the early 1950s and 1960s – when African nations began demanding an end to colonialism. Various African nations rose intellectually, physically, and politically to counter colonial presence.

10.2 Colonialism and European Supremacy

Colonialism goes beyond racism and might be better understood in the context of supremacy and subjugation. Monarchies, dating back to 3000–4000 BC in Egypt, were based in hierarchy – they involved, among other things, valuing and devaluing, ruler and being ruled, a lesser and a greater. Determining who shall be the ruler and who should be a subject is an even more fascinating phenomenon as it involves the concept of supremacy, i.e., the running conviction that one group is superior (culturally, socially, politically, and economically) over the other, that one group matters more than other groups (Bonds & Inwood, 2016). Supremacy is the intentional and conscious repression of others inspired by a fixed-false belief of superiority. From Before Christ (BC) to modern day, considering how European nations occupied entire African nations and subdued African people, is nothing short of European supremacy (Bonds & Inwood, 2016; Elphick, 1983; Frederickson, 1981; Kantrowitz, 2020; Meer, 2019). European supremacy has grave implications in the perpetuation of trauma on and in several generations of Africans. This chapter will highlight trauma in colonial Angola, and Kenya as well as South Africa during apartheid, because of colonial overreach and explores semblances of healing with transition to democracy, an apology with reparations and a truth and reconciliation commission respectively.

10.3 Angola, Africa

Diogo Cão, a notable Portuguese navigator, considered the first European explorer to sail along the west coast of Africa, and surveying the majestic Congo River, landed in the coast of Angola in 1492 (Lewis, 1908; Missinne, Davis, & MacGaffey, 1970; Ravenstein, 1900; Wheeler, 1975). He led the embryonic group of Portuguese settlers into Angola in 1492. His arrival became the harbinger of the subsequent pillage of Angola's human capital in the form of slaves that were distributed to Brazil and other posts along the North American and South American seaboard.

The Portuguese would then continue non-stop, the pillage of Angola's natural resources for the enrichment of the Portuguese metropolis, for nearly five centuries (Adelman, 1975; Clarence-Smith, 1979; Henriksen, 1973). African territories located along Africa's western seaboard generated great interest in the discussions among attendees of the Berlin Conference. Angola, the crown jewel of Portugal in Africa, and Congo, now DR Congo, were the foci of the negotiations. It is noteworthy to mention that King Leopold II (of Belgium) obtained rights to what is now deemed Congo territory (a country that borders Angola) while in attendance at the Conference of Berlin. Both Diogo Cão and King Leopold II were great proponents of European colonialization of the continent of Africa. These two stakeholders of African colonialism are good examples of the persistent, harmful presence of European colonial forces in Africa from the fifteenth century to the twentieth century.

10.4   Portuguese Influence in Angola

When the Portuguese expedition, led by Diogo Cão, landed in the northern coast of Angola in 1492, they initially met the residents of the commanding Kingdom of Kongo. By then, the Bakongo Kingdom was a well-established ruling entity subdivided into six provinces and included the powerful state to the south, called the Ndongo Kingdom (Broadhead, 1979; Thornton, 1977). The Bakongo Kingdom exercised a formidable commercial dominance over its subjects. Trade steered in the kingdom involved agricultural goods and the exploration of mineral wealth. Initially, Portugal began a cordial relationship with the powerful Kingdom of Kongo, engaging the kingdom in the sale of firearms, in exchange for minerals, and ivory. Through the process of time, the Portuguese introduced religion within the kingdom. Consequently, the Bakongo King himself not only became a convert of Christianity but also introduced a governance framework in the kingdom that mimicked structures of European states.

Portugal colonization of Angola territory began in earnest, circa 1575 (Boxer, 1963). Portuguese explorer Paulo de Novais had just arrived in Angola leading an expedition of families of early colonists and a contingent of four hundred soldiers that were sent to safeguard the new Portuguese settlements (Ball, 2018; Heywood & Thornton, 2019). By then, the Kingdom of Ndongo, under Ngola (King) Kiluange was emerging (Santos & Subtil, 2017). By fostering a series of alliances with important neighboring states, Ngola Kiluange succeeded in delaying Portuguese expansion and dominance of its territories, for several decades. However, the Portuguese concocted a way to destabilize the alliance, and eventually Ngola Kiluange was not only captured but beheaded.

10.5 Queen Njinga Mbande Pushes Back against Portuguese Colonial Powers

In later years, another formidable authority rose within the ranks of the tenacious Ndongo Kingdom. Queen Njinga Mbande (*Rainha Njinga Mbande*) grew up in the immediacy of her father, himself a king (Heywood, 2019; Miller, 1975; Thornton, 1991). At a young age, she quickly marshalled the art of war as well as formidable diplomatic skills. As astute as she was, she quickly understood her place in history, and her insightfulness soon propelled her to prominence. As queen, she had the foresight to rebuild old alliances that her father had failed to consolidate in a timely manner. She managed to bring together previously warring kingdoms into a mega-alliance of states that included the states of *Ndongo, Congo, Matamba, Dembos, Cassange*, and *Kassama*. This cohesive amalgamation of native states managed to impact decisive blows to Portuguese colonial forces, forcing them to retreat to their own sanctuaries, the coastal towns they controlled. Portugal became one of the wealthiest European nations. Angola, its breadbasket, supplied the Portuguese metropolis with precious natural resources that included rubber, diamond, iron, ivory, coffee, cotton, and fish. It is easy to understand that from 1575 through 1975, Angola's economic empowerment was seriously handicapped during colonial rule. If anything, Portugal's political, social, and economic power was sustained by the unyielding pillaging of Angola's resources. Portugal's colonialization of Angola came at the expense of Angola's upward social, political, and economic mobility.

At the onset of the 1960s, the Portuguese colonial authorities imposed the forceful cultivation of cotton to the native population of the Cassange region, near Malange, located in the Angolan heartland. The native population was being coerced into surrendering a large share of their cotton harvest to the Portuguese authorities (Pitcher, 1991). At the same time, the authorities levied an exorbitant, unfair poll tax (a major direct tax, solely imposed on indigenous cotton farmers). Concurrently, Angolans were growing dissatisfied with the ongoing, harsh working conditions imposed by Portuguese commercial interests. One such culprit business entity was *Companhia Geral de Algodoes de Angola* (Furtado, 2017; Keese, 2013). Workers at the Portuguese-Belgian consortium demanded better working conditions. Failure by the management of COTONANG to accommodate the workers' demands led to a 2-week uprise that began on January 4, 1961, and would come to be known as the *Baixa de Cassange Revolt* of 1961 (Alves, 2017; Cann, 2012; McVeigh, 1961; Stone, 1999). The Portuguese responded to the mass protests, with indiscriminate air raids, that would subsequently kill thousands of men and women in Cassange and surrounding areas. Further up north, in the northern district of Uige, the Portuguese conducted arbitrary bombings that killed thousands of native Angolans that were employed in the coffee plantations and had been deemed sympathizers of the rebellion in Cassange.

10.6   Angolan Independence

For many historians, the Cassange Revolt of 1961, and the deliberate, random killing of native Angolans, by the Portuguese, thereafter, is deemed as the leading cata-
lyst to Angolans' quest to end colonial oppression in the country and move toward
independence (Jerónimo, 2008; Stone, 1999). Important to note here is the selfish
demarcation of the African continent at the Conference of Berlin which was damaging to families, legacy, and culture, and its effects can be seen even still today in
many parts of Africa. Angola's fight for independence lasted almost two decades,
from 1961 to 1975. Upon gaining independence from Portugal on November 11,
1975 (after nearly 500 years of oppression), many of Angola's institutions were left
in shambles from healthcare, education, employment, and housing. The stressed
conditions of the war for independence bled into a civil war in Angola that initially
lasted for 16 years (1975–1991). The war between the warring Angolan factions had
acquired an international dimension, as it had involved regional military powers –
Cuba – and the apartheid regime of South Africa. In a broader sense, the Angolan
civil became a proxy war between the two superpowers – the United States and the
Soviet Union. As the external stakeholders – Cuba and South Africa – reached a
landmark agreement in 1988 (December 22, 1988) through the New York Accords
(McFaul, 1989), the United Nations quickly understood that there was a short window to pursue a negotiated peace settlement and move away from the ongoing political and military strife Angola had experienced since independence. On May 31,
1991, the Angolan sides signed a historical Peace Agreement in Bicesse, Portugal,
that called for the immediate cessation of hostilities and the holding of free and fair
elections in Angola in September 1992. Angolans went ecstatically to the polls, for
the first time on September 29 and 30, 1992, but the peace was short-lived because
a contested presidential election soon took the country back to the resurgence of yet
another civil war that persisted for another 10 years. Finally, on April 4, 2002, a
Memorandum of Understanding was signed between the Angolan Government and
the National Union for the Total Independence of Angola (UNITA), which ended
the Angolan civil war, once and for all.

In 2002, the country began in earnest the daunting process of rebuilding the
major infrastructures that had been destroyed during the long civil war. Angolans
went to the polls again in 2008 and 2012, and the ruling party Movimento Popular
de Libertação de Angola (MPA) further consolidated its stronghold on power. In
2017, President Jose Eduardo Dos Santos, who had held the presidency for 38 years,
finally decided to vacate his seat. Angola held yet another presidential election in
2017, and the party in power chose a new leader to give continuity to its 42-year
governance.

Angolans have endured a lot of trauma. They have endured many forms of conflict, and for many decades their liberties were under assault, by several stakeholders.

Angola had been involved in war from around 1961 until 2002, and so the trauma
and profound loss its citizens have endured cannot be underestimated. The country
went through a 14-year war of liberation that was immediately followed by a

37-year-old civil war. Both the rebuilding and the healing process since independence have not been easy. How should any country be expected to reconstitute itself,
in a span of two decades, after 500 years of a debilitating colonial subjugation and
the disruption caused by a 37-year-old civil war? The answer is, it could not possi-
bly withstand and overcome so easily the trauma of centuries of systemic oppression under Portuguese colonization, the enslavement of over five million of its
descendants that were forcefully kidnapped from their villages and hamlets to be
sold in slave markets that fed the need for cheap labor in cotton and coffee plantations in the Americas. Angolan slaves, like other slave cargo, travelled in inhumane,
poorly ventilated slave ships, where many died in the high seas (Collins, 2019; Eltis,
1977; Miers, 1998).

Today, the marks of colonialism are still present in Angola and are living reminders, in the form of old bunkers and buildings that the Portuguese constructed to
house and market slaves. While some may call it history, others call them trauma
triggers and reminders. The traumatic residue of colonialism was notable; on the
edges of independence in 1975, literacy rates were suboptimal, for instance (Simon,
1998). The Angolan education system that was crafted in Lisbon, Portugal, by the
fascist regime of Prime Minister Salazar without any local input was woefully inadequate (Cairo, 2006; Duffy, 1961). Equally and unfortunately, it was based on racial
segregation, as evidenced that the Native African population did not have equal and/
or consistent access to the colonial and educational services. There are still structural challenges (Agadjanian & Prata, 2002; Boslego, 2005; Gastrow, 2017; ROZÈS,
2001) and realities that the country is working to mitigate, to include but not limited
to healthcare, education, housing, and the economy (Boslego, 2005; Duffy, 1961;
Gastrow, 2017). Because of so much death and loss, whole generations have been
lost to death and displacement as millions of Angolans live outside of the country,
the compounded trauma of being refugee in another country is worthy of an entire
book and important to note here (Hansen, 1981). The sequelae of civil war meant
that the Angolan population was and is considerably younger with approximately
over 50% being age 14 and under. Angola is rich in resources with a GDP of approximately 104 billion but limited employment of and access to technology to optimize
and diversify economy (an example is oil, the country exports unprocessed oil and
then must buy the refined oil back at a higher price because the country doesn't have
effective refinery technology) (Frynas & Wood, 2001; Jenkins, Robson, & Cain,
2002; Pike, 2015). Before independence, Angola was the second leading exporter of
coffee in the world (Birmingham, 1988; van Dongen, 1961) – with independence
and lack of technology, they are no longer. Agricultural practices in Angola were
disrupted, and the reasons are multifactorial (Rocha, 2002).

Currently, Angola's population has crossed the 30 million mark, and illiteracy
(while notably improved), healthcare, economic, and education infrastructure are
still daunting to overcome. 500 years of colonial- and war-related trauma cannot be
resolved in 30 years, healing must not be rushed, but the conditions for healing must
be established and prioritized. There must be acknowledgment of the detrimental,
traumatizing impact colonialism and civil war have had and continues to have on
this country (and many countries subjected to colonization and civil war) (Ayalon,

1998; Barber, 2014; Cliff & Noormahomed, 1993; McIntyre & Ventura, 1995; Pearce, 2012; Rudenberg, Jansen, & Fridjhon, 2001) and its journey to heal from within. Safe, secure, and thoughtfully executed democratic elections in 2017 in Angola brought with it improved hope for healing and change.

10.7   Kenya, Trauma and Healing

The British Empire ruled The Colony and Protectorate of Kenya from 1920 until The Independence Republic of Kenya gained independence on December 12, 1963. Kenya was not colonized by the British Empire for as long as Angola had been colonized by the Portuguese. The British Empire's motivation for colonization centered around the desire to amass socioeconomic and political power. Agriculture and farming climate were prominent and economic drivers in Kenya, and the country possessed an abundance of raw materials. White British settlers began to occupy farm land and dominate the farming industry. Local Kenyans took note of the land grab and reduced economic opportunities that emerged from White British settler presence. Initially, the natives attempted to negotiate with colonialists on issues such as land sharing and farming profits; after multiple attempts and in the context of unsuccessful negotiations and lost economic opportunities for local Kenyan farmers, tensions rose. Around 1952, a group of Kenyan farmers, predominantly of the Kikuyu tribe, joined arms with a secret farmers society called the Mau Mau. Until then, members of the underground society had not only been economically displaced by the British settlers, but their presence had been challenged by disgruntled White farmers and their allies within the ranks of British colonial security structures. This sort of affairs is widely referred to and emphasized in the literature as having given rise to the Mau Mau Rebellion of 1952. One of the foremost goals of the Mau Mau Uprising was above all to reduce British presence in the colony, so that local Kenyans could benefit from their own subsistence farming. The Mau Mau Revolt lasted roughly 8 years, i.e., from 1952 to 1960. Even though the Mau Mau in the end failed to achieve their ultimate goals, nevertheless they waged an initial successful campaign that, for 8 years, slowing and in some ways halting British advancement. The Kenya death registries from 1952 to 1960 highlighted thousands of deaths and Mau Mau casualties with a notable proportion of death facilitated by public hangings, abuse, and torture (Anderson, 2012; Colonial office London, 1959). It has often been ascertained that official percentage of Kenyans that were hanged had been dubiously understated by the authorities. Of note (and indicating the mismatch in resources), in the eight-year conflict, only 32 White settlers were killed. The death disparity is unreal. The Mau Mau Rebellion ended in 1960, and 3 years later, Kenya gained independence.

Many historians contend that the Mau Mau Rebellion, and its aftermath, was a watershed moment in pre-colonial Kenyan history (Berman, 1991; Buijtenhuijs, 1973; Newsinger, 1981; Wa-Githumo, 1991). The Mau Mau Uprising had many ramifications, one of which was that it created, within the psyche of native Kenyans, an urgency to get rid of the murderous colonial masters. That newly intuitive desire within the Kenyan population, to seek freedom from the colonial oppressors, gave Kenyan, British anti-colonial activists added strength and impetus to seek independence from the British colonial establishment.

The conditions under which Kenyans were placed by the British during the Mau Mau Revolt left an indelible psychological mark. The Kenyan National Commission on Human Rights (KNCHR) is an independent watchdog institution established by the 2002 Kenya National Commission on Human Rights (Gilbert, 2011; Kindiki, 2004). The KNCHR brought to light the torture and abuse of Kenyans by British colonial forces during the Mau Mau Uprising. At the height of the Mau Mau Rebellion in 1952, Elkins asserts that the British were determined to civilize Kenyans as a means of neutralization (Elkins, 2000). The KNCHR provided an account of the British Empire's soldiers treatment of Kenyans during the Mau Mau Rebellion which at the time included but were not limited to execution, torture, maiming, inhumane detention conditions and camps, malnutrition, castration of men, beating, and sexual assault and raping of Kenyan women (Atwoli, Kathuku, & Ndetei, 2006). The trauma was profound and pervasive. A study by Atwoli et al. (2006) specifically investigated the prevalence of PTSD in Mau Mau concentration camp survivors/veterans in Kenya. This cross-sectional study included 181 Mau Mau concentration camp survivors/veterans; based on DSM IV-TR criteria the time and upon formal assessment, over 66% of survivors met formal criteria for PTSD (Atwoli et al., 2006). Individuals exposed to war-like conditions are at risk for the development of PTSD (Harder, Mutiso, Khasakhala, Burke, & Ndetei, 2012). A study by Jenkins et al. (2015) investigated the probability of PTSD in a rural area of Kenya and its associated risk factors. This is another cross-sectional study that gathered data from a household survey on mental disorders and accompanying risk factors. The study revealed that 48% of Kenyans had experienced a severe trauma with an overall prevalence rate of approximately 11% of probable PTSD (Jenkins et al., 2015). A 2012 study by Jenkins and colleagues had previously noted a pattern of high incidences of trauma in rural districts of Kenya (Jenkins et al., 2012).

In 2013, with strong advocacy of the Kenyan National Commission on Human Rights (KNCHR), Mau Mau survivors, and their lawyers, the British Government issued a formal apology for the trauma that had been inflicted upon Kenyans during the Mau Mau Revolt. The British Broadcasting Corporation (BBC) on June 6, 2013, run a story titled, "Kenya's Mau Mau Uprising: Victims Tell Their Stories." The BBC, as a background to the story, stated that William Hague, the British Foreign Secretary had expressed regret and that there would be compensation for Kenyans tortured during the Mau Mau Uprising (BBC News – Kenya's Mau Mau uprising, 2013a). According to the BBC, three elderly Kenyans – Paulo Nzuli, Jane Muthoni Mara, and Wambugu Wa Nyingi – had given detailed accounts of their ordeals, at the hands of British authorities to the British High Court. The surviving claimants had made categoric, appalling statements on the abuses that they have been subjected to, which the Court had found legitimate (BBC News – Mau Mau Torture victims to receive compensation, 2013b; Warner, 2013). The British acknowledged the harms that had been done by way of violent, inhumane tactics that resulted in chronic and persistent trauma of Mau Mau survivors and their families (Elliott, 2016; BBC News – Kenya's Mau Mau uprising, 2013b).

The British admitted to de-prioritizing human rights; the deleterious impact of the detention camps, prisons, and gallows; and the raping of Kenyan women. It was concluded that British colonial powers were systematically cruel and vicious (BBC News – Mau Mau Torture victims to receive compensation, 2013a; Warner, 2013). The apology also came with a commitment to building a monument to honor the Mau Mau fighters and for older Kenyans who were able to show that they had been tortured by British security officers, reparations at approximately 14 million pounds (BBC News- Mau Mau Torture victims to receive compensation, 2013a; Warner, 2013). Multiple news stations covered the reactions of Kenyans who were in receipt of the ruling and apology and plan for reparations – it was met with sighs of relief, tears, and sense that the true healing could start (BBC News – Mau Mau Torture victims to receive compensation, 2013a; Warner, 2013). This felt like a form of justice, and scholars have spoken to power of healing through justice (Yamamoto & Serrano, 2012).

10.8   South Africa, Apartheid, White Supremacy, Truth, and Reconciliation

Oliver & Oliver, 2017 outline the unique colonization history of South Africa by breaking it down between unofficial colonization, official colonization, and internal colonization (Oliver & Oliver, 2017). Accordingly, official colonization by the Dutch began in 1652. Subsequent infighting between the Dutch and the British ended with the defeat of the Dutch. In 1795, the Cape Colony became a British colony. It was subsequently returned to the Dutch in 1802. Subsequent infighting between the Dutch and the British ended with the defeat of the Dutch and the establishment Cape Colony in 1806 by the British. It was that same Cape Colony that attained a fully sovereign nation state of the British Empire in 1934. A 1960 referendum in South Africa brought an end to the British monarchy rule over South Africa. On May 31, 1961, by way of the outcome of the referendum, South Africa was elevated to the status of the Republic of South Africa.

Unofficial colonization was described as Black groups from the north entering South Africa and the subsequent subdivision of the country into four distinct societies with two being ruled by British and two by the Afrikaners.

On the other hand, internal colonization is what took place in the period 1961–1994, when the country embraced "White" democracy. This period was characterized by the internal colonization of White Afrikaners and the rise of the apartheid regime of South Africa (Oliver & Oliver, 2017). South Africa is beautifully positioned in terms of sea access, and it was one of the trade routes to India, making it appealing to the British. Around the mid-1800s, South Africa was determined to be an untapped source for diamonds and gold, increasing the attraction of European nations. Providing brief historical context into the lead into the apartheid: circa 1816–1826, 1860–1911, thousands of Indian workers and traders came from India, and during this same period, diamonds and gold were discovered in South Africa. In 1912, the Native National Congress now known as the African National Congress (ANC) was founded. Several discriminatory laws were passed in South Africa that prohibited Black South Africans' participation in political life and the nation's governance and limited the possibilities of social, political, and economic upward mobility. The 1913 Land Act prohibited Black South Africans from purchasing land outside of reserves and making it illegal for them to work as sharecroppers. All those unfair laws were aimed at limiting upward mobility, for Blacks, in several sphere of South Africa's political, social, and economic life.

Several South African civic groups vehemently opposed the Land Act. The African National Congress (ANC) was one of the several outgrowths of the opposition to the Land Act and other discriminatory policies.

In 1914, The National Party (the party that ruled the country during apartheid from 1948 to 1994) was established. While the Union Act of 1934 professed South Africa to be an independently sovereign state, it is important to emphasize here that the British Monarchy did not fully dissolve/abdicate its status until May 31, 1961, when South Africa became the Republic of South Africa, which then gave rise to the apartheid regime (Boraine, 2000; Elphick & Giliomee, 1979; Guelke, 1989; MacCrone, 1937; Worden, 1985).

The grab for South Africa centered around a quest for power and wealth much like in the case of Angola and Kenya. In the case of South Africa, there is the well-documented traumatic history of apartheid – Oliver and Oliver (2017). From 1948 to the early 1990s, a small White minority called Afrikaners (South African ethnic group with Dutch, German, and French roots, an extension of European settlers in the country) ruled South Africa's predominantly Black population.

10.9   Apartheid

The National Party was the dominant political party in South Africa, in power during the nearly 50-year stretch of institutionalized racist laws and policies enveloped in White Supremacy. Apartheid was marked by law-sanctioned segregation based on skin color, which were enforced by an all-White government. The apartheid was a form of state-sanctioned segregation and racism as manifest by marriage bans between Whites and other racial/ethnic groups and more specifically disallowed sexual relations between White South Africans and Black South Africans. Equally, in 1950, the Population Registration Act was passed requiring all South African racial and/or ethnic groups be identified and stratified by race. This Registration Legislation was so divisive resulting in the severing of families as it was possible that a child, mother, or father could be individually identified as being from different racial/ethnic groups.

The description of internal colonization is a critical one as it gives some context to the rise and consolidation of apartheid and its sinister plots for the minority government of South Africa to be taken as a serious independent nation among other nations in a forum like the United Nations.

When the Dutch colonized South Africa, they carried with them their White supremacist ideas and values. Historical records emphasize and confirm attitudes of European superiority and ideas about slavery among the Dutch (Bonds & Inwood, 2016; Elphick, 1983; Frederickson, 1981; Kantrowitz, 2020; Meer, 2019). Dutch attitudes of White supremacy, subjugation, and segregation infiltrated South Africa. While apartheid happened in the interim period, while South Africa was still under the grips of the British Empire, the constructs of apartheid can be traced back to the late 1700s when the Dutch Empire embarked upon South African land (Bonds & Inwood, 2016; Elphick, 1983; Frederickson, 1981; Kantrowitz, 2020; Meer, 2019).

It is worth mentioning that the notion of apartheid was gaining root in South Africa, when the Civil Rights Movement was gaining ascendency in the United States and the fight against segregation, in the Jim Crow South, was accelerating. The opposition to apartheid forces was robust; Nelson Mandela was a prominent leader in the anti-apartheid movement and in the African National Congress. He was such an effective civil rights activist that the apartheid regime arrested him and his closest associates in 1962 on charges of sedition. At the historical Rivonia Trial (October 9, 1963, to June 12, 1964), Mandela and 15 political associates were sentenced to life imprisonment for conspiracy to overthrow the state (Marshall, 2016). Mandela would serve almost 30 years in prison and split his incarceration tenure as a prisoner of conscience at the notorious Robben Island, Pollsmoor Prison, and Victor Verster Prison.

While Mandela was imprisoned, the calls for the abolition of apartheid were persistent and robust. The United Nations Security Council demonstrated opposition to apartheid in several of its resolutions along the years. Also, anti-apartheid protests erupted in Soweto in 1976, over the death of Steve Biko, a political activist that had been savagely tortured and murdered by the apartheid security forces. Consequently, in 1976, the UN Security Council moved to impose an embargo on the sale of weapons to South Africa, which was followed by economic sanctions imposed by the United States and the United Kingdom in 1985 (South African History On-line, 2015).

The concerted political and social pressure at home and abroad finally brought South African leaders to their knees and reconsider their position on apartheid. After Mandela's release from prison, the intense work of ending apartheid began in earnest. Several apartheid laws were repealed, and political dialogue began between the ANC and the Government of President Frederik de Klerk. Subsequently, sanctions were lifted, and the process of establishing a democratic, free, multi-ethnic society began to unfold.

On April 27, 1994, South Africa held its first democratic, multi-racial elections, with the ANC, under Mandela won 62.25% of the vote. On May 10, 1994, Nelson Mandela, the anti-apartheid activist, lawyer, and former prisoner of consciousness, was inaugurated President of South Africa, under a theme of national unity, healing, and forgiveness. He was finally released from prison on February 11, 1990, as a result of the steadfast demands of Black South Africans, whose cries found resonance in political activists from across the world, as well as several United Nations Security Council Resolutions that excoriated the apartheid regime time and again for its despicable racial policies and its illegal occupation of Namibia. Many political analysts also credit Frederik de Klerk, the last apartheid South African President, as a visionary, for he foresaw the release of Nelson Mandela to temper the looming threat of a racial civil war in South Africa.

10.10   Trauma of Apartheid

Several studies have been conducted on the deleterious impacts and aftermath of apartheid in South Africa (Hirschowitz & Orkin, 1997; McKay, 1997). Hickson and colleagues (1991) studied the impact of apartheid on children in South Africa. The study revealed that apartheid had deleterious impact on Black children in South Africa. Hickson highlights the trauma associated with poverty, racism, violence, growing up in a segregated society, and political uncertainty. The psychological toll of apartheid on Black youth in South Africa was profound (Hickson & Kriegler, 1991; Straker, 1989), and the trauma of apartheid is ever present (Adonis, 2018; Arcot, 2015; Atwoli, Stein, Williams, et al., 2013; Dawes, 1990; Kagee & Price, 1995). Around 1995, the Truth and Reconciliation Commission was established to investigate human rights violations during apartheid (Chapman & van der Merwe, 2008; McKay, 1997).

10.11   Truth and Reconciliation

The Commission was chaired by Archbishop Desmond Tutu who presided over hearings as early as 1996. The hearing itself was traumatic as thousands of survivors rendered accounts of torture, death, families being separated, and needless suffering at the hands of the National Party. Upon 2 years of hearing the stories, the Commission deemed that apartheid was indeed a crime against humanity and determined that the government needed reform; it named individual perpetrators of violence, and it called for reparations (Chapman & van der Merwe, 2008; McKay, 1997).

This was the beginning of a semblance of justice and helped Black South Africans start to think about what a journey to healing might look like.

Angolan, South African, and Kenyan government recognized a historical truth – a person, system, and society cannot get to reconciliation in the absence of truth. Extending this sentiment, safety must be created (safety established through acknowledgment of harm) in order to get to truth, and truth is the prerequisite for reconciliation. Racism, colonialism, White supremacy is trauma, its continued presence structurally and systemically is trauma compounded. Healing and reconciliation flow through truth and justice. The pervasive and prolonged trauma of colonialism, European supremacy, and civil war is a common thread that weaves through the three countries highlighted in this chapter. They also share in their hope for the possibility of transformative healing – Angola with a newfound democracy, Kenya and reparations for Mau Mau survivors, and South Africa's truth and reconciliation commission offers a window into what the beginning of healing can look like.

References

Adelman, K. (1975). Report from Angola. *Foreign Affairs, 53*(3), 558–574. https://doi.org/10.2307/20039527.

Adonis, C. K. (2018). Generational victimhood in post-apartheid South Africa: Perspectives of descendants of victims of apartheid era gross human rights violations. *International Review of Victimology, 24*(1), 47–65. https://doi.org/10.1177/0269758017732175.

Agadjanian, V., & Prata, N. (2002). War, peace, and fertility in Angola. *Demography, 39*, 215–231. https://doi.org/10.1353/dem.2002.0013.

Aghie, A. (2004). In C. Landauer (Ed.), *Imperialism, sovereignty and the making of international law*. Cambridge: Cambridge University Press.

Akeredolu-Ale, E. O. (1975). *Underdevelopment of indigenous entrepreneurship in Nigeria*. Ibadan: Ibadan University Press.

Alves, T. (2017). Reporting 4 February 1961 in Angola: The beginning of the end of the Portuguese empire. In J. Garcia, C. Kaul, F. Subtil, & A. Santos (Eds.), *Media and the Portuguese empire*. Cham: Palgrave Studies in the History of the Media. Palgrave Macmillan. https://doi.org/10.1007/978-3-319-61792-3_13.

Anderson, D. M. (2012). British abuse and torture in Kenya's counter-insurgency, 1952–1960. *Small Wars & Insurgencies, 23*(4–5), 700–719. https://doi.org/10.1080/09592318.2012.709760 .

Arcot, R. (2015). The traumatic state of psychology: An investigation of the challenges psychologists face when aiming to help trauma survivors in post-apartheid South Africa. *Independent Study Project (ISP) Collection*. 2042. https://digitalcollections.sit.edu/isp_collection/2042

Atwoli, L., Kathuku, D. M., & Ndetei, D. M. (2006, July). Post-traumatic stress disorder among Mau Mau concentration camp survivors in Kenya. *East African Medical Journal, 83*(7), 352–359. https://doi.org/10.4314/eamj.v83i7.9446.

Atwoli, L., Stein, D. J., Williams, D. R., et al. (2013). Trauma and posttraumatic stress disorder in South Africa: Analysis from the South African Stress and Health Study. *BMC Psychiatry, 13*, 182. https://doi.org/10.1186/1471-244X-13-182.

Ayalon, O. (1998). Community healing for children traumatized by war. *International Review of Psychiatry, 10*(3), 224–233. https://doi.org/10.1080/09540269874817.

Ball, J. (2018). Staging of memory: Monuments, commemoration, and the demarcation of Portuguese space in colonial Angola. *Journal of Southern African Studies, 44*(1), 77–96. https://doi.org/10.1080/03057070.2018.1403265.

Barber, B. K. (2014). Research on youth and political conflict: Where is the politics? Where are the youth? *Child Development Perspectives, 8*(3), 125–130. https://doi.org/10.1111/cdep.12074.

BBC News. (2013a, June 6) *Mau Mau torture victims to receive compensation – Hague*. Retrieved from https://www.bbc.com/news/uk-22790037 on February 3, 2021.

BBC News. (2013b, June 6). *Kenya's Mau Mau uprising: Victims tell their stories*. Retrieved from https://www.bbc.com/news/uk-22797624 February 16, 2021.

Beidelman, T. O. (2012). *The culture of colonialism: The cultural subjection of Ukaguru.* Bloomington: Indiana University Press.

Berman, B. J. (1991). Nationalism, ethnicity, and modernity: The paradox of Mau Mau. *Canadian Journal of African Studies/Revue canadienne des études africaines, 25*(2), 181–206. https://doi.org/10.1080/00083968.1991.10803888.

Bernhard, M., Reenock, C., & Nordstrom, T. (2004, March). The legacy of Western overseas colonialism on democratic survival. *International Studies Quarterly, 48*(1), 225–250. https://doi.org/10.1111/j.0020-8833.2004.00298.x.

Birmingham, D. (1988). Angola revisited. *Journal of Southern African Studies, 15*(1), 1–14. https://doi.org/10.1080/03057078808708188.

Bond, P. (2006). *Looting Africa. The economy of exploitation.* London: Zed Books.

Bonds, A., & Inwood, J. (2016). Beyond white privilege: Geographies of white supremacy and settler colonialism. *Progress in Human Geography, 40*(6), 715–733. https://doi.org/10.1177/0309132515613166.

Boraine, A. (2000). *A country unmasked: Inside South Africa's truth and reconciliation commission.* Oxford/New York: Oxford University Press.

Boslego, J. (2005, Winter). Angola's agony. *Harvard International Review, Cambridge, 26*(4), 6.

Boxer, C. R. (1963). *Race relations in the Portuguese colonial empire.* London: Oxford University Press.

Broadhead, S. (1979). Beyond decline: The kingdom of the Kongo in the eighteenth and nineteenth centuries. *The International Journal of African Historical Studies, 12*(4), 615–650. https://doi.org/10.2307/218070.

Bueno de Mesquita, B. (2007). Leopold II and the Selectorate: An account in contrast to a racial explanation. *Historical Social Research, 32*, 203–221.

Buijtenhuijs, R. (1973). *Mau Mau: Twenty years after, the myth and the survivors.* The Hague: Mouton and Co..

Cairo, H. (2006). "Portugal is not a small country": Maps and propaganda in the Salazar regime. *Geopolitics, 11*(3), 367–395. https://doi.org/10.1080/14650040600767867.

Cann, J. P. (2012). Baixa do Cassang: Ending the abuse of Portuguese Africans. *Small Wars & Insurgencies, 23*(3), 500–516. https://doi.org/10.1080/09592318.2012.661613.

Chamberlain, M. E. (1999). *The scramble for Africa.* London: Longman.

Chapman, A. R., & van der Merwe, H. (2008). Introduction: Assessing the south African transitional justice model. In A. R. Chapman & H. van der Merwe (Eds.), *Truth and reconciliation in South Africa: Did the TRC deliver?* (pp. 1–19). Philadelphia: University of Pennsylvania Press.

Clarence-Smith, W. G. (1979). The myth of uneconomic imperialism: The Portuguese in Angola, 1836–1926. *Journal of Southern African Studies, 5*(2), 165–180. https://doi.org/10.1080/03057077908707999.

Cliff, J., & Noormahomed, A. R. (1993). The impact of War on Children's health in Mozambique. *Social Science and Medicine, 36*, 834–848.

Collins, G. M. (2019). Edmund Burke on slavery and the slave trade. *Slavery & Abolition, 40*(3), 494–521. https://doi.org/10.1080/0144039X.2019.1597501.

Colonial office London. (1959). *Further documents relating to the deaths of eleven Mau Mau detainees at Hola Camp in Kenya.* Nairobi: Kenya National Archives.

Craven, M. (2015, March). Between law and history: The Berlin conference of 1884-1885 and the logic of free trade. *London Review of International Law, 3*(1), 31–59. https://doi.org/10.1093/lril/lrv002.

Dawes, A. (1990). The effects of political violence on children: A consideration of south African and related studies. *International Journal of Psychology, 25*, 13–31.

Driver, F. (1991). Henry Morton Stanley and his critics: Geography, exploration and empire. *Past & Present, 133*, 134–166. https://doi.org/10.2307/650769.

Duffy, J. (1961). Portuguese Africa (Angola and Mozambique): Some crucial problems and the role of education in their resolution. *The Journal of Negro Education, 30*(3), 294–301. https://doi.org/10.2307/2294318.

Elkins, C. (2000). The struggle for Mau Mau rehabilitation in late colonial Kenya. *The International Journal of African Historical Studies, 33*(1), 25–57. https://doi.org/10.2307/220257.

Elliott, B. (2016). *Africans resist colonialism: The Mau Mau story*. Boston University Pardee School of Global Studies African Studies Center. Retrieved from https://www.bu.edu/africa/outreach/teachingresources/history/the-mau-mau-rebellion/ February 16, 2021.

Elphick, R. (1983). A comparative history of white supremacy. *The Journal of Interdisciplinary History, 13*(3), 503–513. https://doi.org/10.2307/202948.

Elphick, R., & Giliomee, H. (Eds.). (1979). *The shaping of south African society 1652–1810*. Cape Town: Longman.

Eltis, D. (1977). The export of slaves from Africa, 1821-1843. *The Journal of Economic History, 37*(2), 409–433. Retrieved February 22, 2021, from http://www.jstor.org/stable/2118764.

Ewans, M. (2002). *European atrocity, African catastrophe: Leopold II, the Congo Free State and its aftermath*. London: Routledge Curzon.

Frankema, E., Williamson, J., & Woljer, P. (2015). *An economic rationale for the African scramble: The commercial transition and the commodity price Boom of 1845–1885*, NBER WP 21213.

Frederickson, G. M. (1981). *White supremacy: A comparative study in American and south African history*. New York: Oxford University Press.

Frynas, J. G., & Wood, G. (2001). Oil & war in Angola. *Review of African Political Economy, 28*(90), 587–606. https://doi.org/10.1080/03056240108704568.

Furtado, T. (2017). On private coercive power in Angola: Towards a comparative approach. *Portuguese Studies Review, 25*(1), 151–175. 25p.

Gastrow, C. (2017). Cement citizens: Housing, demolition and political belonging in Luanda, Angola. *Citizenship Studies, 21*(2), 224–239. https://doi.org/10.1080/13621025.2017.1279795
.

Gilbert, J. (2011). Indigenous peoples' human rights in Africa: The pragmatic revolution of the african commission on human and peoples' rights. *The International and Comparative Law Quarterly, 60*(1), 245–270. Retrieved February 17, 2021, from http://www.jstor.org/stable/23017106.

Gondola, D. (2002). *The history of Congo*. Westport: Greenwood Press.

Guelke, L. (1989). The origin of white supremacy in South Africa: An interpretation. *Social Dynamics, 15*(2), 40–45. https://doi.org/10.1080/02533958908458473.

Hansen, A. (1981). Refugee dynamics: Angolans in Zambia 1966 to 1972. *International Migration Review., 15*(1–2), 175–194. https://doi.org/10.1177/0197918381015001-219.

Harder, V. S., Mutiso, V. N., Khasakhala, L. I., Burke, H. M., & Ndetei, D. M. (2012). Multiple traumas, postelection violence, and posttraumatic stress among impoverished Kenyan youth. *Journal of Traumatic Stress, 25*(1), 64–70. https://doi.org/10.1002/jts.21660.

Henriksen, T. (1973). Portugal in Africa: A noneconomic interpretation. *African Studies Review, 16*(3), 405–416. https://doi.org/10.2307/523512.

Heywood, L., & Thornton, J. (2019). In search of the 1619 African arrivals: Enslavement and middle passage. *The Virginia Magazine of History and Biography, 127*(3), 200–211. Retrieved February 17, 2021, from https://www.jstor.org/stable/26743946.

Heywood, L. (2019). *Njinga of Angola: Africa's warrior queen*. Cambridge, MA: Harvard University Press.

Hickson, J., & Kriegler, S. (1991). Childshock: The effects of apartheid on the mental health of South Africa's children. *International Journal for the Advancement of Counselling, 14*, 141–154. https://doi.org/10.1007/BF00117733.

Hirschowitz, R., & Orkin, M. (1997). Trauma and mental health in South Africa. *Social Indicators Research, 41*(1/3), 169–182. Retrieved February 4, 2021, from http://www.jstor.org/stable/27522261.

Jenkins, P., Robson, P., & Cain, A. (2002). Local responses to globalization and peripheralization in Luanda, Angola. *Environment and Urbanization, 14*(1), 115–127. https://doi.org/10.1177/095624780201400110.

Jenkins, R., Njenga, F., Okonji, M., Kigamwa, P., Baraza, M., Ayuyo, J., Singleton, N., McManus, S., & Kiima, D. (2012). Prevalence of common mental disorders in a rural district of Kenya, and socio-demographic risk factors. *International Journal of Environmental Research and Public Health, 9*, 1810–1819. https://doi.org/10.3390/ijerph9051810.

Jenkins, R., Othieno, C., Omollo, R., Ongeri, L., Sifuna, P., Mboroki, J. K., Kiima, D., & Ogutu, B. (2015). Probable post traumatic stress disorder in Kenya and its associated risk factors: A cross-sectional household survey. *International Journal of Environmental Research and Public Health, 12*(10), 13494–13509. https://doi.org/10.3390/ijerph121013494.

Jerónimo, M. (2008). *Angola: "Baixa De Kassanje" Massacre turns 47 years*. Angola Press Agency via all Africa. Retrieved 5 January 2008.

Jewsiewicki, B. (1977, Autumn). The great depression and the making of the colonial economic system in the Belgian Congo. *African Economic History, 4*, 153–176.

Kagee, A., & Price, J. (1995). Apartheid in South Africa: Toward a model of psychological intervention. *Journal of Black Studies, 25*(6), 737–748. Retrieved February 4, 2021, from http://www.jstor.org/stable/2784762.

Kantrowitz, S. (2020). White supremacy, settler colonialism, and the two citizenships of the fourteenth amendment. *The Journal of the Civil War Era, 10*(1), 29–53. https://doi.org/10.1353/cwe.2020.0002.

Katzenellenbogen, S. (1996). It didn't happen at Berlin: Politics, economics and ignorance in the setting of Africa's colonial boundaries. In P. Nugent & A. I. Asiwaju (Eds.), *African boundaries: Barriers, conduits and opportunities* (pp. 21–34). London: Pinter.

Keese, A. (2013). Searching for the reluctant hands: Obsession, ambivalence and the practice of Organising involuntary labour in colonial Cuanza-Sul and Malange districts, Angola, 1926–1945. *The Journal of Imperial and Commonwealth History, 41*(2), 238–258. https://doi.org/10.1080/03086534.2013.779116.

Kindiki, K. (2004). On the independence of the Kenya National Commission on Human Rights: A Preliminary Comment. *East African Journal of Human Rights & Democracy, 2*, 120.

Lawrence, P. (1980). The beginnings of European colonialism: A review article. *Oceania, 51*(1), 53–59. Retrieved February 16, 2021, from http://www.jstor.org/stable/40330496.

Lewis, T. (1908). The old kingdom of Kongo. *The Geographical Journal, 31*(6), 589–611. https://doi.org/10.2307/1777621.

MacCrone, I. D. (1937). *Race attitudes in South Africa: Historical, experimental and psychological studies*. London: Oxford University Press.

Marshall, H. (2016, December). The Courtroom as a Space of Resistance: Reflections on the Legacy of the Rivonia Trial. *African Studies Quarterly, suppl. Special Issue: China-Africa Relations: Political and Gainesville, 16*(3/4), 176–177.

McFaul, M. (1989). Rethinking the "Reagan doctrine" in Angola. *International Security, 14*(3), 99–135. https://doi.org/10.2307/2538933.

McIntyre, T. M., & Ventura, M. (1995). *Children of War: A Study of PTSD in Angolan Adolescents*. Paper presented at the 103rd Annual Meeting of the American Psychological Association, 12 August, New York.

McKay, A. (1997). The survivors of apartheid and political violence in Kwazulu-Natal. In B. Rock (Ed.), *Spirals of suffering: Public violence and children* (pp. 277–320). Pretoria: HSRC Publishers.

McVeigh, M. (1961). The bullets of civilization. *Africa Today, 8*(7), 5–8. Retrieved February 17, 2021, from http://www.jstor.org/stable/4184235.

Meer, N. (2019). The wreckage of white supremacy. *Identities, 26*(5), 501–509. https://doi.org/10.1080/1070289X.2019.1654662.

Michalopoulos, S., & Papaioannou, E. (2014). National Institutions and subnational development in Africa. *Quarterly Journal of Economics, 129*(1), 151.213.

Michalopoulos, S., & Papaioannou, E. (2016). The long-run effects of the scramble for Africa. *American Economic Review, 106*(7), 1802–1848.

Miers, S. (1998). Slavery and the slave trade as international issues 1890–1939. *Slavery & Abolition, 19*(2), 16–37. https://doi.org/10.1080/01440399808575237.

Miller, J. C. (1975). Nzinga of Matamba in a new perspective. *The Journal of African History, 16*(2), 201–216. JSTOR, www.jstor.org/stable/180812.

Missinne, L., Davis, R., & MacGaffey, W. (1970). Brief communications and letters. *African Studies Review, 13*(1), 145–154. https://doi.org/10.2307/523702.

Newsinger, J. (1981). Revolt and repression in Kenya: The "Mau Mau" Rebellion, 1952–1960. *Science & Society, 45*(2), 159–185. Retrieved February 17, 2021, from http://www.jstor.org/stable/40402312.

Odukoya, A. O. (2018). Settler and non-settler colonialism in Africa. In S. Oloruntoba & T. Falola (Eds.), *The Palgrave handbook of African politics, governance and development*. New York: Palgrave Macmillan. https://doi.org/10.1057/978-1-349-95232-8_10.

Oliver, E., & Oliver, W. H. (2017). The colonisation of South Africa: A unique case. *HTS Theological Studies, 73*(3), 1–8. https://doi.org/10.4102/hts.v73i3.4498.

Pearce, J. (2012, July). Control, politics and identity in the Angolan civil war. *African Affairs, 111*(444), 442–465. https://doi.org/10.1093/afraf/ads028.

Pike, J. "Cabinda". Global Security. Retrieved 23 January 2015.

Pitcher, M. A. (1991). Sowing the seeds of failure: Early Portuguese cotton cultivation in Angola and Mozambique, 1820–1926. *Journal of Southern African Studies, 17*(1), 43–70. https://doi.org/10.1080/03057079108708266.

Ravenstein, E. (1900). The voyages of Diogo Cão and Bartholomeu Dias, 1482-88. *The Geographical Journal, 16*(6), 625–655. https://doi.org/10.2307/1775267.

Rocha, J. (2002). The costs of the conflict in Angola. *South African Journal of International Affairs, 9*(2), 1–16. https://doi.org/10.1080/10220460209545387.

Rodney, W. (1972). *How Europe underdeveloped Africa*. London: Bogle-L'Ouverture Publications.

Rozès, A. (2001). ANGOLAN DEADLOCK. *African Security Review, 10*(3), 17–31. https://doi.org/10.1080/10246029.2001.9628111.

Rudenberg, S. L., Jansen, P., & Fridjhon, P. (2001). Living and coping with ongoing violence: A cross-national analysis of Children's drawings using structured rating indices. *Childhood, 8*(1), 31–55. https://doi.org/10.1177/0907568201008001003.

Santos, A., & Subtil, F. (2017). Literature against the empire: Narratives of the nation in the textbook *História de Angola* and in the novel *Yaka*. In J. Garcia, C. Kaul, F. Subtil, & A. Santos (Eds.), *Media and the Portuguese empire* (Palgrave studies in the history of the media). Cham: Palgrave Macmillan. https://doi.org/10.1007/978-3-319-61792-3_17.

Simon, D. (1998). Angola: The peace is not yet fully won. *Review of African Political Economy, 25*(77), 495–503. https://doi.org/10.1080/03056249808704331.

South African History On-line (2015, July 16). *The Nelson Mandela Presidency – 1994 to 1999*. Retrieved from https://www.sahistory.org.za/article/nelson-mandela-presidency-1994-1999 last updated July 20, 2020.

Stanley, F. M. L. (1989). *The making of an African explorer* (411 pp). London: Constable.

Stone, G. (1999). Britain and the Angolan revolt of 1961. *The Journal of Imperial and Commonwealth History, 27*(1), 109–137. https://doi.org/10.1080/03086539908583049.

Straker, G. (1989). From victim to villain: A 'slight' of speech? Media representations of township youth. *South Africa Journal of Psychology, 19*(1), 20–27.

Thornton, J. (1977). Demography and history in the kingdom of Kongo, 1550-1750. *The Journal of African History, 18*(4), 507–530. Retrieved February 17, 2021, from http://www.jstor.org/stable/180830.

Thornton, J. K. (1991). Legitimacy and political power: Queen Njinga, 1624-1663. *The Journal of African History., 32*(1), 25–40. https://doi.org/10.1017/s0021853700025329.JSTOR182577.

van Dongen, I. S. (1961). Coffee trade, coffee regions, and coffee ports in Angola. *Economic Geography, 37*(4), 320–346. https://doi.org/10.2307/141997.

Viaene, V. (2008). King Leopold's imperialism and the origins of the Belgian colonial party, 1860–1905. *The Journal of Modern History, 80*(4), 741–790. https://doi.org/10.1086/591110.

Wa-Githumo, M. (1991). The truth about the Mau Mau movement: The most popular uprising in Kenya. *Transafrican Journal of History, 20*, 1–18. Retrieved February 17, 2021, from http://www.jstor.org/stable/24520300.

Warner, G. (2013, June 9). *Britain apologizes for Colonial-Era torture of Kenyan Rebels*. National Public Radio. Retrieved from https://www.npr.org/2013/06/09/189968998/britain-apologizes-for-colonial-era-torture-of-kenyan-rebels on February 3, 2021.

Wesseling, H. L. (1996). *Divide and rule: The partition of Africa, 1880–1914*. Amsterdam: Praeger.

Wheeler, D. (1975). *The International Journal of African Historical Studies, 8*(2), 357–359. https://doi.org/10.2307/216689.

Wolfe, P. (2006). Settler colonialism and the elimination of the native. *Journal of Genocide Research, 8*(4), 387–409. https://doi.org/10.1080/14623520601056240.

Worden, N. (1985). *Slavery in Dutch South Africa*. Cambridge: Cambridge University Press.

Yamamoto, E. K., & Serrano, S. K. (2012). Reparations theory and practice then and now: Mau Mau redress litigation and the British high court. *Asian Pacific American Law Journal, 18*. University of Hawai'i Richardson School of Law Research Paper No. 3488414, Available at SSRN: https://ssrn.com/abstract=3488414.

Index

A
Adams, John, 18–19
Adverse Childhood Experiences
    (ACEs), 110–111
African colonialism, 154
African National Congress (ANC), 161
Amygdala, 14, 36
Angolan Independence, 156–158
Apartheid, 161
Articles of Confederation, 16–18

B
Black Americans, 80, 81

C
Cardiovascular health disparities, 123
Civil Rights Movement, 42
Coast of Angola, 153
Colonialism, 151, 153, 157
Constitution, 16
COVID-19
    death rates, 143
    disproportionately impacted, 142
    economic recession, 139
    life-threatening condition, 137
    pandemic, 145
    vaccinations, 144
Culturally Informed Adverse Childhood
    Experiences– C-ACEs, 113

D
Declaration of Independence, 16
Diencephalon, 5
Discrimination, 43

E
Economy *vs.* health and safety, 140
Education
    for Black Americans, 81
    Department of Education, 80, 81
    health determinants, 84–86
    history of, 79–80
    No Child Left Behind (NCLB) policy, 82
    poverty, impact of, 83
    Reconstruction era, 80
    socioeconomic inequality, 82
    Title I of the Elementary and Secondary
        Education Act, 82
European supremacy, 153

F
Fear
    and brain, 5–8
    ecology of, 2
    ecosystem, impact on, 2
    fear-on-fear interactions, 3
    during Great Depression, 1
    and Hoover, Herbert, 38–40
    and Johnson, Lyndon B., 51

© The Author(s), under exclusive license to Springer Nature Switzerland AG 2021
A. Moreland-Capuia, *The Trauma of Racism*,
https://doi.org/10.1007/978-3-030-73436-7

Fear (*cont.*)
McCarthy and socially constructed
fear, 41–44
and Nixon, Richard, 37–38, 51
and Obama, Barack, 53–54
and politics, 36
and poverty
brain development, impact on,
67–68
definition, 66
economic downturn, 65–67
environmental injustice, 70
homelessness, 69, 70
low skills, 70–71
and nutrition, 68–69
and racism, 65
stress, 71–72
unemployment, 65
unemployment and
underemployment, 70–71
and Reagan, Ronald, 52–53
and Roosevelt, Franklin D., 40–41
social constructivism, 44–47
stress, 35
and Truman, Harry, 49–50
and Trump, Donald, 54–56
in US (*see* United States)
Fear and trauma, 107
Franklin, Benjamin, 20
Frontal and temporal lobes, 15

G
Great depression, 38

H
Hamilton, Alexander, 20
Healthcare system, 119
cancer detection, 124
cancer treatment, 125
cardiovascular health disparities, 123
discrimination and racism, 123
pain management, 122
providers and clinicians, 128
structural components, 127
Herrnstein, Richard, 48
Hoover, Herbert, 38–40
Human behavior, 5

I
Implicit Association Test (IAT), 64

J
Jefferson, Thomas, 16, 21
Johnson, Lyndon B., 51

K
Kenya, 158
Kenyan National Commission on Human
Rights (KNCHR), 159

L
Law enforcement and policing systems, 91
anticipatory anxiety and fear, 97
attitudes toward police and fear, 99
behavior modification, 98
classical conditioning, 98
during COVID-19, 92
during Reconstruction era, 95, 96
extremism and supremacy, 97
fear conditioning, 98
police-involved deaths, 93
shootings by police based on sex and
race, 94
slave patrols, 95
twentieth-century policing, 96
Learned fear-related behaviors, 45

M
Madison, James, 21
Mau Mau Rebellion, 158
Medulla oblongata, 6
Midbrain, 5
Murray, Charles, 48

N
Nixon, Richard, 37–38, 51
No Child Left Behind (NCLB) policy, 82

O
Obama, Barack, 53–54

P
Politics and fear, 36
Portugal colonialization, 154, 155
Posttraumatic stress disorder (PTSD), 113
Predator and prey
antipredation behavior, 3
behavioral patterns, 2

curly-tailed lizard, 4
direct killing, 3
feeding times and patterns of racoons, 2
non-native tree-dwelling green anole, 4
physiologic and behavioral changes, 4
Psychoanalytic theorist, 136
Public Health Service (PHS), 141

R
Racial discrimination
    mental health treatment and
        diagnosis, 126
    systematic review, 121
Racism, 107
    ACEs, 110
    C-ACEs, 113
    DSM-5 framework, 113
    ethnoviolence, 114
    housing disparities, 110
    neither liberty nor safety, 115
    Philadelphia ACE study, 112
    PTSD, 113
    structural impact, 109
    wage disparities, 110
Reagan, Ronald, 52–53
Roosevelt, Franklin D., 1, 40–41

S
Scholastic Aptitude Testing (SAT)
    scores, 83
Scramble for Africa, 151–153
Shakespeare, William, 63
Social constructivism, 44–47
    Bell Curve suggestion, 48
    Birth of a Nation (film), 47
    Black women, 48
    and narrative, 49
    power of false negative narratives, 47

Spanish flu of 1918, 140
Stress, 71–72

T
Title VI of the Civil Rights Act, 82
Trauma, 15
Trauma of Apartheid, 163
Truman, Harry, 49–50
Trump, Donald, 54–56
Truth and reconciliation, 163–164

U
United States
    Adams, John, 18–19
    Chinese Exclusion Act, 26–27
    COVID-19 public health crisis, 13
    founding documents, 16–18
    Franklin, Benjamin, 20
    Hamilton, Alexander, 20
    inhumanity of slavery, 23–24
    Jefferson, Thomas, 21
    laws, policies, and practices, 24–25
    Madison, James, 21
    Washington, George, 19–20

V
Vaccination disparities, 144
Vicarious trauma, 143
Vitamin D deficiency, 69

W
Washington, George, 19–20

Z
Zinc deficiency, 69